CHAMBER OF COMMERCE
ADMINISTRATION

E. W. Stephens Publishing Company
Columbia, Missouri

CHAMBER OF COMMERCE ADMINISTRATION

Second Revised Edition, 1951

Edited by

S. G. WENNBERG

Professor of Marketing, School of Business and
Public Administration, University of Missouri,
Columbia, Missouri

A Textbook Published by and for the
NATIONAL INSTITUTE
for Commercial and Trade Organization Executives. Founded in 1921. Conducted under the auspices of Chamber of Commerce of the United States, American Chamber of Commerce Executives, American Trade Association Executives, Northwestern University.

Compiled Under Supervision of Textbook Advisory Committee

GEORGE W. CATTS, Chairman
Executive Manager
The Chamber of Commerce of Kansas City
Kansas City, Missouri

RALPH BRADFORD
International Vice President
Chamber of Commerce of the United States
Washington, D. C.

JOHN C. BEUKEMA
Secretary-Manager
Greater Muskegon Chamber of Commerce
Muskegon, Michigan

WILLIAM H. BOOK
Executive Vice President
Chamber of Commerce
Indianapolis, Indiana

BEN B. LAWSHE
Manager, Commercial Organization Department Chamber of Commerce of the United States
Washington, D. C.

S. SPENCER SHAW
Manager, Northern Central Division Chamber of Commerce of the United States
Chicago, Illinois

Contributing Editors

JOHN C. BEUKEMA
Secretary-Manager
Greater Muskegon Chamber of Commerce
Muskegon, Michigan

WILLIAM H. BOOK
Executive Vice President
Chamber of Commerce
Indianapolis, Indiana

D. W. CAMPBELL
General Manager
Chamber of Commerce
Long Beach, California

SCOTT R. DeKINS
Vice President and Assistant General Manager
Chamber of Commerce
St. Louis, Missouri

CARL R. DORTCH
Director, Bureau of Governmental Research
Chamber of Commerce
Indianapolis, Indiana

LLOYD FOSTER
Executive Vice President
Chamber of Commerce
Birmingham, Alabama

R. H. GODDARD
General Secretary
Chamber of Commerce
Worcester, Mass.

DWIGHT B. HAVENS
Manager
Chamber of Commerce
Rochester, Minnesota

MARVIN HURLEY
Assistant General Manager
Chamber of Commerce
Houston, Texas

BEN B. LAWSHE
Manager, Commercial Organization Department
Chamber of Commerce of the United States
Washington, D. C.

ALFRED McVAY
Secretary-Manager
Chamber of Commerce
Walla Walla, Washington

LESTER MILLIGAN
Secretary
Chamber of Commerce
Mason City, Iowa

FRANK K. SHAW
Industrial Engineer
Atlanta Chamber of Commerce
Atlanta, Georgia

FRED E. SPERLING
General Secretary
St. Paul Association of Commerce
St. Paul, Minnesota

RAY H. WEISBROD
Executive Director
Milwaukee Association of Commerce
Milwaukee, Wisconsin

Copyright 1951 by National Institute for
Commercial and Trade Organization Executives
832 First National Bank Building, Chicago, Illinois

Ben B. Lawshe

*This book
is dedicated to*

Ben B. Lawshe

WHO HAS SERVED FAITHFULLY FOR MANY YEARS ON THE FACULTIES OF NATIONAL INSTITUTE AND THE REGIONAL INSTITUTES THROUGHOUT THE UNITED STATES.

HIS WISE COUNSEL AND SYMPATHETIC UNDERSTANDING HAVE HELPED MANY CHAMBER OF COMMERCE EXECUTIVES TO BETTER SERVE THEIR ORGANIZATIONS AND THEIR COMMUNITIES.

FOREWORD

This textbook on Chamber of Commerce administration will be more helpful to the student if he understands how it has been written. Many present-day Chamber executives have contributed manuscript material as contributing editors, while others, during the last quarter of a century, have unknowingly made valuable contributions through their work and experience. This textbook first was published by the National Institute in 1927 and completely revised in 1942.

A Textbook Advisory Committee was created in January, 1948, by the Board of Managers of the National Institute and charged with the responsibility of rewriting the 1942 edition in the light of present-day conditions. Fifteen experienced Chamber of Commerce executives of proven ability were asked by this committee to provide material for various chapters as contributing editors. S. G. Wennberg, Professor of Marketing, School of Business and Public Administration, University of Missouri, was retained by the committee to edit this material into textbook form effective for teaching purposes.

The manuscripts of the contributing editors were reviewed by two or more members of the Textbook Advisory Committee before being turned over to the Editor together with written comments by the reviewers. In order to eliminate duplication and provide uniformity, Professor Wennberg rewrote most of the material furnished by the contributing editors.

The Editor's manuscript, as prepared for the publisher, was then reviewed in its entirety by Ben B. Lawshe, Manager of the Commercial Organization Division of the Chamber of Commerce of the United States. Such minor changes as seemed advisable to Mr. Lawshe and to the Chairman of the Textbook Advisory Committee then were made before the copy was given to the publisher.

This textbook is primarily for the student of Chamber of Commerce administration who has had little or no experience. To the seasoned manager it may seem elemental, and a mere outline of what might be developed on a given subject. The book will find its greatest use in the National Institute and the various regional institutes for Chamber of Commerce executives. It is expected that instructors using this book will greatly expand the various subjects by lectures. Not all phases of a given subject are covered, and it is reasonable to expect that before this 1951 edition is revised new techniques in Chamber of Commerce administration will have been discovered.

This third edition of Chamber of Commerce Administration is a complete revision of the 1942 edition edited by Marvin Hurley, then General Manager of the Chamber of Commerce of Lincoln, Nebraska, and now Assistant General Manager of the Chamber of Commerce of Houston, Texas. Those familiar with the 1942 edition will recognize the contribution which it has made to the new edition. The work of Mr. Hurley and his associates is gratefully acknowledged.

Sources of material have included former editors, manuscripts furnished by contributing editors, courses presented at the National and regional institutes, reports of the American Chamber of Commerce Executives annual meetings, proceedings of the Southern Association of Chamber of Commerce Executives, the Commercial Organization Department of the Chamber of Commerce of the United States, and reports and publications of commercial organizations throughout the country. It has not seemed practical to indicate the sources of specific material. Rather, we have followed the accepted practice among Chamber of Commerce executives that experiences and ideas of one person are available to all others in the profession.

The student should not be disturbed if he finds his instructor differing from views expressed in Chamber of Commerce Administration. While this book expresses the views of experienced executives and the majority opinion of successful Chamber of Commerce managers, it is expected that some good instructors may differ from these views. Such differences should stimulate discussion and thinking on the part of the students.

Duplication of material in different chapters has been avoided insofar as possible. Chapter XII on governmental affairs and Chapter XIII on civic activities are closely related.

These two chapters were first combined by the Editor under the caption, "Civic and Governmental Affairs", but later separated by the Textbook Advisory Committee into two chapters so that the material would be better adapted to institute instruction.

The members of the Textbook Advisory Committee express their appreciation to the many who have contributed to the 1951 edition of Chamber of Commerce Administration. We are especially indebted to Professor S. G. Wennberg who edited this book, to the School of Business and Public Administration, University of Missouri which gave sympathetic encouragement in this work because of its contribution to the public good, to the contributing editors, and to Marvin Hurley and his associates who published the 1942 edition.

If this book helps a struggling Chamber of Commerce executive to meet some of his daily problems, if it contributes toward the improvement of Chamber of Commerce management, it will have served its purposes.

GEORGE W. CATTS, *Chairman*
Textbook Advisory Committee

Chamber of Commerce of Kansas City
Kansas City, Missouri
January 1, 1951

TABLE OF CONTENTS

FOREWORD 7-9

Chapter I

The Organization

HISTORICAL ORIGIN: Origin of the term; early American chambers; the modern chamber evolves 17
THE MODERN CHAMBER: Flexibility; dynamic character; fundamental principles; trade associations and chambers of commerce 21
PRINCIPLES OF ORGANIZATION: Articles of association; constitution and by-laws 23
ORGANIZATION STRUCTURE: Membership; board directors; elected officers; committees; manager and his staff; departments; subordinate and affiliated organizations ... 26
SUMMARY 32

Chapter II

Program of Work

PLACE AND FUNCTION: Program fundamentals; policies in program building; types of projects 34
BUILDING THE PROGRAM OF WORK: Opportunist plan; program-of-work committee; projects committee; president's conference; round table method; referendum method; operating manual 38
MECHANICS OF PROGRAM PREPARATION: Record and analysis of suggestions; writing the program; formal adoption and publicity 46
USE OF PROGRAM OF WORK: Program follow-up; performance 49
SUMMARY 51

Chapter III

Meetings

PLACE AND FUNCTION OF MEETINGS: Make possible membership participation; develop thought and judgment; uncover and develop leadership; serve as medium of communication; meetings are newsworthy 52
PREPARING THE MEETING: Calling the meeting; checking attendance; cancelling meetings; place of meeting; physical arrangements; speakers; preparing the content .. 54

11

CONDUCTING THE MEETING: Introduction of members; assisting the chairman 60
AFTER THE MEETING: Minutes; follow through 62
SPECIAL PROBLEMS: Board of directors' meetings; annual meetings; general membership meetings; special meetings; luncheon and dinner meetings 64
SUMMARY 68

Chapter IV

Committees—Appointment and Management

TYPES OF COMMITTEES: Administrative and project; investigating and executing; standing and special; subcommittees 70
COMMITTEE PERSONNEL: Techniques of selection; appointment 73
THE CHAIRMAN: Board members as committee chairmen; appointment 75
COMMITTEE MEETINGS: Frequency; agenda and committee service; conduct; meeting the issue; reporting to the board 77
SUMMARY 80

Chapter V

Membership

PROBLEMS OF MEMBERSHIP: Prospect file; ethical standards; membership agreement 81
MEMBERSHIP RELATIONS: Assimilating the new member; billing methods; collecting unpaid dues; suspensions . 86
RESIGNATIONS: Letter of acknowledgment; personal follow-up; board action 88
MEMBERSHIP COMMITTEES AND CLUBS: Importance of membership committee; experience with membership clubs 89
MEMBERSHIP CONTESTS. ONE-DAY CAMPAIGNS. INTENSIVE CAMPAIGNS: Charting the campaign; organization structure and campaign leadership; campaign publicity; educational and speaking programs; subscription quotas; advance solicitation; building the team organization; assignment of prospects; training the worker; the worker's kit; kick-off meeting; report meetings; turning campaign into victory 91
SUMMARY 112
APPENDIX: CHARTING THE MEMBERSHIP CAMPAIGN 114

Chapter VI

Fiscal Operations

SOURCES OF REVENUE: Membership dues; special subscriptions; service charges and miscellaneous income; rents, club facilities and dining rooms; publications and directories; public funds 120
THE BUDGET: Preparing the budget 129
OTHER FINANCIAL POLICIES AND PRACTICES: Reserve fund; collection of income; control of expenditures; payment of bills 135
RECORDS AND REPORTS: Accounting records; audits and reports 139
SUMMARY 141

Chapter VII

Publicity

PURPOSES OF PUBLICITY: Merchandising the program; keeping members sold; promoting specific projects; advertising the community 143
FUNDAMENTALS OF GOOD PUBLICITY: Selection of audience; selection of appeals; selection of media; general principles 146
INTERNAL PUBLICITY: House organs; special bulletins; mail to members; reports 149
THE NEWSPAPER: Value of support; values in news; writing the copy; relations with the press 154
RADIO PUBLICITY: 158
PUBLIC RELATIONS: 159
COMMUNITY PUBLICITY: The product; scope of campaign; tourist promotion; convention activity 160
SUMMARY 165

Chapter VIII

Office Administration

ELEMENTS OF OFFICE MANAGEMENT: An example of efficiency 167

CONDITIONS FOR ECONOMY AND EFFECTIVENESS:
Quarters; office arrangement; equipment and supplies;
general appearance 169
COMMUNICATIONS: Personal contacts; telephone contacts
and practices; correspondence 171
FILES AND FILING METHODS: Requisite principles; bases
for filing systems; methods of filing; operating the filing
system; general rules 177
OFFICE ORGANIZATION, RULES, AND PROCEDURES:
Organization; personnel relations; miscellaneous rules
and regulations 181
SUMMARY 185

Chapter IX

Commercial Activities

RETAIL TRADE ACTIVITIES: Organizing for retail trade
activities; determining the retail trade area; analyzing
the retail market; retail trade promotion; meeting retail
competition; financing retail activities 186
WHOLESALE TRADE ACTIVITIES: Organizing and financing wholesale trade activities; wholesale trade areas;
wholesale trade promotion 198
FOREIGN TRADE ACTIVITIES: Sources of foreign trade
information; helping exporters and importers 203
SUMMARY 208

Chapter X

Industrial Activities

LOCATION FACTORS: Location factors can be developed;
community attitude; zoning and planning for industry .. 210
PLANNING INDUSTRIAL ACTIVITIES: The industrial
survey; making the survey; using the survey; the time
element; coordination with other agencies and programs .. 215
SERVICE TO ESTABLISHED INDUSTRY: Planning service activities; industrial relations; taxation and industry;
sales promotion; aid to marginal industry; aid to small
businesses; traffic bureau services; miscellaneous services . 220
DEVELOPING LOCAL INDUSTRY: Industrial financing
plans; incubator buildings; technical assistance; direct
sponsorship 224

ATTRACTING NEW INDUSTRY TO THE COMMUNITY:
Finding prospects; dealing with prospects; appealing to
prospects 226
SUMMARY: 231
APPENDIX: THE INDUSTRIAL SURVEY 231

Chapter XI

Agricultural Activities

DEVELOPING AGRICULTURAL ACTIVITIES: The informal committee; organizing for the program; building the program; financing the program 239
THREE MAIN ACTIVITIES: Town-farm gatherings; work with youth organizations; agricultural fairs and expositions 244
REPRESENTATIVE AGRICULTURAL PROGRAMS: Programs of small and medium-sized chambers; programs of large chambers 248
GENERAL FARM PROBLEMS 254
SUMMARY 254

Chapter XII

Governmental Affairs

THE EXPANDING ROLE OF GOVERNMENT: Needed: A Voice for Business 256
PROBLEMS OF LOCAL GOVERNMENT: The necessity for sound community development; the desire for public improvements; the selection of public personnel; social welfare and public relief; the tax problem; efficiency in government 258
THE NEED FOR FACTS: The role of the Chamber of Commerce; cooperating with public officials; informing the public 260
CITIZENS' CONSTANT INTEREST: Develop interest; rewards may not be spectacular; the value of routine interest; a word of warning 263
LEGISLATION—STATE AND NATIONAL: Forming a committee on legislation 265
SUMMARY 268

Chapter XIII

Civic Activities

DEFINITION: Why engage in civic activities; scope of civic activities; guides to participation in civic affairs; practical limitations in the civic field; things upon which success depends; actual results the final goal 270

PROCEDURE FOR CIVIC ACTIVITIES: Effective committee service; need for authoritative information; publicity for civic projects; ability to secure public support; responsibilities of the manager; cooperation with other agencies; organizing a project 277

PUBLIC WELFARE ACTIVITIES: Education; charity and character building; recreation; community chest; health and sanitation; housing 285

MUNICIPAL SERVICES. CITY PLANNING: Street Traffic 291

SAFETY ACTIVITIES: Traffic safety; industrial safety; public safety 296

TRANSPORTATION ACTIVITIES: Aviation; highways; local transportation; railroad, bus and truck service; postal service 297

SUMMARY 298

Chapter XIV

The Manager and His Job

THE JOB: The content of the job; as a career; salary; manager or assistant; how to get the job; should there be a contract? 300

THE MANAGER: Basic requirements; self-improvement; associations of executives 310

SOME PROBLEMS: Public speaking; calling on members; health 313

IN CONCLUSION 315

Chapter 1

The Organization

THE URGE to build cities is elemental. It is one of the oldest instincts of man, and it has persisted through the ages. Chambers of commerce are organized primarily to give expression to that instinct. Wide and varied as their activities are, their first and foremost function is to build the city by increasing its population, wealth, and standard of living.

Although of European origin, the modern chamber of commerce is esssentially an American institution. Its development and success in this country are solidly based on the fact that it fills an important place in our institutional structure. In a real sense, the chamber is an *epitome of the free enterprise system*. It incarnates the American idea of progress and growth. It provides the agency through which men may voluntarily pool their energies to accomplish collectively those things for the general welfare that no individual can do alone. And it affords a means for the development and expression of business opinion.

Chambers of commerce are basically *local institutions*. They embody, as no other agency, the urge for community progress. Their genius lies in organizing and directing the energies of those men in every community who believe that their city has a place in the sun and are determined to find that place. Chambers of commerce must necessarily have widely varied programs to serve the diversity of interests among their membership. But the prime purpose of the chamber is, and must always continue to be, the original objective of building the commerce and industry of the community.

To achieve that objective the chamber has two principal fields of activity:

1. Increasing the wealth and prosperity of the community by facilitating the growth of existing businesses and fostering new ones.

2. Employing the wealth thus created in establishing and improving the civic, educational and cultural facilities of the community in order to attract more business and industry.

The organization that fails to function in these particulars is not a true chamber of commerce. Moreover, it falls short of exploiting its greatest appeal to its members. A good chamber member is fundamentally a *city builder*. Whatever a member may expect from his chamber in the way of personal service or service to his type of business, his first demand is that it shall protect and develop the best interests of the community as a whole. His enthusiasms are centered and he finds his greatest personal satisfaction in performing those chamber services that help his city to grow and prosper, so that his business may grow and prosper.

HISTORICAL BACKGROUND

As long as commerce has existed, traders have probably banded together. The first purpose of their associations was, perhaps, that of seeking common protection against enemies and marauding bands of robbers. Later they established codes to govern the conduct of trade, and still later they attempted to exert influence on legislation. But these early associations of traders have little in common with the modern chamber of commerce which is, in fact, a twentieth century product.

Origin of the Term

The first known use of the term chamber of commerce occurred in Marseilles, France, where such an organization was established by the city council toward the close of the 17th century. The oldest chambers in the British Isles are those of Glasgow (1783), Edinburgh (1785), Leeds (1785), and Manchester (1794). It was not until 1881 that a chamber of commerce was established in London.

The imperial ambitions of Kaiser William I of Germany gave great impetus to the chamber of commerce movement in that country. Perceiving the usefulness of such organizations in promoting trade and training young men for commercial careers, especially overseas, Bismarck encouraged their establishment in principal German cities. Other European countries promptly followed Germany's example.

The European or continental chambers of commerce have, however, little in common with the modern American organization. Although they are associations of business men, they operate frequently as quasi-public agencies, vested with certain administrative and judicial powers with respect to trade. These powers may include establishment of codes governing commercial practice; arbitration of disputes; issuance of certificates of origin, price and value; promulgation of rules of navigation; and supervision over other commercial bodies. Under highly centralized governments, the chambers have been used as agencies for directing and controlling economic activity in behalf of the central planning authority. This was true, for example, in Nazi Germany where regional and local chambers virtually exercised powers of life or death over individual concerns.

The Early American Chambers

The oldest chamber of commerce on the American continent is that of the State of New York, organized in 1768 and chartered by King George III in 1770. The second oldest is the Charleston, S. C., chamber formed in 1773. The New Haven and Philadelphia chambers were organized shortly thereafter. By 1870, the number of local chambers had increased to forty.

The early American chambers, like their European prototypes, were associations of tradesmen organized for the protection and promotion of commerce. The establishment of the New York state chamber, for example, was a direct result of the obnoxious Stamp Tax Act, passed by Parliament in 1765. Forced to organize in self-defense to fight the act, New York tradesmen quickly perceived the advantages of such association. The statement on organization of the New York chamber declared:

"Mercantile societies have been very useful . . . for promoting and encouraging commerce, supporting industry, adjusting disputes relative to trade and navigation, and procuring such laws and regulations as may be necessary for the benefit of trade in general".

In their role as associations of businessmen the early chambers of commerce undertook to promote the sale of goods. They organized markets, made and enforced rules of trade, protected goods in transit, and even operated their own trading floors. But their activities were limited to those directly connected with commerce. The emergence of the chamber of commerce as a true community organization came much later as businessmen began to realize that their own prosperity depended upon the development of a prosperous, healthy and happy community.

The Modern Chamber Evolves

From 1890 on the growth of the chamber movement in the United States was rapid. In this year 1950 there are probably 4,000 such organizations in the country. The growth was, however, more than one of numbers. The chamber of commerce of today has little in common with the old "board of trade" and "booster club" of half a century or more ago. The change is more than one of refinement; the basic philosophy of chamber operations has changed.

Prior to 1912, most local chambers were primarily interested in attracting new industries to their community. Civic and commercial development took second place. Gradually chambers came to recognize that industrial growth was dependent on civic and commercial development as well. In fact, so much emphasis was placed on civic problems that many chambers began to assume the character of civic associations. Their membership was all-inclusive of every element in the community and their program was largely one of promoting public facilities. By 1925, it was perceived that chambers, in order to be true to their purpose, must remain primarily *business* organizations, and express the point of view of business. The importance of *balance* in the chamber of commerce program began to be recognized.

Another major change took place with the advent of the New Deal in 1933. Governmental affairs on federal, state and local levels became major items in the chamber of commerce program. The chamber became the interpreter of government to business and, conversely, of business to government. In this field of activity the chamber of commerce is assuming growing responsibilities and achieving increasing usefulness.

THE MODERN CHAMBER OF COMMERCE

The modern chamber of commerce has been variously defined. Among the more familiar definitions are:

> "Chambers of commerce are men working together to make their community a better place in which to live and make a living".
>
> "Chambers of commerce are organizations of the forward-looking citizens of a community—principally businessmen and women—interested in promoting the civic, commercial and industrial welfare of the community and in expressing business opinion".
>
> "Chambers of commerce are voluntary organizations of the business elements of a community and others who share their viewpoint, organized for the purpose of improving the conditions under which trade and industry are conducted and to promote the general welfare of the community".

Flexibility of the Chamber

Any definition of the chamber of commerce must be general rather than specific because chambers differ widely in organization and structure as well as in methods of operation and character of activities. Such diversity is explained by the fact that chambers are organized to meet local needs and local objectives which vary greatly based on such factors as size of the community, character of population, and nature of the local economy. A chamber of commerce in a rural community without industry necessarily operates along lines different from those of its metropolitan neighbor. The former, with a mixed merchant-farmer membership, may function through frequent membership meetings and confine its activities to farm-city relations. The latter, concerned with a far broader range of problems, may function through a board of directors and a highly developed committee organization. It may employ the services of a manager and a highly departmentalized staff.

Regardless of these differences in structure and program, both are true chambers of commerce in that they develop and express business opinion and concentrate their efforts on promoting the best interests of the community along civic, commercial and industrial lines. It is this flexibility of the modern chamber of commerce—its ability to adapt itself to any local circumstance—that is the great source of the chamber's strength and general appeal.

Dynamic Character of the Chamber

Chambers of commerce are not static organizations. They are highly dynamic, capable of meeting local emergencies as they arise, without sacrifice of regular functions. Their history has been one of constant modification to meet the demands of the new day without surrendering essential principle. The modern chamber is a highly skilled organization, with definite techniques embodying the same "know-how" in the field of community development as American industry and trade have achieved in the fields of production and distribution. Those who administer it, are rapidly attaining professional status.

Fundamental Principles

The first law of chamber operation is that it must be responsive to and reflect accurately the thinking of the local community, and particularly its business element. Like men, cities are individuals, each having its mode of thought and living. It is fundamental that each chamber should incorporate the spirit of its own community. Only in this way can it develop and retain public confidence and be useful.

Secondly, the chamber must provide a vehicle for the expression of community aims and aspirations. It must develop a program of activities and a committee structure to give effect to these aims and translate them into reality.

Third, it must always remain predominantly a business organization serving the business interests of the community. The chamber of commerce should refrain from attempting to speak for *all* people, for in that event it would lose its identity as the *voice of business*. This principle does not conflict with the generally accepted doctrine that the chamber must devote itself to community progress because enlightened business today knows that: *If it isn't good for the community as a whole, it isn't good for business.*

Trade Associations and Chambers of Commerce

Historically, trade associations trace their origin to the guild movement of the mediaeval period. Their growth in this country, beginning in 1890, has closely paralleled that of the chambers of commerce. The two institutions are, however, fundamentally different.

The trade association has been defined as "a voluntary non-profit organization of business competitors, usually in one branch of the manufacturing, distributing or service fields, the objective of which is to assist its members and its industry in dealing with mutual business problems in several of the following areas: accounting practices, business ethics, commercial research, industrial research, standardization, statistics, trade promotions, and relationships with government, labor and the general public".

The first distinguishing characteristic of the trade association is, therefore, that it generally draws its members from a single branch of industry or trade. A second distinction lies in the fact that the trade association renders specific services of a business character to its membership. In contrast to the chamber of commerce, it concerns itself only rarely with purely civic problems.

These distinctions should be kept clearly in mind because the public is sometimes confused about the functions of the two types of organization. It may demand trade association services of a chamber of commerce which is not equipped to render them. Or a trade association may embark on a program of community betterment that lies more properly in the chamber field.

Chambers are frequently called upon to organize local trade groups that are to function through committees served by the chamber staff. The practice is especially common in communities where the trade group is too small to stand alone and must rely on the chamber for support. Many chambers have, for example, well-organized groups of retailers in various lines—such as clothing, department or variety stores—that operate as trade associations under chamber *imprimatur;* i. e., with the chamber providing necessary staff and facilities. Generally speaking, however, chambers should refrain from intruding in the field of organized trade groups unless there are compelling reasons for doing so.

PRINCIPLES OF ORGANIZATION

There are two types of chamber of commerce organization: the corporate form and the non-incorporated voluntary association. From a legal point of view, the voluntary associations are partnerships. The members assume, therefore, partnership liabilities for anything the chamber does; i. e., they may be held responsible for its debts. Hence, this type of chamber organization is usually found only in small and quasi-rural communities.

Metropolitan chambers are almost without exception organized as corporations, usually as non-profit corporations. The statutes of all states make provisions for the organization of such corporations and define the fields in which they may operate. Non-profit corporations are customarily granted certain privileges and immunities, the most important of which are exemptions from state corporation and income taxes. On the other hand, their powers are strictly circumscribed. The chamber that wishes to enjoy the immunities of a non-profit corporation must, therefore, be careful to operate within the limits of the authorization granted it.

Ever since the first Revenue Act, chambers of commerce have also been exempted from the payment of federal income taxes. The rule is, however, subject to certain limitations. The Bureau of Internal Revenue has held that the true character of an organization must be determined from the activities in which it is engaged and not from its name. Hence, the mere fact that an organization calls itself a chamber of commerce does not necessarily relieve it of tax liability. The Bureau has further held that an organization which engages in business ordinarily carried on for profit, is not exempt even though its income is only sufficient to make the business self-sustaining. A chamber of commerce that operates a credit bureau or a traffic department from which it has income, may therefore endanger its tax-exempt status. In ruling thus, the Bureau proceeds on the principle that these activities compete with services offered by private enterprise operated for profit and subject to taxation. Furthermore, a chamber of commerce cannot spend a substantial part of its revenues for the purpose of influencing legislation or engage in other overt political activity without becoming taxable. As long as a chamber of commerce operates strictly within its own field, however, it will remain tax exempt under the Federal Revenue Act.

Articles of Association

In order to incorporate a chamber it is necessary to file so-called *articles of association* with the secretary of state or other state official, as provided by statute. An attorney should be employed for this purpose.

The articles of association usually specify the name of the association, the purpose for which it is organized, principal office or place of business, resident agent, term of existence, names of incorporators, numbers of trustees or directors and their names, qualifications for membership, and such other *minutiae* as the statute may require. When approved the articles of association virtually constitute the charter under which the chamber operates.

Constitution and By-Laws

At the organization meeting it is necessary to adopt a constitution and by-laws. In recent years there has been a tendency for chambers of commerce to dispense with the constitution, or basic organization agreement, and to employ the by-laws to define the character, purpose and methods of operation of the chamber.

Where both are used the constitution should state the name of the organization, its object, the character of its membership and the nature of its government. It should make provisions for annual and special meetings, define fiscal powers, provide for referenda and amendments, and lay down other fundamental principles of the organization. The by-laws, on the other hand, should define the methods by which these principles are to be achieved and safeguarded. They should deal with such matters as membership qualifications, dues, resignations and expulsions; methods of voting; election of directors; methods of filling vacancies; officers and their duties; bonding requirements; committees; meetings of the board of directors, quorum; fiscal year; audits; amendments and the like.

By-laws should not be too rigid. They should constitute the framework of the edifice, not the entire building. The board of directors should be given wide powers to establish policies. The board that finds itself continuously hampered by checks and balances, cannot operate effectively. Too rigid by-laws must result in loss of the flexibility that has always been the hallmark of the successful chamber of commerce.

ORGANIZATION STRUCTURE

The organizational structure of the chamber of commerce comprises many parts, each of which has its place and function. Among the most important are: the membership, the board of directors, the officers, the chamber committees, and the manager and his staff. The present section will discuss each of them briefly.

Membership

One of the foremost problems of the chamber of commerce is that of building a sound membership structure. In a real sense, the membership *is* the chamber of commerce. Chamber membership is normally open to all "forward-looking citizens" of the community. But this principle has its limitations. Thirty years ago the strength of a chamber was frequently measured by the size of its membership; i. e., by the ratio of members to the total population of the community. Accordingly, many a chamber launched intensive and indiscriminate membership campaigns. Many a small businessman who had not the slightest concept of what a chamber of commerce was like or how it functioned, was persuaded to join—often under duress—only to drop out in a year or two with dues unpaid.

Here are a few acid tests that should be applied to every membership application:

1. The applicant should be able to afford such a membership.
2. He should be able to contribute something in addition to his dues; i.e., he should be able and willing to think and act constructively on community problems.
3. He should be in a position to benefit from the chamber's efforts. Such benefits need not necessarily be direct; they may also be the indirect benefits that accrue to every business through the growth and progress of the community.

The chamber should strive for a balanced membership. This implies a proper ratio between corporate and individual members. Generally speaking, a chamber is strongest when from 50 to 60 per cent of its dues income comes from corporate support; i. e., from the principal business institutions of the community. Such support usually takes the form of a single, continuous subscription—part of which may be applied to pay the dues of the principal officers of the corporation at the individual dues rate. The balance goes to a so-called "activities fund" or "sustaining fund". This is only one of many devices employed to ensure equitable support—on the twin bases of ability to pay and benefits derived. The principal advantages of a substantial income from corporate sources are:

1. It provides the chamber with an assured income requiring a minimum of membership maintenance.
2. It reduces collection costs materially.
3. It helps sell the small businessman, who is more ready to subscribe when he knows that large enterprises are assuming their full share of support.

It is, however, equally important that the chamber should have a representative group of individual members among small businessmen, professional people and others. Without this group the chamber cannot be representative and truly the "voice of business" in the community. Furthermore, it is this group that must furnish the bulk of committee personnel to carry out the chamber's varied program of activities. The development of a balanced membership is, therefore, an important objective requiring constant study and effort.

As a democratic institution, the chamber door is normally open to everyone seeking affiliation. As a practical matter, however, there are occasions when a member is a liability rather than an asset. This is particularly true of those individuals and businesses that operate in a shadow zone; i. e., those whose operations are legally or ethically subject to question. Their affiliation may become a source of embarrassment—as, for example, the vendor of questionable securities.

Board of Directors

Much has been said and written on the subject of how the board of directors should be constituted and elected, but little unanimity of opinion has developed. Pope's couplet still applies:

"For forms of government let fools contest,
Whate'er is best administered is best."

Here are a few simple rules that are generally applicable:

1. The board of directors should be properly representative of the membership at large rather than dominated by particular cliques or groups.
2. The predominant interest of each board member should be the welfare of the community as a whole rather than that of special groups.
3. Board members should have sufficient prestige to command general respect.
4. They should combine the qualities of loyalty, vision, ability and sound judgment with willingness to serve.

A board should be neither too large nor too small. A median bracket may be a board of from 12 to 18 members. Small boards may act more expeditiously, but they often fail to reflect membership opinion, particularly on controversial issues. A large board tends to become a debating society. The size of the board is properly a matter of community preference, based on the need for giving proper representation to all interests that have something at stake.

Many chambers elect board members by or from trade groups. The practice has proven an effective method of ensuring each group some representation on the board. Generally speaking, however, it is not the best procedure. It may lead to the election of mediocre men with a limited community outlook. The fact that board members represent particular groups may result in log-rolling and the development of a program of activities aimed at promoting the special interests of these groups. If this should happen, the general program of the chamber must inevitably suffer. Selection of men on their individual merits has, by and large, proved to be the surest method of obtaining a board that will command the confidence of the community as a whole.

The directors should act collectively, and not as individuals. The director who interferes in administrative details, works directly with department heads rather than through the manager or, by his officiousness, hampers the manager in the discharge of his duty, is doing serious injury to the chamber.

The function of the board of directors is to direct; i. e., to determine policy. It is the legislative body of the chamber, and not its executive branch. A clear understanding should always exist between the board and the management as to what constitutes policy-making and what is administration. The board should scrupulously avoid interference in administrative detail. On the other hand, although the manager may and should recommend new policy whenever he thinks it needful, he should never initiate such policy without board approval.

The board of directors determines the program of work and authorizes special activities. It is also responsible for chamber finances, and its functions include consideration and approval of the general budget as well as the appropriation of funds for special purposes. The board either appoints or approves the selection of committee personnel. It devotes a considerable portion of its time to the review of committee reports and recommendations. It appoints the manager and approves the selection of department heads.

Board meetings are usually held monthly or fortnightly; sometimes as frequently as once a week. The by-laws of some chambers provide for an executive committee to function during the interim between board meetings. The executive committee is usually composed of the chamber officers and a few of the more active and representative directors.

Questions of policy are sometimes submitted by the board of directors to the membership, either at the annual meeting or by the referendum method. The by-laws should specify whether such referenda are binding on the board and, if so, the number or percentage of votes required to make them mandatory.

Elected Officers

The elected officers of the chamber of commerce are those common to most corporate organizations.. They include a president, one or more vice-presidents, a secretary and a treasurer. Their respective functions are those usually assigned to such officers.

The president presides at the meetings of the board of directors and the organization as a whole. He provides much of the direction, initiative and drive that are necessary to ensure that the chamber functions in such a way as to win popular support. He counsels frequently with the manager and makes necessary contacts with members, government officials, and others who have business with the chamber. He does his utmost to harmonize discordant elements. A sagacious, conscientious and devoted president is one of the best guarantees of successful chamber operation.

In large and complex organizations with two or more vice-presidents, each of them may assume responsibility for particular activities or departments. As a general rule, however, the main duty of the vice-president is that of acting for the president in his absence. The manager is often named secretary, holding the title of secretary-manager. In that dual capacity he keeps the records of the chamber as well as looks after its administration. The treasurer is frequently named chairman of the finance or budget committee.

Committees

Committees are the heart of the chamber organization. They are the agency through which projects are initiated and carried to completion. They are the means whereby the members are actively enlisted in chamber service. A chamber's strength and influence can usually be measured by the character of its committees and by the amount and quality of the work done by them.

A chamber of commerce uses both standing and special committees. They may be either administrative or project committees. Administrative committees are those concerned with the internal affairs of the chamber, such as the committee on committees, and the finance, membership, program of work and publicity committees. Project committees, on the other hand, are those engaged in various activities for community development such as retail promotions, conventions, local and state taxation, fire prevention, education, new industries and the like.

The Manager and His Staff

The manager, by whatever title he is known, is in charge of administration. He is responsible to the board of directors. Successful operation of the chamber depends largely upon his personality, vision, acumen and business ability. A board of directors, even though manned by the ablest men of the community, can devote only a limited amount of time to chamber affairs. The day-to-day operation of the chamber is the responsibility of the manager. His duties include such diverse functions as supervision of staff, service to committees, relation with the public and press, conduct of negotiations, and correspondence. Unless the manager is versed in the principles of chamber administration, is skilled in human relations, has the ability to motivate and inspire, and knows the possibilities of his community—its advantages and disadvantages—the chamber will falter and fail.

It is the manager's duty to see that the chamber is properly organized; that its by-laws are workable and in accordance with sound practice; that a program of work is developed and a committee organization is created to execute it; that regular meetings are held and that they are properly planned and productive. In short, it is his duty to see that the chamber functions. He supervises also the staff and establishes the duties and responsibilities of each department. He maintains close and cordial relations with the membership, and assists in recruiting for committee service those individuals who are most able to contribute to the chamber program. He serves the committees and the board of directors by delineating issues and supplying facts and analyses. He is careful, however, to refrain from making policy. He knows when to speak and when to be silent.

Departments

The organization of metropolitan chambers is frequently departmentalized. Each department renders highly specialized services to the membership and occasionally to the public at large. Among such departments are: traffic, industrial, research and statistics, wholesale distribution, retail credit, foreign commerce, tourist and resort, and several others. They are usually organized to meet specific needs and may be supported by special assessments on those who use their services. More often, however, the services are taken into consideration in fixing the general rate of dues to be paid by those members who may be expected to benefit from them. The departments are generally headed by specialists. For example, the head of the traffic bureau may be a man certified to practice before the Interstate Commerce Commission and the state public service commission.

Some of the smaller chambers may act as agents for the state by selling auto licenses, hunting and fishing licenses, and the like. The purpose is usually that of securing additional income.

Subordinate and Affiliated Organizations

Many chambers of commerce operate subordinate or affiliated organizations. Some include the local junior chamber of commerce as a divisional activity. Some have a women's division. Some have highly articulated trade bureaus serving groups of retailers, truckers and other mercantile or service groups.

The junior chamber of commerce has a rule that when a member reaches the age of 36 years, he must terminate his membership. Many chambers of commerce welcome the junior graduate into the senior body, usually with some ceremony. In a few cases they give a year's free membership as an inducement.

SUMMARY

1. The chamber of commerce has its origin in man's desire to build and improve his city, and thereby enlarge his own trade opportunities. It must remain true to this purpose.

2. Associations of men engaged in trade or manufacture have existed since the dawn of history, but the modern chamber of commerce is a relatively recent development.

3. There are two principal types of chambers of commerce, the American or voluntary association; and the Continental or quasi-governmental body.

4. Chambers of commerce are fundamentally community organizations, composed of business and professional men engaged in various lines of activity. They differ from trade associations in that the latter primarily serve a single line of trade and industry.

5. The four principal fields of activity of a chamber of commerce are commercial, industrial, agricultural and civic.

6. Chamber dues rates are predicated on the principle of "ability to pay". Hence the basic individual dues rate is usually supplemented by some form of sustaining fund, largely subscribed to by corporate members.

7. The chamber of commerce is customarily organized as a non-profit corporation. The by-laws should set forth the manner of government and mode of operation.

8. Boards of directors are legislative bodies. Administration is customarily vested in a paid executive who carries out policies established by the board.

9. Chambers function principally through committees, who also help to maintain liaison with membership.

10. A sound program of work is an essential part of chamber organization.

Chapter II

Program of Work

THE PROGRAM of work is the operations plan of the chamber of commerce. It is a schedule of today's activities in the light of tomorrow's needs. Because they operate in familiar fields, some organizations do not feel the need for a formalized program. But a progressive chamber breaks new ground every day. Because it is a leader rather than a follower, it is forever confronted with new problems and new tasks to be done. By programming its work the chamber seeks to ensure that its resources are allocated and its efforts are expanded in such a way as to serve the community best.

PLACE AND FUNCTION

A chamber of commerce needs to offer no excuse for the planning phases of its activities. A farmer, if he is a good farmer, plans his crops well in advance of planting time—sometimes planning the rotation of his crops for years in advance. A builder follows a set of plans in the construction of any type of structure. In the early days of highway construction, stretches of road were improved without any thought of their relationship to an overall program, but today every major highway job fits into a definite pattern. The schedule followed by a train or a plane is a plan. Likewise, planning is essential to efficient chamber of commerce operation.

The fundamental purpose of the program of work is to help the chamber of commerce fill a more useful place in the community. More specifically, it contributes toward this end-result, because:

    1. The program of work charts the future course of activity. By establishing guide posts, it directs the thinking and channels the energies of the chamber toward specific goals. And by weighing these goals, one against the other, it promotes balanced activity.

2. It furnishes a check-chart of performance. From year to year, the record of accomplishments may be checked against the established goals to measure progress.
3. It serves as a challenge to the membership to meet its obligations to the community. It helps, therefore, to mobilize the manpower of the community for definite accomplishments.
4. It helps to coordinate the activities of the membership for effective concerted action.
5. Properly evolved and agreed upon, it helps to sell the chamber to its membership and to the community at large.

Program Fundamentals

In the final analysis, the building of a program of work for a chamber of commerce is nothing more nor less than community planning. In building its program, the chamber must, therefore, have in mind the interests of the community as a whole. It must not allow itself to become a mere agent of minority groups and special interests. This must be the basic tenet of all program building.

There are other guide posts that are fundamental to successful program work. Some of these may be stated as follows:

1. As far as possible, the program of work should be based on a factual analysis of the community's needs and possibilities.
2. It should reflect sound judgment of values by giving emphasis to those projects of general interest for which the need is greatest and most urgent.
3. It should be flexible enough to accommodate change, and it should be revised periodically in the light of such changes.
4. It should be carefully prepared and presented so as to challenge leadership and hold the support of the community's citizenship.

Policies in Program Building

The by-laws of some chambers of commerce provide for a method of making out the program of work. Some of the methods in common use will be discussed later in this chapter, and some program fundamentals have been indicated, but it is advisable at this point to suggest some of the general policies to be observed in building the program:

1. Activities should be of a business or general community nature.
2. Work now being satisfactorily performed by other organizations should not be duplicated; but cooperation is not to be interpreted as duplication.
3. While a chamber of commerce is primarily a business organization, the social implications of business well-being must be recognized. Business will thrive permanently only where the people of the community live in a satisfactory environment. Consideration should be given, therefore, to all civic and social conditions which contribute to the general wholesomeness of community life.
4. Public issues are clearly within the field of interest of the chamber of commerce; but partisan, political or religious matters are not. Anything resembling partiality toward a special interest is to be avoided.
5. Activities which will encourage and assist local business should be undertaken; but it must be remembered that any community necessarily buys and sells in a large market, and the chamber of commerce program must be constructed accordingly.
6. As the representative of business, the chamber of commerce has no function when business itself is divided on an issue, unless the public interest is involved. Then it should take whatever position the public interest requires.
7. The work of the chamber of commerce is continuous, and projects are included in the program of work regardless of the time required for completion.
8. The financial requirements of a project should be taken into consideration before it is made a part of the program of work.
9. Although ideal in its conception, a project may be wholly impractical and therefore rejected. Only those activities which come within the scope of the chamber of commerce and for which there is reasonable expectation of substantial progress of a constructive nature, should be included.
10. The program of work should be adapted to the particular needs of the local community for the time anticipated in the program and should be subject to revision at least once a year.
11. In order that it may present a complete outline of the activities of the chamber of commerce, the program should include recurring activities as well as those planned for some definite time.
12. The program of work should, on the other hand, be as short as possible and still be comprehensive. The number of projects undertaken at any one time should be kept within the limits of the organization's resources for investigation and effective result-getting action.

A city is not built in a day—nor in a decade. In fact, a community is never completed. There is always something to do; and the number of tasks that need doing is likely to exceed by far the capacity of even the strongest chamber. Selection becomes therefore necessary. The program of work should be based on that understanding.

In selecting projects for the program of work, the first measure should be "need". If there is not a real need for it, leave it out. If there is a need, however, then next consideration should be given to the "purpose". Is the proposed activity for which there is a real need, consistent with the functions of the chamber of commerce? If it is, then use a third measure: its "scope". Does the proposed activity, which is consistent with the purpose of the chamber of commerce and for which there is a need, come within the proper scope of the organization's activities? Or does it more properly fall within the scope of some other organization or community agency? If all projects proposed for the program of work are measured by the yardsticks of "need", "purpose" and "scope", a workable program should result. There are, of course, practical limitations that must also be kept in mind. Are the financial resources and the man power of the chamber of commerce in condition to undertake the activity and with reasonable assurance of success?

Types of Projects

Two broad divisions of chamber of commerce activity should be kept in mind in building the program of work. They are: (1) *internal activities* and (2) *external activities*.

The internal activities have to do with the maintenance of the organization itself. They include such functions as the maintenance of membership, supervision of finances, conduct of elections, and appointment of committees. They are of no value either to the members or to the public except as they contribute to the strength of the body through which the outward forms of service are rendered.

The external activities include all projects that are concerned with the requirements and the welfare of individual members, the membership as a whole and the general public. Obviously, it is the external activities that measure the true value of a chamber of commerce. But that does not mean that the internal activities are less important. It may be by his head and his hands that a man earns his living; but he should not, on that account, neglect his stomach.

Four groups of external activities may be differentiated:

1. Commercial activities
2. Industrial activities
3. Agricultural activities
4. Civic and governmental activities

For the purpose of planning the program, these groups may again be subdivided. There is, however, no standard pattern for further classification. The classification adopted by a particular chamber in constructing its program of work and the emphasis given to each subdivision should reflect local conditions and needs.

BUILDING THE PROGRAM OF WORK

The success of a chamber in building its program of work must depend in part on the method employed. There are innumerable ways of building a program, however, and there seems to be no one method that is best for all chambers and in all circumstances. Rather, a particular chamber should seek to find and use that method which best meets the needs of its organization and the conditions under which it operates. Some of the most commonly used methods are discussed in the following paragraphs.

Opportunist Plan

When this plan is used, the chamber of commerce has no formal program of work. It merely keeps its eyes open for worthwhile, needed services as they become apparent from time to time. Whenever it sees an opportunity to do something constructive, it seizes upon it.

There is no question but that this plan is the simplest. In the past it has been the most commonly used method. Moreover, during periods of emergency when it is impossible to anticipate the legitimate demands that will be made on the chamber, it becomes necessary to follow this plan to some extent, no matter what other method may have been adopted by the organization.

Under the opportunist plan, responsibility for the program rests with the board of directors. Whenever the president or the manager brings to the board of directors an issue or a project that appeals to that body, the board refers it to the appropriate committee for action.

Sometimes a new undertaking of first importance may develop within one of the committees. It becomes then the duty of the committee to report the facts developed and its suggestions to the board of directors, asking either for the board's instructions or that the matter be referred to a more appropriate committee.

The weaknesses of the opportunist plan are not far to seek. Because there is no consistent and organized effort to develop a cohesive program, the activities of the chamber may become haphazard and unbalanced. Important issues may be entirely overlooked; or they may not be brought to the attention of the board of directors until they have become acute problems. As a result of the failure to plan ahead, the board may find itself unable to deal with new, vital issues because the resources of the chamber have already been fully committed.

In spite of these weaknesses, the opportunist plan may work fairly satisfactorily whenever an organization is well established and thoroughly alive in all its parts. Moreover, whether or not it relies primarily on this method, every chamber of commerce is somewhat of an opportunist. It deals with current problems. It must be quick to recognize and act upon new issues as they arise.

Advantages	Disadvantages
It is so simple that little time or energy is consumed in making a program.	The program is largely determined by a small group of individuals.
It leaves practically the entire resources of the organization to be devoted to performance.	Little time or thought is devoted to the program; mistakes in judgment may be expected.
It results in a timely program.	The organization may be led into a course of action to which the majority of the members do not subscribe.
	A program developed in this way has a tendency to be short sighted and unbalanced.

Program of Work Committee

Under this plan a program of work committee is appointed some time in advance of the beginning of each new year. It is the responsibility of the committee to develop and recommend a complete program of activities for the coming year. In so doing it may follow any number of procedures.

The committee may make up the program on the basis of present commitments plus suggestions that are developed in the course of its study. In some departmentalized organizations, each department may be asked to submit its recommended program for the year ahead. These recommendations are carefully evaluated, and the projects selected by the committee are coordinated and incorporated in the overall program.

On the other hand, the committee may develop a tentative program on its own initiative and then submit it to the various sub-divisions of the organization for comments. Still another way is to send a questionnaire or invitation for suggestions to the entire membership. In some cases, suggestions may even be solicited from the public at large through newspaper publicity. Whatever procedure is adopted, however, responsibility for developing and recommending a program for approval by the board of directors, rests with the committee.

Advantages	*Disadvantages*
It permits the use of those who are particularly well qualified to help plan the program of work.	If not carefully handled, the plan may be open to the criticism that a "clique" develops the program of work.
It enables thorough consideration of each suggestion.	A poorly selected committee may burden the organization with a poorly planned program.
There is little chance of overlooking important projects.	The committee may have a tendency to let itself be influenced by self-interest groups.
A well-balanced program may be expected.	Because commitments are made at the beginning of the year and because the plan does not provide machinery for periodic review of the program throughout the year, the program may lack flexibility and timeliness.

Projects Committee

Under this plan, the development of the program of work is a continuous activity. The projects committee is responsible for following and studying the changing needs of the community, and for evaluating the activities of the chamber in the light of those needs. On the basis of such studies it recommends new projects or modifications in the existing program of activities.

Because its work is continuous, the committee is in a position to approach the survey of community needs in an organized and orderly manner, and to develop the facts on which a sound program of work may be built. By seeking counsel and by drawing into conference various groups of citizens, the committee may develop a program that is broad and fundamental.

The recommendations of the projects committee are made to the board of directors for approval and assignment to working committees for execution. There may be times when the board elects to submit various recommendations to a referendum of the membership.

Advantages	*Disadvantages*
This plan recognizes that program building is a continuous problem.	The plan may seem to relieve other groups and individuals of their responsibility for concerning themselves with community issues and program building.
It provides machinery for careful study and evaluation of all projects to be undertaken.	
New needs and issues are likely to be uncovered early as they arise, and no important problem is likely to be overlooked.	It may lead to an over-emphasis on planning with a consequent neglect of performance.
	Because the program changes gradually by accretions, it lacks "news-value" and does not lend itself to publicity.
The plan is likely to appeal to the best minds of the community.	

President's Conference

At the beginning of the year, as soon as the new committees are formed, the president may call a conference of his committee chairmen and fellow officers. The purpose of the conference is to determine the program of work for the ensuing year.

The success of this method depends to a considerable extent on the care with which preparations for the conference are made. Prior to the meeting, the president and the manager should go over the list of committees for the purpose of determining what, in their opinion, are the major activities of each. Each chairman should be asked to prepare a proposed program for his committee and to be ready to express his views on other important activities in which he believes the organization should engage.

The conference should be held at an hour when discussion will not be hurried. Every attempt should be made to secure complete attendance. Skillful handling on the part of the president as chairman of the meeting is required to ensure success of the plan. The manager, acting as secretary for the conference, should record all suggestions for each committee—good, bad or indifferent.

The next step is a meeting of the officers, sometimes referred to as the president's cabinet. This meeting should take place within a few days after the conference, so that the various phases of the discussion will be fresh in mind. At this meeting, each member should be supported with a roster of the proposed projects, listed according to possible committee assignments. It then becomes the responsibility of the president's cabinet:

1. To select and designate a limited number of important projects as the chamber's major program for the year.
2. To assign at least one major project to each committee, and as many other jobs as may be considered advisable.

Only in unusual cases should any activity, proposed and agreed to in conference, be abandoned—and then only for good reason. The cabinet may, however, decide that certain important activities were overlooked by the conference, and incorporate them in its proposed program. The final step is the adoption of the program of work by the board of directors.

Advantages

The plan ensures that the committees which are responsible for carrying out the program, have an important part in making it.

If sufficient time is given to the conference, the plan permits careful weighing of all activities, one against the other, and thorough discussion by diverse interests.

The plan ensures that each committee will have one or more major assignments.

It stimulates enthusiasm on the part of committee chairmen for the program of the chamber.

Disadvantages

The plan requires time and patience.

Unless the president is an exceptionally capable chairman, the conference meetings may drift with the result that important proposals receive only inadequate consideration or no consideration at all.

Unless several conferences are held during the year, there will neither be sufficient check on progress nor opportunity to revise the program.

The conference plan is a popular method of building a program. In organizations with several departments and many committees, however, it is likely to be somewhat unwieldy. Even in smaller organizations, more than one meeting is usually required to develop a sound program. And in order to check on progress and keep the program timely, it is desirable that several conferences should be called during the year.

Round Table Method

The purpose of the round table plan is to bring as many members as possible into active participation in program building. Accordingly, the membership is divided into groups, and group meetings are held at which plans and programs are discussed. In order to ensure that the discussion at each meeting will be as broad as possible, the division of the membership into groups should be at random and without regard to vocation or interests. As a general rule, no group should have more than forty members.

The plan requires considerable time and advance planning. It is advisable to select a number of experienced chamber members to act as chairmen of the meetings. These men should be thoroughly briefed on the purpose and method of conducting the meetings.

At each meeting the chairman should explain its purpose, and the president or manager should be present to discuss the work of the chamber. The meeting should then be thrown open for general discussion, and each participant should be invited to state his ideas. Successful handling of this roundtable portion of the meeting requires tact and skill. Unless the chairman is able to control the meeting, the discussion is likely to wander aimlessly rather than to contribute constructive suggestions and analyses. A carefully planned agenda should prove helpful in guiding the discussion. Inasmuch as the meetings are intended to be purely advisory, the adoption of resolutions should be discouraged.

At the conclusion of a meeting, each member should be asked to write his suggestions on a signed memorandum bearing two or more questions, such as:

1. What do you expect the chamber of commerce to do in order to serve your branch of industry, trade or profession?

2. What, in your opinion as a citizen, is the thing of first importance that the chamber should do for the good of the community as a whole?

The suggestions secured by the questionnaire as well as those made verbally during the meeting must, of course, be classified, analyzed and evaluated. They constitute, however, the raw materials from which the president, his cabinet or some committee appointed for that purpose may construct a program of work.

Advantages	*Disadvantages*
The plan brings the greatest possible number of members into active participation in program building.	The plan is unwieldy for the larger organizations although it may work successfully in the smaller chambers.
It encourages free discussion of issues by all members.	It is difficult to find men capable of acting as chairmen of group meetings. A badly conducted meeting may do far more harm than good.
It promotes understanding on the part of the membership of the chamber, its functions, strength and limitations.	
It helps to sell the chamber and its program to the membership. It helps to develop leadership for the organization because of the training and experience gained by those who preside at the meeting.	The plan requires an undue amount of time for developing the program—time that might better be spent on the projects themselves.
It aids in developing a program that is attuned to membership thinking.	

Referendum Method

The referendum method is frequently used in conjunction with one of the plans already discussed. Used in this manner, it should perhaps be regarded as a device for securing suggestions and ferreting out membership attitudes, rather than as an independent method of program building. In some cases, however, so much emphasis is placed on the referendum as an element in program making that its designation as a separate plan may be justified.

Under this plan the board of directors or the officers of the organization prepare a tentative program which is sent to the members with the request that they vote on the suggestions offered. The members are also encouraged to submit any ideas they may have for chamber activities. The final program is constructed largely in terms of the opinions and preferences expressed by the referendum.

This method may encourage participation in program building by some members who might not otherwise have concerned themselves with chamber activities. There is reason to doubt, however, whether many of the votes cast in such a referendum represent a great amount of thought on the part of the members. It is also common experience that a substantial portion of the membership will refrain from voting at all.

Advantages	Disadvantages
The plan affords every member an opportunity of expressing his opinion.	If the referendum is long, it will not be read; if it is short, it may not afford sufficient information to permit intelligent voting.
It may therefore give a broad indication of the lines along which the thinking of the membership is running.	Unless supplemented by some other method, the plan will hardly provide sufficient thought and planning to ensure a sound, balanced program.
It may uncover definite needs which the officers of the chamber have overlooked.	

The Operating Manual

The plans discussed so far have to do with external activities. There should also be a program for internal activities. Such a program serves to guide the daily operations of the chambers. Once prepared, it helps to reduce lost motion and to give the executive better control over his organization.

Policies and operating rules governing many internal activities may be found scattered throughout such diverse sources as the by-laws of the organization, minutes of board meetings, resolutions adopted by the membership, and policy statements and operating directives issued by the president or the manager. Policies and operating rules relating to other activities may never have been clearly defined. They need to be formalized and reduced to written statements. And all of these matters should be brought together and made available in convenient form in a comprehensive operating manual.

Such an operating manual should cover all important internal activities of the chamber. There should, for example, be a section on finances relating to such matters as budgeting, procedures on income and expenditures, follow-up procedures on collections, preparation of financial statements, and audits. Another section might set forth personnel policies and employment practices. In short, the manual should provide a complete guide for the management of all important internal functions of the organization.

MECHANICS OF PROGRAM PREPARATION

Whatever method or combination of methods is used in developing the program of work, the quality of the final product will depend on the care with which each successive step in the program-making process is performed.

Record and Analysis of Suggestions

A careful record should be made of every program suggestion. A systematic procedure is that of typing a separate card for each suggestion as the proposals are received from various meetings or from a referendum. A standard 3″ x 5″ card will be found convenient. Because it may indicate a particular shade of meaning, the member's exact wording should as far as possible be followed. If one member has made a number of suggestions, a separate card should be used for each. The source of the suggestion and the date on which it is made should always be noted on the card.

The suggestions recorded in this manner should be analyzed not only prior to the adoption of the program for the year, but also from time to time throughout the year. By so doing it is possible to keep the program timely and abreast of membership thinking.

For the purpose of such analysis, the suggestion cards should be sorted into piles of identical or related proposals. This will usually develop the fact that there are several projects in which a large number of members are interested. In addition, there will be a considerable number of undertakings which have been noted by several members, but which are apparently of less popular or general interest. Trailing down from these will be small "stacks" of suggestion cards proposing activities of still less popular interest, until finally there is a group of miscellaneous proposals each of which is suggested by only one or a very few members.

After the sorting process is completed, the next step is classification of the proposed projects. In smaller chambers that are not highly departmentalized, it may be sufficient to classify the suggestions into three groups:

1. Activities for which there is a general demand.
2. Projects of fundamental merit, the need for which is understood by an alert minority, but for which there is not yet popular demand.
3. Activities of less fundamental merit suggested by a limited number of members or by a sectional group.

Because of their popularity, the first group of projects should be considered for immediate adoption. They might well become the major program of the chamber. In spite of their merit, it may be advisable to postpone adoption of the second group of projects until their need is more generally understood. If postponement is decided, these projects might well be included in the forum or discussional program of the chamber. In this way, the merits of the projects may be brought to the attention of the membership at large. The third group, if included in the program at all, should be considered supplementary activities of minor or sectional importance.

In larger and more highly departmentalized organizations, the proposed projects may be further classified according to the division or department under which they most logically fall. In so doing, care should be exercised to ensure that a particular department is not overloaded with work. As a general rule, each department should have but one major project during the year in addition to the recurring activities that are considered the regular functions of the department.

The time factor is another basis for significant classifications, the proposed projects may be further classified accord be completed within the chamber's program year, and others that may require several years. The adoption of long-term projects means, of course, a serious commitment of finances and resources. Moreover, although no project should be rejected merely because it cannot be completed within the year, it is important that the program should contain several activities that can be so concluded. Completions are, of course, far more spectacular than mere progress, however significant and steady. Hence, it is probably true that members—and the public at large—tend to measure the success of the chamber by the number of successful completions, rather than in terms of the progress made on long-range projects.

Writing the Program

In writing the program, the virtues of good English, careful expression and exact statements should not be forgotten. This is particularly important with respect to the major program. Perhaps no other single factor may contribute more to delays, waste of effort and loss of interest in committee work than the failure of the program to define clearly the exact nature of the project assigned. A good program should be short, but it should also be definite and practical. A good program should excite the imagination of men and set those who read it, to thinking about a truly greater city.

Formal Adoption and Publicity

When a proposed program has been completed and has been approved by the program of work committee, the president's cabinet or whatever agency has primary responsibility for program-making, it should be submitted to the board of directors for formal adoption. By such formal action, the organization puts itself on record as promising to undertake certain specific tasks during the program year. The sense of the significance of the program may also be maintained by presenting to the board each month a report on activities and accomplishments, and by publishing each quarter a summary of the monthly reports to the board.

The program of work should, as a rule, be given wide publicity among the membership. Whether it should also be given general publicity is for the individual organization to decide. Some chambers prefer to treat the program as an internal matter, seeking publicity only when projects are finally accomplished. Others believe that the general public deserves to be kept fully informed about the plans of the chamber, and that this policy helps to sell the chamber to the community. Among the results that may be accomplished by publicity are:

1. Members, as well as the general public, will have fuller and more definite information about what the chamber is doing than they otherwise could have.
2. Members of the several committees, who are already committed to doing their part of the program of work,

will have another incentive to deliver performance. Publicity furnishes a positive motivation by emphasizing the significance of the job to be done. Moreover, businessmen do not like to have fellow members and citizens generally know that they failed to do what they agreed to do.

Whether publicity is used or not, the program of work enables the president and the directors to check constantly the progress of major activities.

USE OF PROGRAM OF WORK

The development and adoption of a program of work is only a first, albeit important, step. In the final analysis the usefulness of a program must be measured in terms of the extent to which it contributes to purposeful, effective and balanced chamber activities.

Program Follow-Up

Whenever a committee attacks a new project, it should map its course of action by planning each successive step by which the task is to be accomplished. That is to say, each project becomes itself a starting point and a subject for a detailed subsidiary program of work. "Patterns of Progress", the series of experience-sharing reports published by the Commercial Organization Department of the Chamber of Commerce of the United States, provides excellent examples of specific projects that are worked out in detail. An organization may have a perfect program of work and a sound committee structure, but still fail because the campaign of action was not planned in detail.

For example, the program of work may include an item such as: "Sponsor a Fire Prevention Week Program". This is a specific project, but it means little unless it is broken up into detailed jobs such as: (1) getting mayor to proclaim "Fire Prevention Week"; (2) distribution of fire prevention week posters by fire marshall's office; (3) distribution of home inspection blanks to public schools; (4) station-break announcements for radio stations; (5) announcements for church bulletins; (6) speakers for civic clubs and women's organizations; (7) distribution of information through county and home demonstration agent's office; (8) public exhibit of fire department equipment; (9) regular press releases throughout campaign to all local newspapers and to local **organizations**.

This leads to the conclusion that the development of a program of work does not stop with a mere statement of over-all objectives. Each project must be broken down into its component parts, and the method of attack charted in detail. Each committee should be responsible for mapping this step-by-step procedure for its own projects. It is neither the purpose nor the responsibility of the program of work committee, or the board of directors, to undertake such detailed planning. Responsibility for planning as well as for execution must run through the entire organization.

The organization structure provides the machinery through which the program of work is translated into performance. In order to ensure maximum accomplishments it is, therefore, necessary that the organizational structure should itself be adapted to the tasks to be accomplished. Related activities should be properly grouped together. Lines of responsibility and authority should be clearly defined and thoroughly understood. The diverse elements of the organization must be fitted together in such a way as to eliminate overlappings, duplications and conflicts. The relationships of one organizational element to the others must be exactly stated and clearly understood. And finally, there must be a sharply defined "system" of operations.

Performance

Performance is the final test of the chamber management and the soundness of its program of work. Performance includes three elements: the results, the quality and the cost. The primary objective is to get results—to get the job done. But we may sometimes do a job and still fail in the performance of our mission. The mere fact that a project has been completed affords small reason for rejoicing if slipshod work makes the results of questionable value. Or again, the job may be done and the results may be thoroughly satisfactory; and yet the cost in manpower and money may be out of all reason. Successful performance depends, therefore not only on a sound program of work, but also on a capable organization and an effective system of operations. The management of any chamber of commerce must be constantly on the alert to determine how well the job is being done and how it can be done better.

"Never start something that cannot be finished" is as good a rule for a chamber of commerce as it is for individuals. Tasks which slumber and are forgotten have the brand of incompetence. It is all right to change one's mind occasionally—when convinced that one is wrong—but the habit of letting things slide is fatal. Because a program of work encourages prompt and businesslike performance, it is a necessary agency for effective chamber of commerce work.

SUMMARY

1. If a chamber of commerce is to meet its responsibilities of community leadership, it should have a definite program of work incorporating the best thought of the community and revised at least once each year.

2. A program of work furnishes a course of action and a check-chart of performance. It is a challenge to community responsibilities, brings new man power into the program, and coordinates the membership for effective action.

3. A program of work should be representative and carefully prepared, should take recognition of change and reflect good judgment, and should be based upon careful analysis of the community's needs and possibilities.

4. There are several effective ways of developing a program of work. One method may meet the need most effectively in some communities, while another may serve best in other communities.

5. The completed program should be short, definite, and practical. The schedule of projects should be kept separate from the internal program which guides operating details.

6. Once the program of work is adopted by the board of directors, it should be used in a way that will encourage the most effective results. Projects should be broken down into specific jobs.

Chapter III

Meetings

IT IS THE function of the chamber of commerce to organize and employ the abilities of its members and other public spirited citizens for the purpose of promoting projects of community interest. Much of the work of the organization is done in committee and other group meetings in which the members discuss the problems and opportunities of the community, pool their ideas and work together in order that their collective judgment may be made effective. The success of the meetings—and, consequently, the success of the chamber itself—must depend largely on the care and skill with which they are prepared and conducted. It is therefore essential that the manager should master the techniques of arranging and handling meetings so as to ensure their success.

THE PLACE AND FUNCTION OF MEETINGS

Perhaps more so than any other group, businessmen know the problems and difficulties of securing prompt, intelligent and decisive action through meetings. Group action is almost certain to be slow and ponderous. Discussions may wander or even degenerate into meaningless bickering. Members may be swayed by oratory—by specious arguments rather than by sound reasoning. The temptation to procrastinate and to "pass the buck" is always present. And even if a meeting arrives at sound conclusions, the task of translating them into action may still remain. Group action through meetings is, therefore, no panacea. Yet, such meetings have their place and function; and in an organization such as the chamber of commerce they come to be of paramount importance.

Meetings Make Possible Membership Participation

Meetings constitute one of the most important links between the chamber of commerce and its membership. They make it possible for the individual member to participate actively in the work of the organization. Such participation, in turn, stimulates interest and makes the member feel that he is "getting something" from the chamber. Meetings are the means by which the collective skills and judgment of the membership are brought to bear on community problems.

Meetings Develop Thought and Judgment

The collective knowledge and judgment of the group are superior to those of the individual. It has been said two heads are better than one; likewise, ten are better than two— if they are thinking and working toward a common goal. Meetings make group thinking possible. They serve as a catalyzer to stimulate the development of thought. A suggestion by one member may set off a chain of ideas in the minds of others. In the resulting exchange of views a wide range of experience and knowledge is brought to bear on the problem, and through a process of give and take all its ramifications are explored and evaluated. When finally there is a meeting of minds, the conclusions are likely to represent the best possible judgment of the group.

The decision of the group may be superior to that of an individual also in another respect. The individual is limited not only by the range of information at his command, but also by his inability to eliminate personal prejudice and preconceived notions from his thinking. In a group composed of men of independent minds it is possible to achieve a well-balanced consideration of a problem and to check the impulsive and hasty action that is so often the undoing of busy men. In each group there should be at least one man of the watch-dog type,—sure to be on his feet with an objection or a counter-argument whenever he believes some decision is being made without sufficient information or consideration.

Meetings Uncover and Develop Leadership

A chamber of commerce works in many fields. To do its work well it must command a wide diversity of skills and experience. Meetings make it possible to observe men at work, to learn something about their interests and capacities, and to find new leadership. Moreover, meetings afford the individual the opportunity of developing his leadership abilities. It may be true that the chamber of commerce is not primarily a leadership training institution. Its function is rather that of utilizing the available leadership for the welfare of the community. Nevertheless, the development of leadership capacity is an important by-product of organized effort. Through participation in group activity men acquire the ability to analyze problems and present their views in argument and counter argument. They learn how to get along with others, how to give and take, and how to lead. The chamber of commerce and the community are thereby the gainers.

Meetings Serve as a Medium of Communication

Information, plans or ideas can be conveyed by letter, report, telephone conversation or any other means of communication. A meeting, however, affords the opportunity for thorough discussion and explanation. Consequently, it may convey an idea or a body of information far more clearly than any other method of communication. Moreover, meetings may do more than merely impart stark information. They may engender enthusiasm and provide the inspiration needed to stimulate each member to go out and get his job done.

Meetings serve not only as a medium for communicating information from the chamber to the membership. They are equally effective in making the wishes of the membership known to the chamber management. They serve to develop new ideas to crystalize group thinking, and to achieve common policy on important issues.

Meetings Are Newsworthy

Meetings afford an opportunity for publicity. They are newsworthy. They call attention to the activities of the chamber, and they contribute something to the chamber's effort to sell its services to the community.

PREPARING THE MEETING

The manager should plan and make arrangements for all meetings, either personally or through someone assigned the responsibility. The exact steps will, of course, depend upon the type and size of the meeting. For all meetings, however, successful planning and preparation require careful attention to every detail. Nothing must be overlooked or left to chance. Some of the essentials of successful planning are discussed in the following paragraphs.

Calling the Meeting

A good attendance is the first essential of a successful meeting. If the purpose or attraction of the meeting is one of wide appeal, attendance is likely to be good. Even in such a case, however, attendance cannot be taken for granted. It must be stimulated—and the manager should never forget that, when the meeting hour has arrived, nothing can be done to correct the failure to promote attendance.

The call to the meeting should generally be in written form. Such a written notice serves as a constant reminder. The member may have it before him on his desk, or he may instruct his secretary to make a note of the meeting. The call should be sent well in advance of the meeting day. Usually a week or ten days is sufficient. The notice should state the purpose, hour, date and place of the meeting. When the call is made more than a week in advance, it may be advisable to omit mention of the day of the week on which the meeting is to be held. By so doing the possibility is avoided that some member will notice only the day—and not the date—and then show up a week early. The call to the meeting should be signed by the president or the chairman, rather than by a paid member of the staff.

If a large and representative attendance is desired, the meeting may require more publicity than that afforded by a simple notice. The call to the meeting should itself be more elaborate, perhaps printed. The story of the meeting should be featured in the official publications of the chamber, and additional publicity might be secured through press and radio. A personal telephone campaign is often used to build attendance. Each member of a "telephone committee" or of the staff, is given a list of from five to ten members whom he is supposed to call for the purpose of urging their attendance. This plan is usually resorted to when the purpose of the meeting is to raise money or otherwise without appeal. It is likely to be most effective when each member of the telephone committee calls his own friends and business associates. At best, however, the campaign can reach only a relatively small number of members.

The manager should maintain a "meeting book" in which all meetings are entered. Before calling a meeting he should check the time and place to make sure that there is no serious conflict. A meeting schedule or a bulletin board is advisable in smaller organizations. Many larger chambers publish a daily bulletin listing the meetings of the day.

Checking Attendance

If a full attendance or a quorum is necessary, it is always a good idea to telephone each member the day of the meeting to check whether or not he will attend. If a quorum is in doubt, the manager or the chairman may succeed in prevailing upon some members to attend even though they did not originally plan to do so.

A telephone check also serves other purposes. The response of the member to the inquiry is likely to indicate his interest—or lack of interest—in the meeting. A careful record of the telephone responses is, therefore, a valuable tool for evaluating the usefulness of the member for future committee service. The telephone check also makes it possible to know the exact number of participants and consequently, to make the best possible room arrangements. If the group is so large that a telephone check becomes burdensome, a returnable reservation card, attached to the call to the meeting, may serve as a satisfactory substitute. The card should be so worded as to cause the member who is not planning to attend, to state his reasons. A telephone check should be made in the case of those members who fail to return their reservation cards.

Cancelling Meetings

Once a meeting has been called it should not be cancelled except for good and sufficient reason. If, however, it becomes evident that a quorum cannot be mustered and that no business can be transacted, then the meeting should be cancelled or postponed. Those faithful in attendance should not be permitted to waste their time in a meeting that serves no purpose.

If it becomes necessary to cancel or postpone a meeting, every effort should be made to notify all participants. Notices should be sent even to those who have indicated that they would not be present. They may have changed their plans in the last minute. Every precaution should be taken to ensure that the notice of cancellation reaches the member personally. No member is likely to feel kindly toward the chamber if he comes to a meeting that has been cancelled. It makes no difference that the fault is in fact that of his secretary who failed to relay the cancellation message to him.

Place of Meeting

If accommodations permit, it is desirable that meetings should be held in the quarters of the chamber of commerce. Several advantages may be gained by so doing. Usually, the atmosphere of the chamber quarters is "right" and conducive to effective work. Members of the staff are available whenever needed, and files are accessible for quick reference. Moreover, if the presence of the manager or the president is required at two or more meetings that are held at the same time, he may go quickly from one to another.

If the meeting must be held elsewhere, the place selected should be central, convenient to the participants, adapted to the purpose, quiet and free from interruptions. If it is necessary to secure the attendance of some person who finds it difficult to attend meetings away from his place of business, it may be possible to schedule the meeting in his office. Not only does this ensure the attendance of the particular person, but—if he is an outstanding man in the community, with a name that draws—it may also stimulate the attendance of others. In no circumstance, however, should such consideration be extended merely to satisfy the vanity of some pompous individual.

Physical Arrangements

The physical arrangements of the meeting place are another factor that bears on the success of the meeting. The room should be well lighted and comfortably ventilated. A room that is too hot, too cold or poorly ventilated, is a handicap to any meeting. To a meeting that has been called for the purpose of serious work, such conditions may be disastrous. The committee that "goes to sleep" in a stuffy room might as well not be in session.

Tables and chairs should be so arranged as to contribute to the efficiency of the meeting. If the size of the group permits, a long table with the chairman at the end, or a horseshoe or circular table will be found most satisfactory. Several smaller tables scattered over the room tends to break up the unity of the meeting. Chairs should be as comfortable as possible, preferably with full or half arms. Folding chairs should be avoided, even in large meetings. Chairs should be so arranged that the fewest possible number of members face windows or look into a glare of light. For large meetings seating capacity should be ample. For smaller groups it is better to add chairs, if necessary, rather than to have several chairs vacant.

There are a host of other details to which the manager, or his assistant, must pay attention. If the meeting is a deliberative one, he should furnish paper, pencils and ash trays. If the matters to be discussed are in written outline, a folder containing the outline—and any other necessary documents—should be placed in front of each person as soon as he is seated. It may be a simple thing, but if the folder carries the name of the member, that fact may add a bit to his self-esteem and make him feel more at home in the meeting. Visual aids—such as charts, graphs and maps—should be so constructed, arranged and placed that they can be readily seen and explained.

For larger groups the manager should always provide gavel and lectern. If a public address system is to be used, it ought to go without saying that someone should check it before the meeting to see that it is in working order. Yet, countless meetings have been delayed and thrown into confusion because someone neglected to do the obvious.

Speakers

The attraction of many meetings is an address by some speaker. Because his performance may make or break the meeting, care must be exercised to ensure that the man selected has something to say, that he knows how to say it, and that his topic is of interest to the group. If the speaker is also able to lay claim to prominence, so much the better. A well known name goes a long way to ensure good attendance. But if the speech is a failure, there is not much consolation in the fact that the speaker is a successful businessman, a captain of industry or an eminent scientist.

The speaker should be secured well in advance of the meeting, usually by written invitation. The letter of invitation should explain the nature of the meeting, suggest the general subject to be discussed, and indicate the reasons for the chamber's choice of topic and speaker. Without being flowery or unctuous, the invitation should convey the suggestion that the chamber would consider it a privilege to hear the speaker. The letter should also give information about the expected attendance. If the invitation is correctly handled, there need be little or no expense for traveling and honorarium.

A speaker, whether or not he is paid, is the guest of the chamber and should be treated accordingly. It is up to the manager to see that hotel reservations are made for him, that local transportation is provided, and that his stay is otherwise made pleasant. Everything possible should be done to ensure the success of his engagement. Information and photographs should be obtained well in advance to ensure adequate publicity, and every effort should be made to secure the attendance promised. Perhaps one of the most common sins committed against a speaker is that of overloading the program with items of business, announcements and other preliminaries so that the audience becomes restive and tired even before he has a chance to begin. This sort of behaviour is an inexcusable breach of common decency and fair play. Yet everyone who has ever donated his time and services to civic clubs, chambers of commerce and similar organizations, knows that the practice is only too common.

Preparing the Content of the Meeting

It is the responsibility of the manager to work with the chairman in planning the program and preparing all matters that are to come before the meeting. If it is one of a series—as in the case of many deliberative meetings—he should first carefully review the minutes of previous meetings to make sure that all items requiring further action by him, his staff or a sub-committee, have been attended to. He should then plan the next steps. He should assemble all information, data, papers and reports for which there may be a call. If any new matter is to be presented, he should make sure that he has completed all preliminary work and that it is in good form. Statements on any new proposals should be clear, concise and convincing. The manager should not forget that a well-prepared presentation commands respect and confidence, expedites deliberations and tends to strengthen the chances of favorable action.

In making his preparations the manager should work closely with the chairman. One of his foremost responsibilities is that of making sure that the chairman is fully informed about all matters to come before the meeting, and that he has a complete understanding of their ramifications. At the same time it is essential that the manager should know the chairman's point of view so that there will be no conflict in presentation of any proposition. He should, therefore, sit down with the chairman to plan in detail the agenda and the strategy of the meeting. Together they should go over all data, papers and reports. The manager who fails to coach his chairman, has failed in his responsibility as manager. It may be simpler to take the lead in a meeting than to brief the chairman; but the manager who does so, violates the very spirit and purpose of the chamber of commerce and jeopardizes effective group action. The chances are that such a manager will not long remain in chamber of commerce service.

CONDUCTING THE MEETING

The chairman—and not the manager—is responsible for conducting the meeting. Its success must, therefore, depend to a considerable extent upon his skill and leadership ability. Nevertheless, the manager can, quietly and unobtrusively, contribute a great deal to the meeting. The importance of careful planning, preparation and coaching has already been stressed. In addition, there are many things the manager can do during the meeting to make it run smoothly, pleasantly and effectively.

Introduction of Members

The manager should be on the alert to greet each member as he comes into the room and make sure that he is introduced to any fellow member he may not know. A meeting need not be interrupted to introduce a late-comer, but he should be introduced at the close of the meeting. Proper introductions are important for several reasons. They make each member feel at home. The meeting becomes, therefore, friendlier and more pleasant. Moreover, the discussion is likely to be freer and more to the point when each member knows the names and backgrounds of his fellow members. And finally, most members prize the contacts and friendship that chamber of commerce work makes possible. They are an important part of the reward for the time and effort that the members give to the organization. It is up to the manager to make sure that such contacts are facilitated.

Assisting the Chairman

From the time when the chairman calls the meeting until it is adjourned, he should be in control. Individuals wishing to speak should be required to address the chair. Private conversation between members should not be permitted when someone else has the floor. Discussion should be held firmly to the matters before the group and should not be allowed to wander. Debate should not be stifled, but no member should be permitted to monopolize the meeting. This is a matter for the chairman to handle in a friendly but firm manner. Many a meeting has been ruined because one man was permitted to talk too much. The successful meeting is one in which all present participate. The wise chairman will, therefore, ask questions of a retiring member in order to draw him into the discussion.

When several items of business are to be brought before the meeting, the chairman can greatly expedite the discussion by stating—or asking the manager to state—each proposition clearly and concisely. When this is done, a motion is often made disposing of the matter immediately and without debate. On the other hand, if a proposition is badly stated or incompletely explained, all sorts of questions may be raised. Because the issue is not understood, much of the discussion may be meaningless or at cross purposes. As a result, time is wasted and a desirable action may have to be postponed.

Although the chairman should be in full charge of the meeting, the manager may be of great assistance to him. As secretary, the manager should be seated next to the chairman so that they can readily confer. Suggestions made quietly by the manager may help the chairman through many a difficult situation. By "feeding" the chairman papers and information as they are needed, the manager may help to keep the meeting moving smoothly and, at the same time, enable the chairman to give undivided attention to the discussion. And by calling on the manager to restate motions or to supply pertinent facts, the chairman may retain continuous control of the meeting without seeming to monopolize it.

In his capacity as secretary the manager should, of course, keep accurate notes on all motions and actions so that he may later prepare the minutes of the meeting. As a rule, however, it is advisable to dispense with the formal reading of the minutes of a previous meeting. To the member who was present at that meeting, there is nothing quite as boring as a long-winded account of what took place. If the approval of the minutes should be a matter of record—as in the case of a board of directors' meeting—it is a good idea to send copies to all members well in advance of the next meeting. The minutes may then be approved without reading.

AFTER THE MEETING

Group action can seldom accomplish more than merely establish policy, make recommendations or outline a course of action. It is the responsibility of the manager to see that the decisions of the group are carried out and made effective. The value of even the most successful meeting may be lost if he fails to follow through. On the other hand, even a mediocre meeting may be made significant by decisive and effective implementation. The most important work of the manager begins, therefore, *after* the meeting is adjourned.

Minutes

The minutes of a meeting are important not only because they afford a permanent record of the business transacted, but also because they may constitute the basis and authority for subsequent action. They should, therefore, be promptly and accurately prepared while the details of the meeting are still fresh in the memory of the manager. The minutes should show the name of the group; the date, time and place of the meeting; the name of the presiding officer, and the names of all others present. In the case of meetings of the board of directors, committees and other regularly constituted groups, it may also be advisable to record the names of those members who were absent. The minutes should show all actions taken and motions passed, together with the name of the person making each motion. It is not usually necessary to record the name of the seconder. Minutes need not be voluminous. No effort should be made to quote everyone who comments during the meeting. On the other hand, important points, reasons and arguments upon which an action is based, should be made matters of record.

All minutes should be preserved in such a manner as to

ensure their safety and permanency at the same time as they are made readily accessible for future use. Some chambers keep all minutes of all meetings in a single volume, or series of volumes, chronologically arranged. A more common practice, however, is that of maintaining a separate minute book for each group. Such a book needs to be nothing more elaborate than an ordinary loose-leaf binder in which new minutes can be inserted as they are prepared. A binder has obvious advantages over a file folder.

Follow Through

With the minutes prepared, it is up to the manager to make sure that the decisions of the meeting are translated into significant activity. Even the soundest recommendations or the most carefully worded resolution may be of little value unless it is supported by subsequent action. An illustration may serve to emphasize the importance of effective follow-through. A chamber, let us say, has decided to oppose a bill before the state legislature and has passed a resolution accordingly. If nothing more were done, the opposition would hardly be very effective. It is up to the manager to see that the correctly worded resolution is sent, with a letter of transmittal, to the chairman and the members of the legislative committee before which the bill is pending. If the chamber has so decided, he may request that a delegation be invited to appear before the committee. He may arrange for conferences with the senators and the members of the house representing the city of the chamber. He may seek the support of press and radio by sending them copies of the resolution and telling them the story of the chamber's opposition. While all of this is going on, he may make a behind-the-scene study to determine who are back of the bill and why they want it enacted. With such knowledge, an effective campaign might be organized to build public sentiment against the bill.

Although the responsibility for decisive follow-through rests squarely with the manager, it does not follow that he, or some member of his staff, must personally do eveything that has to be done. The appearance of the manager and his staff before a committee of the legislature, for example, would hardly be very effective. Nor may the manager be the best man to make the behind-the-scene study of legislative motives. A sub-committee might be appointed for that purpose. Regardless of who is to do the work, however, it is the duty of the manager to make all necessary preparations, to assist, and to check to see that the work is done.

The work that is assigned by a committee or other group to a sub-committee or the chamber staff, may sometimes require considerable time for its completion. If, in such a case, the principal group does not plan to hold a meeting until the work is completed, it is a good practice to keep its members informed by mailing them periodic progress reports. The practice helps to keep the group alive and to ensure continued interest. Moreover, if the work is to be done by a sub-committee, the practice affords the manager a reason for calling on its chairman for a report on the work accomplished. The practice serves, therefore, two purposes. It facilitates control at the same time as it furnishes a spur and incentive for the sub-committee to complete its assignment.

SPECIAL PROBLEMS

Up to this point the discussion has been concerned with problems that are more or less common to all chamber meetings. A chamber of commerce conducts, however, a number of different types of meetings, each of which offers its own peculiar problems. Some of them will be discussed in the following sections.

Board of Directors' Meetings

The meetings of the board of directors are, in a sense, the most important meetings of the chamber of commerce. It is in these meetings that policy is determined and action authorized. They are also one of the foremost responsibilities of the manager. It is his duty to see that they are well arranged, that the agenda is carefully planned, and that all matters to come before the board have been fully prepared.

It is a fundamental principle of chamber of commerce operation that the work of the organization should as far as possible be delegated to committees. Such delegation is made by the board of directors. The committees, in turn, study the matters assigned to them and submit their findings and recommendations to the board for consideration and action. Sound as this system is, it may give rise to conflicts and even abuse. A strong and active board may, for example, succumb to the temptation of doing work that should properly be delegated to a committee. Even worse, in acting upon a proposition it may disregard the findings of the committee and base its decision on nothing more substantial than its own snap judgment. A weak board of directors, on the other hand, may go to the other extreme and function only as a "rubber stamp". In such a case the chamber of commerce may quickly find itself enmeshed in conflicting policies, each of which is urged by a different committee.

The manager can do a great deal to ensure that the system work as it is intended that it should. If necessary, he should tactfully urge the board of directors to make full use of the committee organization before it acts. Whenever a controversial issue is to be considered, he should make sure that the committee chairman is present at the meeting of the board to explain and defend his report. If a board decision should run counter to the recommendations of a committee, he should make sure that the position of the board is fully explained to the chairman and the members of the committee. If, on the other hand, a board is too prone to accept any and all recommendations without careful review and consideration, he should step in to fill the breach by calling the attention of the board to important considerations which it may have neglected to take into account. It is obvious, however, that if a manager is to do these things successfully, he must act tactfully, diplomatically and intelligently.

The manager can also contribute to the efficiency of the board by working with the chairman in planning and arranging its meetings. Careful thought should be given to the preparation of the agenda. Propositions that are not likely to develop lengthy discussion and those requiring no formal action should be handled first. If the board meets at luncheon, time may be conserved by the presentation of less important matters between courses. Care should be taken, however, not to spoil the enjoyment of the meal. The manager should never forget that the board of directors is his boss, and that his professional skill, industry and integrity are judged largely by his contacts with the members of the board and by the way he handles its meetings.

Annual Meetings

The by-laws of most chamber of commerce provide for an annual meeting. In some cases the by-laws require the transaction of such business as election of officers, presentation of reports and similar matters to take place at such meeting. On the whole, however, it is better that the annual meeting should be a festive occasion with a limited amount of business transacted. It may be the occasion for honoring the retiring officers and for recognizing signal achievement. An outstanding speaker and good entertainment may add to the enjoyment of the meeting. But it is hardly the proper time for lengthy reports.

If a review of the past year is called for, every effort should be made to make it interesting. This may be done by dramatizing the presentation by means of motion pictures, by the use of charts and posters descriptive of the chamber's activities, by honoring the men who have made conspicuous contributions to their success, and by any other means that is unique and effective. Such a review, when well done, may impress the members even though it adds little that has not already been brought to their attention through the chamber's regular publicity efforts. Nevertheless, it should not be forgotten that most members are more interested in looking ahead than in gloating over past achievements. An outline of the plans for the coming year is, therefore, likely to evoke more enthusiasm and interest than a review of the past record.

General Membership Meetings

Except at the annual meeting, few chambers of commerce attempt to transact business at general membership meetings. Most chambers are so large that a meeting of the total membership becomes unwieldy. Moreover, experience has shown that it is difficult to secure a representative attendance. Action is often hasty, based on incomplete facts and inadequate consideration. If the issue before the meeting is a controversial one, the danger exists that a minority group may organize and succeed in pushing through its views. Because of these difficulties, most chambers have abandoned general meetings for business purposes. If it becomes necessary to secure the opinion of the entire membership on an important issue, these chambers rely upon a mail referendum. Moreover, many of the organizations that still conduct business at general meetings have adopted the rule that no question can be voted upon in such a meeting unless it has been studied and reported upon by a committee.

Some chambers of commerce, particularly in smaller communities, hold regular membership meetings for other than business purposes. They may be weekly, monthly or quarterly luncheon meetings, addressed by prominent speakers. They may also be conducted as open forum meetings at which important problems of the community or the nation are outlined by a leader and discussed by the members. Regular membership meetings may be of value in attracting and holding members. If they are to be successful, however, they require considerable time and effort—energy that might be better devoted to more important functions.

Special Meetings

Situations arise from time to time when it is desirable to arrange special meetings. The occasions for such meetings are legion. They may, for example, be called to welcome the executives and key men of a new factory, to celebrate the completion of an important chamber project or to honor a civic leader. Some meetings may be limited to the chamber's own membership while others may be thrown open to members of other organizations or to the general public.

Meetings of this kind may be sponsored entirely by the chamber of commerce, or the chamber may be one of several cooperating organizations. The willingness and the ability of the chamber to work with other groups in such matters help to establish its position of leadership in the community. On the other hand, the chamber must guard against the danger of becoming the city's meeting-arranging impresario. The special meetings compete for the time of the chamber's staff and membership. Too many of them may, therefore, lead to neglect of other activities.

Luncheon and Dinner Meetings

Luncheon and dinner meetings—whether large or small—pose a host of problems, ranging from the selection of the menu to the arrangement of the program. Many of these problems have already been discussed in the preceding sections. In summary, however, it may be worth while to quote a set of rules that has been evolved from the experience of many chambers of commerce.

1. Don't hold a luncheon or dinner meeting in too small a room, or in a room that cannot be properly ventilated. Don't wait to see about ventilation until the program is well under way.
2. Don't locate the head table in front of the kitchen where waiters must constantly go around it—or near

the main entrance where late-comers and early-leavers must pass in front of it.
3. If the group is large, don't use a U-shaped table. For a small group it is informal and effective; but if the group is large, it divides the group in two and forces the speaker to address the empty space between.
4. Be careful about whom you invite to sit at the head table, and give some thought to the seating arrangement. Use place cards.
5. To avoid confusion and to introduce a bit of ceremony, assemble those invited to sit at the head table outside the room and escort them to their places in an organized group.
6. It is not always necessary to introduce the men at the head table; but if it is done, it should be done briefly and in such a manner as to suggest why they have been selected for the place of honor. Be sure that the presiding officer has a complete list of names, arranged in the order of seating, giving all information necessary for the introductions.
7. Watch the lighting. The speaker must be seen, and he should see the audience; but be sure the lights don't abuse the eyes of the audience.
8. If there is an orchestra, have it play when the dining room is opened. Have them pack up their instruments and retire before the speaker of the evening is introduced, and not while he is speaking.
9. Don't have too many speakers or too long a program. Don't, under any circumstances, introduce unscheduled speakers on the program. When a program has been carefully planned, nothing is more likely to ruin it than mistaken hospitality to a visiting celebrity or near-celebrity who, if invited to "say a few words", is apt to take up half an hour or more. If he is bad, it ruins the meeting; if he is exceptionally good, it ruins the scheduled speaker—or may do so. In any event, a bargain is a bargain and a program is a program; neither should be tossed aside lightly.
10. The staff man in charge of arrangements should be the least conspicuous person at the meeting. The presiding officer should know where he sits, and he should be alert to any call from the presiding officer.
11. Don't permit a bell boy, a telephone or anything else to interrupt the program—and don't do it youself by passing notes or running to the head table.

SUMMARY

1. Meetings are necessary to enable the membership of a chamber of commerce to pool their ideas and work together to accomplish collectively what individual members cannot accomplish alone.

2. Meetings provide a medium for disseminating information, sampling the opinion of the membership, providing for desirable publicity, and for creating new ideas for future growth of the community.

3. A good attendance is the first essential of any meeting. All means to assure a good attendance should be applied before the hour of the meeting—it is then too late.

4. The mechanics of a meeting are important to its success. All advance preparations are the responsibility of the chamber manager or staff member serving as secretary of the committee.

5. A successful meeting depends largely upon the knowledge and effectiveness of the chairman. His adequate preparation in advance of the meeting is the responsibility of the manager.

6. Finally, the "follow through" after a meeting is over is all-important. It justifies the time spent by the committee members in meeting. The chamber manager is responsible for checking on all work assigned at the meeting to see that the work planned is followed through effectively.

Chapter IV

Committees—Appointment and Management

MEMBERSHIP in a chamber of commerce is more than an investment of money. It is the pledge of interest and energy to the development of a better community. It is likewise an opportunity for men to sharpen and refine their talents, to wield influence through ideas and accomplishment, and to share the rewards of community service.

The chamber of commerce functions through its committees. They are the instrument through which the talents and energies of its members are enlisted, organized and directed into community service. Committee activity makes it possible for the individual member to participate in the affairs of the chamber. It is the means by which his interest is captured, promoted and preserved. Committees are the membership in action, and the organization through which the program of work is carried out. The success of the chamber of commerce depends, therefore, upon the amount and the quality of its committee activities.

The first requirement of effective use of the committee method of operation is that each committee should have a definite purpose and function. Assignments must be more than high-sounding generalities. They must be specific, outlining the task of the committee in as exact terms as possible. Too many committees have floundered and failed because no one took the trouble to define the problems with which they were supposed to deal. Without a clear delegation of responsibility and authority, two or more committees may find themselves working in the same field or at cross purposes. In either event, the result is inevitably wasted effort, loss of interest and a progressive deterioration of the reputation and standing of the chamber in the community.

TYPES OF COMMITTEES

Because of the wide scope of its activities, the chamber of commerce employs many types of committees. Some are concerned with the internal operations of the organization, others undertake investigations or make studies of community problems, while still others are responsible for projects that require action or execution. Most committees are, however, appointed by the board of directors and responsible to it. They may recommend policy, but they do not determine it; they may act, but only within the limits of the board's authorization. Control of the organization is vested in the board of directors, under whose jurisdiction the committees operate.

Administrative and Project Committees

There are two distinct types of committees: *Administrative* and *project*. Committees of the first type concern themselves with the structure of the organization. They are responsible for such things as maintaining adequate quarters, supervising elections, setting up the budget, and preserving and expanding the membership. The project committees, on the other hand, plan and carry to completion the activities outlined in the program of work. An example might be the development of closer working relations between the businessmen on Main street and the farmers in the trade area, or the development of adequate recreational facilities for the community. Both types are of equal importance: the administrative committees preserve the body of the organization; the project committees make possible the concrete accomplishments that assure the endorsement and support of the community.

Investigating and Executing Committees

Project committees may be further divided on the basis of their function into *investigating* and *executing* committees. The investigating committee makes a careful study of a community problem or a proposed chamber project. It seeks to define the problem, to find and weigh alternative methods of solution, to measure their costs, to discover ways of financing necessary improvements, and to assay their effect on the community. When all sides of the problem or project have been thoroughly investigated, the committee makes its recommendations to the board of directors. The executing committee, on the other hand, is responsible for performance. It analyzes its task in terms of the goal to be reached, plans the attack, follows through each step until the project is completed, and then reports the accomplishment to the board.

Both types of committees are committees of action. Nevertheless, their functions require different abilities. Investigation demands technical competence to know what to look for, patience to dig out the facts, an open and analytical mind to evaluate their significance, and imagination and inventiveness to find a solution. Execution, on the other hand, requires vision to plan an attack, ability to organize it, and initiative, energy and persistence to carry it through. Few men possess all these capacities. Careful selection of committee members becomes, therefore, necessary. In some cases it may be advisable to employ a different group of individuals to perform each of the two functions; in others the knowledge and interest gained in the process of investigation may be sufficient reason for retaining the same members to carry the project through to completion.

Standing and Special

No committee should exist without purpose. Inactive committees sap the manpower resources of the chamber and kill its reputation for getting things done.

A program of work includes recurring activities as well as projects that are unique and of a "one-time" nature. The former should generally be assigned to *standing committees*. Such a committee may operate for years because its work carries over from one administration to the next. For example, the budget committee must continuously provide for and safeguard the financial requirements of the organization. Its membership may change, but the committee continues to operate because its function persists.

On the other hand, there are matters that require special handling and immediate but short-lived performance. A project of this kind might properly be referred to a *special committee* created for the particular purpose. The membership of such a committee must frequently possess particular qualifications. Consequently, the board should handpick the members, assign the task, and then dismiss the committee as soon as its report of accomplishment has been approved.

Subcommittees

There are circumstances when the use of subcommittees is advisable. If, for example, the problem assigned to a committee is complex and many-sided, time may be saved and more rapid progress made by having subcommittees study its various facets. A subcommittee may also be used to help the chairman make the necessary preparations for a meeting. For example, in preparing for a meeting of the national affairs committee of a chamber, the chairman might appoint a subcommittee to study and brief a bill pending before the Congress of the United States. Such a practice makes it possible to explain the bill to the full membership of the national affairs committee, assure intelligent discussion, and secure action with a minimum of delay.

COMMITTEE PERSONNEL

The committee is a working unit with a task to perform. Its strength is determined by the composite qualifications of its members. All its members should have an interest in the work of the committee. Each member should be imbued with a spirit of cooperation and loyalty to the group and its chairman. But there should also be a diversity of talents so that a variety of skills, experiences and points of view may be brought to bear on the problem. One may quite accurately predict the success of any committee on the basis of its leadership and the interests, knowledge and capacities of its members; likewise one may safely conclude that the success of any chamber of commerce will be governed by the sum total of its effective committees.

Techniques of Selection

There are several techniques that may be used effectively in selecting committee personnel. Some organizations canvass the entire membership by sending each member a returnable card on which he may indicate his preference for committee service. Others print a coupon, listing all committees, in the monthly bulletin and request members to fill in their selection and return the coupon to the president. Still other organizations assign the function of personnel selection to a committee on committees. The committee on committees analyzes the functions of each committee and makes the assignment of personnel on the basis of the interests and capacities of each member. Some organizations permit each chairman to pick the members for his committee. And, finally, in most organizations the president makes the selections. In all cases when the membership is selected other than by the board, the appointments should be subject to its approval.

Each method has its advantages. When members are assigned to committees in accordance with their expressed preferences, it is reasonable to expect maximum interest and willingness to work. The fact remains, however, that the best men are frequently also the busiest and the most reluctant to assume any committee responsibility. A returnable card or coupon is seldom enough to enlist their services. Moreover, when reliance is placed on expressed preferences, the danger always exists that too many members may want to serve on the same committee, while other committees go begging. A balanced distribution of preferences is rarely found. It becomes, therefore, the task of the committee on committees or the board of directors to try to induce members to give up their choices and to serve on less popular committees.

When each chairman is empowered to select his own committeemen, there is a danger that he will pick his own friends rather than men who are especially qualified for the job. On the other hand, the chairman's knowledge of the committee objectives may enable him to build the strongest possible team. It might reasonably be expected that when members of the board of directors make the selection, they would strive to place on each committee the very best timber available. But even directors suffer from the frailties of common humanity. They may unconsciously develop a self-perpetuating clique. When this happens, the membership and the community in general lose interest in the chamber because it offers no opportunity to share the responsibilities and rewards of a dynamic organization.

One of the largest and most successful chambers attributes its attainments to the committee service of the most important men in town. It strives to limit committee membership to top executives of business because these men are well informed, influential and accustomed to decision making, and because they lend prestige to the committees. The practice is excellent—except for two things. First, the mere fact that a man has been successful in his own business does not necessarily make him an expert—or even a capable worker—on any of the many varied problems with which the chamber deals. As a matter of fact, for many projects the chamber may have to go outside its own membership to find qualified personnel. City, county and state officials, for example, frequently possess technical knowledge that is of essence to effective committee work. And secondly, the practice overlooks the fact that the successful men upon whom the organization depends, were once untried newcomers who were given a chance to prove their worth. If the chamber is to continue to grow and prosper, it needs to make room for the man on his way up.

Regardless of the method of selection, the goal should always be that of securing a competent and efficient working team. The manager can and should be of assistance in the proper selection. For this purpose he should make an effort to know personally as many members as possible. He should observe them at work, and he should make his recommendations objectively and free from personal bias.

Appointment

Appointment to committee service is a distinct compliment. It should be formalized by a letter from the president. The letter should outline the exact duties of the committee; point out its relation to the program of work of the chamber as a whole; and give the name, title and address of the chairman. Moreover, the president should request and receive acceptance of the appointment from the committee appointee before his name is placed on the roster.

The tenure of committee service should be for the duration of the project for special committees, and for one year for standing committees. The appointment for the duration of a project insures the efficiency that comes with continuity of personnel, while the yearly appointments enable the board of directors and the manager to observe each member at work. They can ascertain which members display interest by regular attendance and participation. Each year's committee experience should serve as the basis for succeeding appointments.

THE CHAIRMAN

The chairman is to the committee what a captain is to a ball team. His function is to explain the task, lay out the attack, line up the team, and advise and inspire as the play moves from phase to phase. He should exhibit leadership, vision, enthusiasm and community spirit; and he should command the respect, confidence and loyalty of his committeemen.

He should possess a superior knowledge of the committee project. His knowledge of committee procedure and parliamentary law should enable him to control and direct his group in a forceful, business-like manner. A poor chairman may not only ruin committee action, but destroy interest in future committee service.

Board Members as Committee Chairmen

There are two schools of thought on the question of whether committee chairmen should be selected from the membership of the board of directors. Some chambers prefer to use directors as chairmen whenever possible, while the majority favor the selection of non-board members. Each policy has its advantages and disadvantages. The appointment of a director as chairman emphasizes the importance of the committee. Moreover, a director-chairman knows the activities of all committees. Hence, he is in a position to guide the work of his own group so that it meshes into the other chamber activities. Conflicts and duplication of efforts are therefore reduced to a minimum.

On the other hand, a director serving as chairman may unduly push his pet projects or promote his own interests. Thus, as chairman he is largely influential in shaping the findings and recommendations of his committee, and as director he is in a position to press their adoption by the board. The appointment of non-board members as committee chairmen avoids this danger. Moreover, this policy serves the purpose of broadening participation and delegation of responsibility. It makes possible the selection of the best qualified man for the chairmanship of each committee.

Some chambers attempt to secure the advantages of both policies by following a compromise practice. They seek broad participation and independence of committee action by the selection of non-board members as chairmen. At the same time, they ensure coordination of activities by assigning a director to serve as advisor for each committee.

Appointment

The selection of committee chairman should be made by the president upon the advice of the committee on committees and the manager. All appointments should be confirmed by the board of directors. The appointment to committee chairmanship is a signal honor. It is an expression of confidence, a recognition of ability and a challenge to service. It warrants a bit of ceremony. The appointment should be made by the president in personal conference with the prospective chairman. Such a man-to-man visit affords the president the opportunity to explain the nature of the project and to emphasize the importance of the committee's function. It enables him to gauge the attitude of the candidate. If there is any doubt about his willingness or ability to accept the obligation, he should be given an opportunity to decline the appointment. A member should not be pressed into acceptance of a chairmanship against his better judgment. And under no circumstance should the first announcement of the appointment be conveyed to him as a *fait accomplis* by letter or in the press. Such a practice is inconsiderate. It leads to misgivings and to light acceptance of an important obligation.

COMMITTEE MEETINGS

The techniques of planning, preparing for and conducting meetings have already been discussed in the preceeding chapter. The purpose of the present section is, therefore, merely to call attention to some problems that apply more specifically to committee meetings.

Frequency

The frequency of meetings varies widely from one committee to another. There is no hard and fast rule. In the case of some committees, meetings may be scheduled irregularly as the progress of work dictates. In the case of others, a more regular meeting schedule may be worked out to suit the pattern of action.

Regularity is, of course, an advantage to be sought. When meetings are held to an orderly and invariable schedule, a fuller attendance may be expected at the same time as the problem of calling the meetings is reduced to a minimum. The mere quest for regularity is, however, never an excuse for calling a meeting for which there is no need.

Regularity does not necessarily mean inflexibility. For committees charged with annual events—such as clean-up drives, community chest campaigns and the like—the schedule may be accelerated so that weekly or even daily meetings are held just prior to and during the event, while few if any meetings are called during the balance of the year. Even these committees may, however, profit by a schedule of regular meetings from which deviations are made when necessary. The practice gives emphasis to the element of time, to the importance of planning, and to the chairman's duty of keeping the committee alive.

Agenda and Committee Service

As in the case of all other meetings, the agenda should be worked out well in advance of the committee meeting by the chairman in cooperation with the manager. Because of the large number of committees and meetings, the manager may not be able personally to attend to all of them. In such cases, he should make sure that he is represented by a capable staff assistant. As a very minimum he should furnish each committee with adequate secretarial service. Moreover, the manager should keep himself fully informed about the work of every committee. He should always hold himself in readiness to lend an assisting hand to any committee that might run into difficulties.

Conduct

Successful conduct of committee meetings depends primarily on dispatch and direction. Respect for a few simple rules will do much to marshall committee activity:

1. Begin and end all meetings on time.
2. Review previous action—but make it brief.
3. Read the agenda.
4. Keep the meeting moving, alive and interesting.
5. Avoid lengthy sessions.

The chairman must never lose sight of his key position. His duty is not only that of controlling and directing discussion. He must also stimulate participation by all members by seeking their opinions and comments. The meeting is not intended to serve as a stage on which the chairman or the manager may parade his stellar qualities. Its purpose is to enlist the activity and support of every member. Nothing is more deadening to committee action than a one-man show.

Meeting the Issue

As a leading organization concerned with the progressive development of the community, the chamber of commerce will be forced to face highly controversial issues. It may be the route of a new highway, the zoning of an industrial area, the issuance of bonds for a public building, new taxes or any other proposal that involves some segment of the community or impinges on vested interests. The chamber should not falter in taking a stand in controversy. It must display courage of leadership. In fact, its strength and survival will depend largely upon the role it plays in fostering sound community development.

There are, however, certain principles which every chamber should observe whenever it is dealing with a controversial issue. The first and foremost is that no chamber should take a stand on such an issue before it has been thoroughly studied by a competent committee. Every phase of the problem should be carefully analyzed. Representatives of opposing views should be invited to present their positions. When civil departments are concerned, officials should be asked for their opinion as well as for technical information. When final hearings are concluded, the committee should feel assured that no stone has been left unturned. The board should have reasonable assurance that the committee's recommendations represent its most carefully considered judgment.

It should not be forgotten that the judgment of a committee can be no better than its collective ability to develop and evaluate pertinent information. This fact emphasizes the importance of a second principle: that the membership of every committee must be selected on the basis of competency and in such a manner as to give fair and adequate representation to all contending sides.

Reporting to the Board

Committees are only advisory to the board of directors. When a committee has concluded its investigation, it should report its findings and recommendations to the board whose responsibility it is to decide upon the stand that the chamber is to take. All such reports should be written, fully documented, and carry all exhibits of pertinent information necessary to the board's decision. The report should be presented by the committee chairman. If the subject is complex or controversial, the chairman should be accompanied by key members of the committee. This practice makes available to the board the personal experience of these committeemen and gives them a sense of the value of their participation. Minority reports should generally be avoided, but if no agreement can be reached in committee on an important issue, the use of such a minority report may be the only way in which the committee can bring its assignment to a conclusion.

SUMMARY

1. Successful chamber operation depends upon successful committee action.

2. Committees are membership in action.

3. Committees produce future leaders.

4. The success of committees depends upon the care with which their leadership and members have been selected.

5. Controversial issues are challenges. The chamber of commerce cannot provide leadership if it avoids controversy.

6. Before making any decision, however, the chamber should have all the facts. It is the duty of a committee to dig out, evaluate and weigh such facts.

Chapter V

Membership

IT HAS BEEN SAID that more chamber of commerce managers have failed because they lacked the skills and techniques necessary to attract and hold members, then for any other reason. The truth of this statement may be debatable, but the fact remains that the membership *is* the lifeblood of any chamber of commerce. Members *are* the organization. From them, the active workers are recruited; and from them come the funds with which all operations are financed.

A member may be a large industrial or mercantile corporation carrying many assigned memberships or subscribing heavily to sustaining funds. A member may be the neighborhood butcher or baker, the physician or dentist in the next block, or the wholesale house. A member may be a large hotel or a small restaurant, the printer, the insurance agent, the plumber, the realtor or the beauty shop operator. Their memberships—or the lack of them—may be affected by business conditions, but to a far greater extent they mirror the opinion and confidence of business and professional men in the chamber and its management. As long as the chamber of commerce remains a voluntary institution its membership and financial support will serve as a measure of its success. And as long as members may come and go, the maintenance of membership will remain a major problem of its management.

PROBLEMS OF MEMBERSHIP

The word "membership" is, perhaps, a misnomer when applied to a chamber of commerce affiliation. It is certainly not a membership in the sense in which the term is used in connection with a service club, an athletic club, a country club or any other social or civic organization in which the association is purely a personal one. A membership in a chamber of commerce is a contribution to a cause—an investment in community building. And yet, in recent years there has been a trend away from the once accepted philosophy that a company or a businessman should be a member of the chamber of commerce solely out of civic spirit. Increasingly the question has been asked, "What do I get out of it?" Today, management must be able to answer that question. A membership represents a successful sale of the program of work of the organization—a sale that is made, not in terms of vague generalities, but on the basis of demonstrable advantages to the new member. Unfortunately, most of the benefits that accrue from the activities of the chamber of commerce become available to all members of the business community, whether or not they are members of the chamber. Salesmanship of the highest order is, therefore, necessary to maintain numerical membership and adequate income.

Membership Prospect File

A permanent prospect file, carefully maintained, is essential to successful membership work even in smaller communities. A master card should be made out for each prospect, and reports on calls made by staff members or volunteer solicitors should be entered on the card. The same information should be posted on a companion card of a different color to be used when making solicitations. If the prospect has an in-and-out record, the information on these cards should show who secured the original application and when, the dates and reasons for resignation and other helpful case history. A suggested form of prospect card which seems to meet all needs, is shown in figure 1.

Figure 1
Membership Prospect Card
CONFIDENTIAL

Date_____ No._____
Name_____,_____ Bus._____
Address_____ Exec._____
Zone_____ Phone_____ Rating $_____ Quota $_____
Present: Memb. $_____ Peak Year $_____ In_____
Case History:

Date	Reported by	Remarks	See Again

The search for new prospects is a continuous job, and a job that must be done carefully and thoroughly. Even in small cities it is always amazing how many good and overlooked prospects can be turned up by a diligent study of mercantile rating books, city and telephone directories and other sources. Accuracy is always important, but when the chamber relies on volunteer solicitors to do its membership work, accuracy becomes imperative. Every precaution must be taken not to waste the time or lose the friendship of these volunteers. Names, addresses, telephone numbers and case histories appearing on the prospect cards must be complete and correct. Even one card for a bankrupt firm, a deceased professional man or a company that has gone out of business, can cause the volunteer worker to lose faith in the organization he was so eager to serve. The whole prospect list is likely to be discredited in his eyes—and so is the chamber management.

Who are prospects and who are suspects? That is a difficult question to answer. A business eking out a mere existence may sometimes have an unblemished record of chamber membership extending over many years, while a profitable enterprise may remain out of membership just as persistently or have an in-and-out record. No name of a financially able business or professional man should ever be removed from the prospect file merely because of repeated failures. The chamber of commerce with a large membership built it by consistent and tactful sales efforts leveled at tough prospects. Once they surrender they are likely to remain on the membership rolls, and their surrender may be instrumental in bringing competitors and friends into the membership.

There are certain business and professional segments, however, that should definitely be eliminated from the prospect list. A lawnmower manufacturer with a factory in a distant city may, for example, be listed in the local telephone directory when actually that listing is one of seven or eight maintained by a manufacturer's agent as an index of the companies he represents. The manufacturer's agent is obviously a prospect, if he is not already a member. But the various companies he represents should not be treated as prospects.

Very few of the insurance agencies in even the largest cities are operated by the insurance companies themselves. Nevertheless, local agents constantly launch chamber managers and membership committees on "letter-to-the-home-office" campaigns. They neither will nor should produce results. The local agency may be a highly profitable operation, but in almost every case it is the agent's own business and should carry a chamber of commerce membership as such.

It is likewise a mistake to get membership lists from the local medical and dental societies, the bar association and other professional organizations, and then assume that *all* of the names on these lists represent prospects for chamber membership. The fact is that a great many professional men do not have incomes sufficient to warrant the expense. The sound approach is, therefore, to ask a key man in each group—physician, dentist or attorney—to check the names of those whose professional offices are successful. The same procedure should be used in the case of engineers, architects, morticians and other groups. Such an approach may involve additional effort, but in the long run it pays off. It avoids cluttering up the prospect files, saves postage and other expenses, and keeps the management in good favor with volunteer workers.

Ethical Standards

In the quest for membership the temptation is always present to accept the subscription of any firm or individual that offers to pay membership dues. The wise chamber of commerce, however, is that which maintains ethical standards and scrutinizes every membership application. Prestige, dollars and membership can all be lost by permitting an unethical concern or individual to enjoy the endorsement that is implied by a membership card or the display of a chamber of commerce emblem. Concerns known for sharp business practices should not be admitted to membership; neither should professional men who are not accepted as members by the accrediting organizations of their profession.

The Membership Agreement

Experience has demonstrated that it is advisable to ask the prospective member to complete a membership agreement and not an application form. By its very wording, such an agreement should emphasize the importance of the dollar subscription in support of a program of work rather than the "joining" aspects of the membership. It is particularly important that the agreement should establish the membership on a continuous basis so as to avoid the necessity of repeat calls by a committee or staff member each year to get a renewal. But it is equally important that the member be given the right to revise or cancel the commitment prior to the close of a stated period.

The wording of the agreement is important. It should be so phrased that it can be used for single and plural memberships alike. By stating that the new agreement replaces all membership and sustaining fund subscriptions of prior date, it should make it possible for a company that wishes to increase its support, to do so merely by filling in the new amount as it would a check. Legal terms should be avoided. They are unfriendly, forbidding and unnecessary. Any well-worded agreement will support collection effort and legal action, but it would be decidedly poor policy for any chamber ever to sue a member for nonpayment, no matter how large the amount. A suggested membership agreement, phrased so that the word "application" is not used at any point, is shown in figure 2.

Figure 2

Membership Agreement

MIDDLETOWN CHAMBER OF COMMERCE
MEMBERSHIP AGREEMENT
Date_____19_____

The UNDERSIGNED hereby subscribes and promises to pay annually

_____ Dollars ($_____)
to the Middletown Chambers of Commerce. This agreement replaces all membership and sustaining fund subscriptions of prior date. The right is reserved to revise or cancel by written notice prior to the close of any annual period.

For each unit of $50.00 subscribed the undersigned shall be entitled to one representative with all membership privileges.

Payable in Advance: _____

☐ Annually   Address_____
☐ Semi-annually
☐ Quarterly   By_____

Zone_____ Phone_____ Title_____

Buyer's Guide Classifications_____

Proposed by_____
Seconded by_____

The month of the original agreement should be the anniversary month of the membership. This plan has been found much more satisfactory than the practice of billing all dues at the beginning of the calendar year. The anniversary plan distributes billing, accounting and other membership work over the entire year, and brings in a continuous stream of income. Furthermore, it minimizes the risk that the total income of the chamber may be seriously affected by temporarily adverse business conditions—or temporary disfavor—at the very time when all dues are payable.

MEMBERSHIP RELATIONS

The attitude of a member toward the chamber of commerce and the length of time he will stay with the organization are likely to be determined, first of all, by his estimate of the worth of the chamber's program of work and the efficiency of its management. But his attitude is likely to depend also on a host of little things. His first introduction to the chamber, the manner in which he is billed and the way in which he is treated if his account should become overdue, are some of the more important among these "little things."

Assimilating the New Member

The steps taken to induct the new member into the chamber are obviously of importance. As a minimum the new member should have a formal letter of welcome from the president, even though he may be a neighbor or personal friend. The letter need not be long, but it should express appreciation for the support extended and encourage committee service and active participation by the member. There should be enclosures of a pocket membership card, a roster of the services available to members, and other literature of interest. The president's letter should, if possible, be supplemented by a personal call by a major staff member. At that time the membership plaque or other materials may be delivered.

If the chamber conducts membership breakfasts, luncheons or dinners, a special invitation should be issued to the new member. He should be brought to his first meeting as a guest and introduced, perhaps from the speaker's table. It goes without saying that the new member should be placed without delay on the mailing list for all chamber bulletins and publications, and that his name should be listed in the new member column of the next issue of the bulletin.

Billing Methods

Invoices for membership dues should be mailed about ten days prior to the first of the month when dues are payable. This practice provides ample time for the invoice to clear through the bookkeeper, be approved for payment by the member, and for a check to be made out. In mailing invoices it is a good practice to enclose envelope stuffers containing "flash news" about current activities or future plans. Such news stimulates interest and encourages continuous support. If printed envelope stuffers seem too expensive, a mimeographed card with a little art work is an acceptable substitute.

If the invoice has not been paid by the 20th of the month, it is then time to get a *statement* in the mail, and with it another publicity enclosure. If the membership dues have not been paid by the 15th of the following month, steps should be taken to find out what is wrong.

Collecting Unpaid Dues

Although a period of 55 days has now elapsed since the original invoice was mailed, failure to pay does not necessarily mean that the member is financially embarrassed. That failure may be the member's method of saying that he has resigned. It is not good business practice, but the fact remains that some members lack the courtesy or courage to submit a written resignation—or even to return the invoice with instruction to cancel. Other financially able members may delay payment as a means of registering a complaint. Such a member may be offended by something the chamber has done or failed to do.

A personal collection call will usually bring any complaint out into the open, and may afford the opportunity of removing the cause. Furthermore, because few chambers allow a discount for prompt payment of dues, there are members who postpone payment until they are pressed to do so. Collection calls are therefore likely to produce money. It is poor business to permit membership accounts to become badly delinquent. Not only does such laxity reduce the income of the chamber and reflect upon the efficiency of its management, but as the delinquency mounts it becomes more difficult to collect. The result may be the loss of a member—and a friend. Collection calls should, therefore, be made promptly. Some chambers use a personable young lady for collection work, either on full or part-time basis, and report excellent results.

Suspensions

If it becomes necessary to suspend a member for non-payment of dues, it is best not to notify him that the board of directors has taken such action. It is better to drop the membership quietly and on the friendliest terms possible, leaving the door open for reinstatement at a more favorable time. Most chambers of commerce charge off the delinquent dues of the suspended member and do not expect the account to be paid as a prerequisite to reinstatement.

RESIGNATIONS

Whenever a resignation is received it should immediately be acknowledged by letter. As soon as possible thereafter, a staff member should call on the member in order to ascertain the cause of the resignation and attempt to secure its withdrawal. If the call is unsuccessful, other methods of persuasion should be tried before the resignation is finally accepted.

Letter of Acknowledgment

A member's resignation is entitled to the courtesy of formal acknowledgment. The letter of acknowledgment may be a form letter, but it should always be individually typed and the form should be changed every month or two. It should express genuine regret that the member is contemplating resignation, make it clear that the resignation is not being accepted but will be reported to the membership committee or board of directors, and that someone will discuss the matter with the member. The letter should also urge some current reason why the member might want to rescind his action.

Such a letter of acknowledgment should be sent even when immediate personal follow-up is planned. There is always the possibility that the member may not be available when the personal call is made, and that days or even weeks may pass before the conference can be mutually arranged. After a week or two the member is apt to regard himself as no longer affiliated with the chamber, and the resignation is a closed issue so far as he is concerned. The time for treating a resignation is just as soon as it reaches the office—first by letter and then quickly by personal follow-up.

Personal Follow-up

The first step in the follow-up process is a personal call by the manager or some major staff member. The purpose of the call is to find out what is wrong and, if possible, to set things right. It goes without saying that this is no easy task and that it requires really constructive selling. To be successful the selling job must be specific, to the point, and couched in terms of the interests of the member. In making these calls, the staff member should not ignore the key employees of the member. Many a resignation may be attributed to an over-zealous employee who is anxious to save money for his employer. A talk with such an employee on the activities of the chamber may do wonders.

If the first effort to have the resignation rescinded is unsuccessful, the next step should be that of consulting with the committee member or campaign worker who secured the original application. If any other member might be helpful in securing reinstatement, he too should be consulted. All this should be done before the resignation is submitted to the membership committee. Not until every reasonable effort has been exhausted should the membership committee recommend to the board of directors that the resignation be accepted.

Board Action

Whenever the board of directors considers a resignation the manager should be prepared to report on all efforts to persuade its withdrawal. Moreover, the manager should be on the alert for any resignation trends. The danger always exists that when, on the golf course or at a cocktail party, a member confides in another that he has "cut expenses" by dropping his chamber membership, he may start an epidemic of resignations. Whenever there is an increase in resignations the manager should promptly report the facts to the board. Directors may be expected to be interested in any such trend and, because they and their companies usually have exceptional influence, they are frequently in a position to take effective steps to stem the tide. The time to stop an epidemic of resignations is *before* it takes hold.

MEMBERSHIP COMMITTEES AND CLUBS

The constant help of a powerful and active membership committee or club can be invaluable to any chamber of commerce, large or small. Such a group cannot be built over night, but must be developed slowly by finding and recruiting men who are sold on the chamber of commerce, realize the importance of a strong membership, and are willing to sacrifice the time and effort necessary to secure that membership. These men must be people of standing and influence in the community—men whose efforts are likely to tell. A considerable turnover must be expected in the membership of such a committee. Nevertheless, the average service is frequently of sufficient length to bring about the development of an *esprit de corps* that cements friendships and inspires a high degree of pride of accomplishment. Such clubs often are given a special name such as "Round-Up Club", "Eight O'Clock Club", or other name appropriate to their section of the country. Many members continue their memberships willingly over the years and just as willingly maintain a personal record of continuous production.

Importance of Membership Committees

In the smaller chamber of commerce the staff frequently consists of only the manager and limited stenographic help. The manager's duties may cover all the activities which, in the larger city chamber, are handled by departmental specialists. Under these conditions he has little room for membership work in his busy schedule. His only salvation lies, therefore, in his ability to multiply himself through an active membership committee.

There is another important reason why the manager's voice, face and energy should not be too conspicuous in membership work. With the budget limitations that usually prevail, his interest in membership building may too easily be misconstrued as an interest in securing his own salary. Similarly, any collection work may be regarded as a matter of personal interest rather than as a function vital to the activities of the organization. Even with a strong and active membership committee, however, the manager is by no means relieved of all membership work. He must still take a lead in planning and directing the membership extension program and other efforts designed to produce operating income.

In the larger chambers of commerce conditions are quite different. Most large chambers maintain membership departments with a manager whose main responsibility is the production and maintenance of budgeted income. The department is generally staffed with adequate stenographic and clerical help to handle correspondence and to maintain membership records and prospect files. One or more assistant managers may work as fieldmen making on-the-street sales, collections and membership relation calls. Incidentally, it is considered preferable that these men work on a fixed salary rather than on a commission basis, although an incentive plan combining salary and bonus is also satisfactory.

With such a well-organized membership department, a membership committee may appear superfluous. Such is not the case, however. Because of the vast areas to be covered and the variety of business interests to be reached, it is not possible to provide the man hours necessary to do the job unless volunteer groups are developed to spearhead the work of the paid staff. In order to do its job effectively the department needs the support, influence and prestige that only a strong and active membership committee can provide.

Experience with Membership Clubs

In some cities membership clubs have been so successful that all use of membership committees has been discontinued. In order to permit freedom of action most of these clubs operate more or less autonomously under by-laws established by the members. Names such as *Propeller Club, Contact Club, Dynamo Club, Eight O'Clock Club, Round-up Club* or *Lasso Club* are adopted to lend color and theme to the earnest work of these organizations.

Eligibility for membership follows no set pattern. The founder members are usually men who gained eligibility by recruiting two or more new chamber members during the year prior to that in which the club was organized. In order to retain his membership in the club, however, a worker must qualify anew each year by a continuous record of production. Officers are elected by the club members and usually serve for six months. Most clubs hold monthly luncheon or dinner meetings at which the members are guests of the chamber. In turn, many clubs follow the practice of entertaining new chamber members at gatherings held at intervals of about six months. Because of the favorable experience with these clubs, their number has grown rapidly in recent years.

MEMBERSHIP CONTESTS

Whether they rely upon committees or clubs to spearhead their membership work, most chambers of commerce find it desirable to conduct occasional membership contests. These contests are frequently in addition to the regular annual membership campaign.

Themes and occasions for membership contests are legion. If too many of them are held, however, or if they are too much alike, interest may be expected to lag. It is therefore good practice to limit the number of contests to one or two a year. Interest and rivalry may be stimulated by the award of merchandise prizes. Such prizes may be either purchased or donated by well-wishers, but it is generally agreed that it is poor policy to solicit donations. Some chambers go even so far as to refuse voluntary donations.

Many successful contests offer nothing more tangible than honor and recognition. At the annual banquet of the chamber, for example, a "premium table" may be reserved for those who qualified in the contest. Again, the award may be a fishing trip, a trip to a major baseball or football game, or golf and dinner at a country club—with the chamber paying all expenses. To qualify for such an award, each winner must usually produce two or more membership applications accompanied with checks for a full year's dues. The awards may be rather costly, but the cash receipts from the contest are likely to be three or four times as large as the expense. Furthermore, such contests attract a great deal of attention and help to build an *esprit de corps* among membership workers that can be of lasting value to the chamber.

ONE-DAY CAMPAIGNS

Largely because of the relative ease of enlisting workers for a brief and snappy membership offensive, quite a few chambers of commerce have had consistent success with one-day campaigns. The workers generally assemble at breakfast, set forth on their day of solicitation and reassemble in the evening for reports and a dinner meeting. Although one day campaigns have had a fine success, the term is somewhat of a misnomer. Prospects are usually selected long in advance, many are solicited, and some applications are actually secured before the day of the campaign. Any manager interested in this type of campaign should be forewarned that the planning and advance preparations necessary to ensure success are much more demanding than the simplicity of the name and the brevity of the campaign suggest.

THE INTENSIVE AND COMPLETELY ORGANIZED CAMPAIGN

At one time or another, a chamber may find itself in a position where extraordinary efforts may be necessary. The board of directors may decide, for example, that the chamber must expand its program of work if it is to serve the community satisfactorily, that the the budget is inadequate, and that the dues income must therefore be drasticallly increased. In such a situation the only possible solution may be an intensive campaign to secure new members and to increase sharply the subscriptions of large companies.

Fortunately, such a situation does not arise frequently. When it does come about, however, it is imperative that the manager should know how to deal with the problem. Some chambers have successfully employed the services of professional campaign specialists, but in most cases the manager must assume the entire responsibility for the campaign. As an aid to a manager who faces such a responsibility the remainder of this chapter outlines in some detail the steps necessary in the planning, organization and operation of an all-out effort. Many of the ideas and techniques are also applicable to smaller membership drives and group contests.

Charting the Campaign

A comprehensive campaign seeking increased subscriptions as well as new members is an ambitious undertaking. Ample time must therefore be allowed for preparation. Because a major part of the job of planning, organizing and directing the campaign must fall on the manager and must be added to his already busy schedule, a period of seven or eight weeks from the beginning of planning to the end of the campaign is none too long. The campaign will also require a budget. It must provide adequately for luncheon and dinner meetings, publicity and printing, postage, additional stenographic help and other necessary expenses. The success of the campaign, however, must in the end depend on the support of an organization capable of tackling each of its many phases. Such an organization might include (1) a speakers bureau responsible for educational meetings, (2) a publicity committee, (3) an evaluation committee to establish quotas for corporate subscriptions, (4) an advance subscription committee to solicit large concerns, (5) a national firms committee to seek support from out-of-town companies operating plants or branch establishments in the city, and (6) a sales organization of divisions and teams to concentrate on a prospect list of non-members engaged in every remunerative field of business and the professions.

Once the scope and general plan of the campaign have been decided, the next step is to construct a calendar of day-to-day activities. A long sheet of paper, ruled into columns and rows, will serve the purpose. There should be a column for each day of the campaign period, and a row for each unit of the campaign organization. Beginning with the "victory celebration" and working backwards, every activity of each unit should be scheduled and recorded in its proper row and column. To be of value such a calendar must be detailed. It should not only fix the dates of major events, but also schedule preparatory steps and deadlines of all kinds. It must, of course, be constructed as whole with the activities of each campaign unit meshing into those of all the others. It must also make allowances for the activities of other civic agencies, for national and religious holidays and for local events so as to avoid any conflict that might upset the campaign schedule. When completed, the calendar should represent a step-by-step plan for the campaign, noting and making provisions for every detail. The usefulness of such a calendar as a planning tool and as an instrument of control can hardly be overemphasized. Further suggestions as to its construction and use are therefore given in an appendix to this chapter.

Organization Structure and Campaign Leadership

The operating units of the campaign organization have been briefly mentioned. Something needs to be said, however, about the general structure of the organization; the responsibilities, functions and size of each unit; and the leadership necessary to ensure success of the campaign.

It is not good practice for the president of the chamber to tie himself down in any key position in the campaign organization. Rather, he should hold himself free to move in and lend support and assistance wherever his help is most needed. He should, of course, be an ex-officio member of the campaign executive committee. His presence is also desirable at every campaign meeting. At a good many of them he should speak. His first and foremost duty, however, is that of selecting an outstanding general chairman of the campaign and prevailing upon him to accept the arduous task of that office.

The *general chairman* should head the campaign organization. He should be a man of standing and influence in the community, and a man who has a keen interest in expanding the program of the chamber and enhancing its budget. As general chairman he should be responsible for selecting committee chairmen and securing their acceptance. With the aid of the manager and a campaign executive committee composed of the committee chairmen, he should develop the plan of the campaign and coordinate the activities of the several units of the organization. He should also preside at most campaign meetings.

The *advance subscription committee* is responsible for securing new subscriptions and increased support from the large concerns of the community. Its chairman should therefore be a man of the highest prominence—and a man whose company has a record of liberal financial support of the chamber. He should have the interest, ability and drive necessary to ensure that his personal record of production will be successful. Even more important, he should command the prestige, respect and loyalty necessary to enable him to recruit a committee of the city's most influential businessmen and induce them to work for the success of the chamber. He should know how to inspire his committee and create a spirit of friendly rivalry among its members so that each of them will try to best the production of the others. The total membership of the committee should depend on the number of concerns to be solicited. In order to ensure that every large firm is given adequate, personal attention by the member to whom it is assigned, no member should be asked to assume responsibility for more than five accounts. As a matter of fact, in order to allow for refusals to serve and objections to the assignment of particular firms, it is well to appoint a committee somewhat larger than that suggested by this standard.

The chairman of the *evaluation committee* should be a man of broad knowledge of the financial ability of major companies and one who believes that the value of the chamber's services warrants subscriptions at a sharply increased rate. He should select a committee of five or six men competent to establish and equalize subscription quotas for the larger commercial, industrial and financial concerns of the community.

The *national firms committee* does not need to be large. As a matter of fact, it might be a one-man committee. Its chairman should, however, be a man whose name and company enjoy national reputation. His word should carry weight among national concerns. The principal duty of this man should be that of helping to plan the proper approaches to national firms. He should be willing to lend his personal influence by signing letters, telegrams and special briefs prepared by the campaign headquarters for submission to home offices.

The chairman of the *team organization* should be a dynamic personality—a prominent businessman with a large personal following. He should know how to build and motivate a sales organization, possess a genial personality, be an excellent toastmaster, and have a knack for making report meetings snappy and interesting. The chairman should select and secure the services of division commanders who, in turn, should be responsible for selecting their own team workers. The caliber of the men on each the several levels of leadership must be extremely high because the team workers must themselves be influential businessmen. It should be remembered that it is difficult for any man to command the working cooperation of another individual bigger than himself.

The size of the team organization should be governed by the magnitude of the task ahead. No team worker should be expected to be responsible for more than six prospects. A few enthusiastic workers may ask for as many as 20 or 25 prospect cards, and they should be welcome to them. But there is a great difference between accepting a voluntary offer and *asking* a man to drop his own business in order to work full time for the chamber for a number of days. It should not be forgotten that many prospects require several calls before their application is secured.

Each team should consist of six men—the team captain and five workers. The team captain should, of course, be expected to do his full share of solicitation. Only if he is willing to do so, is he likely to be able to inspire and lead his team. Each team should therefore be able to take care of 36 prospects.

Each division should consist of five teams. By keeping the number small, the division commander will find it possible to keep in close contact with the activities of his teams. He will be able to build the *esprit de corps* necessary for friendly competition and success. No division commander should be required to make solicitations. His job is sufficiently big without that responsibility. Many division commanders will, however, select a personal allotment of cards and turn over their own production to individual workers—either to show appreciation to those who have done an outstanding job or to encourage the conscientious worker who has run into tough luck.

With five teams, each division should be able to take care of from 180 to 200 prospects. The total number of divisions must therefore depend on the number of names in the prospect files. If there are 1200 prospects to be solicited, six divisions should suffice, and the total team organization should call for something less than 200 men.

There is, of course, nothing sacrosanct about such titles as division commander, team captain or team member. Any titles may be used. If a chamber of commerce conducts an annual campaign, however, it is advisable to establish a permanent nomenclature. It is poor policy to have "generals" one year, "admirals" the next, and football terms and titles the following year. Many workers participate in several campaigns, and the use of unfamiliar trick titles is merely confusing to them. If titles are established on a permanent basis, each job takes on significance and its responsibilities become known and understood.

The chairman of the *speakers bureau* should be a man known as an able public speaker. He should have a wide acquaintanceship among men of similar bent. His job is that of assembling a panel of men to address civic, professional and trade organizations on the expansion program of the chamber.

The chairman of the *publicity committee* should be a man whose professional experience as a newspaper man or advertising executive qualifies him to plan and guide the promotional and public relations activities of the campaign. His committee should be small but representative of the media that are to be used in behalf of the expansion program.

A word of warning might be added in conclusion of this part of the discussion. Most experienced campaign managers make it a rule to avoid the use of a co-chairman in any department of activity. The very term suggests a division of responsibility that makes it only too convenient for either or both co-chairmen to shirk their duties of leadership. To a lesser degree the same objection attaches to the use of vice-chairman, vice-commander or lieutenants, unless the organization is very large. The second-in-command is seldom of much aid except as an alibi for the leader who failed.

Campaign Publicity

If the publicity program is to achieve maximum effectiveness, it must be carefully planned well in advance of the campaign. The objectives must be exactly defined; the approach and treatment must be projected; the media selected; and the spacing and impact of newspaper stories, radio time and direct mail pieces decided upon. The success of the publicity—like all other phases of the campaign—must also depend upon a complete and up-to-date prospect list. One of the first steps should therefore be a careful review of the prospect files. Dead names should be removed, new prospects added and the whole list should be appropriately classified.

The publicity program might get under way by mailing several issues of the chamber's regular bulletin to all prospects in the community. The first issues should make no mention of the approaching campaign, but the articles contained in these bulletins should be designed to attract the attention of non-members and to stimulate interest in the chamber as a vital organization serving business and the community. The final issue mailed to non-members should carry a feature story announcing the expansion program, the campaign to finance it, and the names of the campaign leaders.

The importance of the chamber bulletin as a medium of information should not be underestimated. Local newspapers may well edit all selling copy out of press releases. The bulletin may therefore afford the only opportunity of telling the chamber's story completely and in the way it should be told. The bulletin's stories will not be edited for length or for superlatives. Yet, the chamber should never forget the importance of scrupulously truthful stories, wherever they may appear.

In announcing a major campaign it is advisable to give it a capital name rather than to refer to it repeatedly as a mere "membership drive". Possible names are legion. Some examples are: *Middletown Business Development Program, Middletown Opportunity Program,* and *United Middletown Expansion Program.* Challenging slogans can also be used with good effect. Some simple suggestions are: *Keep Middletown Rolling, Let's Keep Middletown Ahead,* and *Let's Secure the Future of Middletown.* Such a name and slogan will be helpful to all forms of publicity, but especially to the attention arresting quality of direct-mail pieces.

The major mailing piece of the campaign need be nothing more elaborate than a broadside telling the story of the chamber, its current activities and its planned program of work. Committees or departments may be played up and their budgets outlined. If the chamber is planning to issue a new buyers' guide or membership directory, now is the proper time to announce it. If offset printing facilities are available, it is possible to make use of photographs, color and art work at very low cost. Money may also be saved by designing the direct-mail piece so as to make the use of envelopes unnecessary. A folded publicity piece with one side spaced for address and post office indicia can be attractive and will save postage and labor as well as envelope costs.

The mailing list for publicity pieces should not be limited to the prospect list, but should also include the entire membership even though only a few members will be asked to increase their annual subscriptions. If the message is addressed primarily to non-members, it is an easy matter to attach a sticker to the copies sent to the members, explaining the purpose of the publicity piece. Most members will be interested in the progress of the campaign. Moreover, if the publicity piece is well done, it will do its share to keep the members sold on the chamber.

If the chamber is weak on memberships among physicians, dentists and lawyers, a folder, small enough to fit into an invitational-sized envelope, is a good door opener. It might ask the question, "What about the Professional Man?" and then supply the answer. It should be remembered, however, that the competition for the reading time of most professional men is extremely keen. The story must, therefore, be told effectively and in as few words as possible. Be sure to refer to these groups as *physicians,* dentists and lawyers, and not as *doctors,* dentists and lawyers. The dentist is also a doctor and he does not like to be denied that recognition. A follow-up letter from the president of a professional organization to its members will help to clinch memberships. It should present a short, convincing sales story and enclose an application card together with an addressed, stamped envelope. Such a letter is advisable because it is particularly difficult for a solicitor to reach physicians and dentists during office hours.

Perhaps the most effective method of employing radio in the publicity program is the use of a series of spot announcements. Each such announcement should be different from the others and should emphasize just one current activity or accomplishment. Station and hour should be chosen so as to ensure that the message reaches the largest possible audience among business and professional men.

If the campaign is merely an annual membership drive, not much newspaper publicity can be expected. If, on the other hand, the campaign is of unusual magnitude and importance, every effort should be made to create situations that will give it news value. The appearance at the "opening breakfast" of a popular campaign worker dressed in nightshirt and nightcap and carrying a lantern and alarm clock, is the type of stunt that will get newspaper publicity and even a photograph. The crowning of a "king for the day" as recognition to the high producer at a report meeting is likely to make the newspapers. No chamber of commerce needs to feel that the use of stunts or "horseplay" is beneath its dignity or that of its campaign workers. Wholesome fun—cleverly done—is always in good taste and can help greatly to make the campaign a success.

The publicity program should be carefully scheduled, and the schedule religiously observed so that publicity pieces are mailed in proper continuity. A full set of literature should reach every prospect before personal solicitation gets under way. The same careful timing must be observed for newspaper releases so that each story has distinctive news value. Names of the chairmen of the various departments of the campaign should be released separately so as to give new leads on news as the campaign progresses.

Educational and Speaking Programs

The first task of the educational program is that of selling the board of directors and the campaign executive committee on the campaign plans. Without the wholehearted and enthuiastic support of these groups the campaign has, of course, little chance of succeeding.

The next step is a joint meeting of the members of all standing committees of the chamber. In almost every organization there are some committees that are practically inactive, but even the members of these committees should be prevailed upon to attend. The meeting should be held prior to any public announcement of the campaign. Its purpose is to present the tentative campaign plans and to seek suggestions and constructive criticisms from the men on whom the chamber relies for active committee work. Ample time should be allowed for discussion from the floor and sound suggestions should readily be incorporated in the campaign plans.

As soon as possible thereafter a meeting should be held with the presidents, secretaries and program chairmen of civic, professional and trade organizations to present the campaign plans to them. The final item on the agenda should be an appeal for speaking engagements. Information should be obtained about the time and meeting place of each organization, the average number in attendance, the speaking dates available and the number of minutes allowed for the delivery of the chamber's message. For this purpose mimeographed forms should be distributed, completed and collected before the meeting breaks up.

The next step in the educational program should be a meeting with the local managers of national firms. The chairman and speakers at this meeting should themselves be managers of national concerns. They should be men who have been active in chamber affairs and whose companies have given liberal support to the organization. At the end of the meeting an information blank should be filled out by all those present. It should call for information about the name and title of the participant, the name of the company which he represents, whether membership support should be taken up with him personally and, if so, whether it should be done by letter or personal call. If he prefers that a letter be sent to the home office, the representative should be asked to supply the name, title and complete address of the executive to whom it should be sent. Immediately following the meeting a letter and a copy of the information blank, together with a stamped envelope, should be sent to every local manager who failed to attend. Incidentally, all letters to national firms—whether addressed to the local manager or the home office—should be written on the business letterhead of the chairman of the national firms committee and signed by him. Copies of all letters and literature sent to a home office should always be sent to the local manager for his information.

If a local manager indicates that he wishes to settle the matter of support in personal conference with a representative of the chamber, his prospect card should be turned over to the advance subscription committee or, if the firm is small, to the team organization for further action. Likewise, one of these two organizations should follow up on any national firm that fails to return the information blank mailed to it. Persistent follow up on such concerns frequently results in substantial subscriptions.

Subscription Quotas

It is the responsibility of the evaluation committee to establish adequate, fair and equitable subscription quotas for all large concerns in the community. Its field of activity should include local as well as national firms, and member as well as non-member companies. Quotas should be based largely upon ability to pay, but they should also take into consideration special services rendered to or benefits enjoyed by particular lines of business or groups of firms. Because the work of the committee must be completed before personal solicitation can get under way, an early meeting should be scheduled.

When the committee meets, each member should be provided with a mimeographed list of all concerns that might reasonably be expected to pay annual dues in excess of a stated minimum, say $100. The names of these companies should be grouped by lines of business so as to permit uniform treatment of all firms in the same or kindred lines. The list should show the commercial rating of each company, as well as its present subscription. It should also provide space for insertion of the quotas agreed upon by the members of the committee.

The committee might best proceed by first considering and establishing the quotas for the largest company in each line of business. This step will serve two purposes. First, it will enable the committee to establish quotas that are equitable as between lines of business; and, secondly, using the quotas of the largest company in each line as a standard, it is fairly easy to set reasonable quotas for all other firms of the group. The quotas may turn out to have little relationship to the current subscriptions of many companies. For example, if budget requirements call for an overall subscription increase of 100 per cent, it may be necessary to set quotas for some firms three or four times as large as their current subscriptions. On the other hand, the committee may find that some companies are already subscribing their full share and that it would be unfair to ask them to pay more. Very substantial quotas may, of course, be established for many concerns which are not yet members of the chamber of commerce. When quotas have been agreed upon by the committee, they should be posted on prospect cards for the confidential information of solicitors.

Advance Solicitation

When the evaluation committee has completed its work, it is time for the advance subscription committee to go into action. It is a good idea, at the organization meeting of the committee, to give each member a mimeographed list showing the names of all companies to be solicited and ask him to check those he is willing to interview. This procedure avoids the haphazard assignments that are inevitable when a long list of company names are read and assignments made on the spot. It permits the manager to make up a master record showing for each company the names of the members who have volunteered to assume responsibility for it. Assignments can then be made carefully in privacy by the committee chairman and chamber manager, perhaps assisted by the general campaign chairman. If several members have selected the same company, the assignment should go to the man who can exert the greatest customer or financial influence—not to the man who is on the receiving end of the company's favor. Some companies for which there are no volunteers, may have to be assigned arbitrarily; but the number of these cases can be reduced by asking each committee member to check about twice as many names as he will actually be assigned. With few exceptions it will be necessary to give a committee member the card of his own organization, but this should not be done until a meeting has been held at which the campaign leaders do a convincing job of selling the chamber's program and needs.

If the work of the advance subscription committee is to succeed, pace-setting will be necessary. Nothing is more effective than being able to announce at the organization meeting of the committee that every company represented on the board of directors of the chamber has subscribed its full quota. If success with other large companies can also be announced, so much the better. This means that work with key companies must start early—even before the advance subscription committee begins its campaign. Because of the time element involved in getting action from national firms, these also should be scheduled for early attention.

It is best to allow almost a week of solicitation before the first report meeting of the committee is held. Large companies do not move quickly and repeated calls may be necessary before results are secured. If the first report meeting should show meager returns, it might have a depressing effect on the campaign. Good news should never be withheld but should be rushed to members by "flash" bulletins. Such news not only serves to encourage and spur members on, but may also be used effectively in inducing other prospects to sign up. Bad news, on the other hand, should be suppressed and "calamity howling" should be avoided. If the steps outlined are followed with proper timing, the work of the advance subscription committee may go a long way to ensure the success of the entire campaign. If, at the opening breakfast of the public phase of the campaign, the committee has completed its work and can deliver an inspiring report, the job of the team organization will seem a cinch.

Building the Team Organization

The job of building the team organization requires a great deal of thought and some technique. If a sound procedure is carefully followed step by step, however, it should not be too difficult to recruit capable workers for all levels of responsibility. An important requisite to success is that the manager should know his membership well enough so that he can offer an ample slate of capable candidates for each job and head off possible selections of incompetent, indifferent or irresponsible men. If, for example, six division commanders are to be appointed, the manager should be prepared to submit to the chairman of the team organization a list of 12 recommended candidates, arranged in order of preference. The chairman should make his selections from this list and secure their acceptances. The names of the men who are not selected as division commanders should be added to the slate of candidates for the next level of jobs, the team captains.

If six divisions of five teams each are to be used, the manager must be prepared to offer a list of 60 to 70 candidates for team captains. The six division commanders should meet with the chairman and, in turn, select a name from the list until it is exhausted. Then, armed with ten or twelve names, each commander should proceed to enroll five captains. Any names he does not use should be turned back to campaign headquarters for possible use by other division commanders who may have had difficulty in securing acceptances.

The names left over after the completion of the selection of team captains should be used by the manager in making up a roster of preferred teamworkers. The roster, containing 250 or 300 names consecutively numbered, should be sent to the team captains in ample time so that they may have the opportunity of studying the list and making tentative choices in advance of a selection meeting. The meeting should be attended by all of the 30 captains. In order to facilitate selection each team should be given a number. Proceeding around a U-shaped table, each captain in turn should make a selection by calling his team number and the number of the candidate of his choice, until each captain is armed with the names of eight or ten desirable workers. As the selections proceed the manager and one or two members of the staff should enter them on a set of master records by writing the appropriate team number opposite the name of each candidate chosen. The team captains need only cross a name off their lists when its number is called.

This method of selecting captains and workers has several advantages. It helps to ensure an even balance of team strength. It gives each captain a "first mortgage" on a definite group of men, thereby eliminating the possibility that three or four captains may try to enroll the same worker—merely to annoy the worker and discourage the unsuccessful captains. It prevents any captain from "jumping the gun" and it discourages the formation of cliques and factions. It helps to ensure that the team organization will represent a cross section of church and social interests as well as of service clubs and other civic organizations.

As soon as the division commanders and team captains have been enrolled, a letter should be sent to every chamber member who is desired as a campaign worker, asking him to volunteer for service by signing and returning a business reply card. The letter should state briefly what the chamber is planning to do, why it is doing it, when the campaign will be held, and how the member may be of assistance. Such a letter will run interference for the team captains who are about to call on the members to ask them to work on teams. It will help to sell them on acceptance, and it will actually get volunteer cards by return mail. The mailing list should, however, be carefully culled. For this purpose, a complete set of envelopes might be run through the addressograph plates and throw-outs made of the members who are wanted elsewhere in the campaign, who are physically unable to perform this sort of service or who have proved themselves undesirable for campaign work. A member should never be eliminated merely because he has lacked interest in the chamber. There is no way of telling whether such interest may not be aroused by the objectives of the campaign, by the quality of its leadership or for some other reason. A complete list of chairmen, division commanders and team captains should appear in the left margin of the letterhead.

A well-written letter sent to a live membership has been known to produce as many volunteers as the team organization requires. The response will, however, depend in part on the chamber's record in previous campaigns. If the worker has never been asked to handle more prospects than those he was told would be his, if the chamber has never extended a campaign beyond the announced closing date and if prospect cards and other aids have been accurate and helpful, most chamber members are usually willing to devote quite a few hours once a year to help build their chamber of commerce and their community. If, on the other hand, the record of previous campaigns has been one of poor leadership, careless preparation, broken promises and failure, it would hardly be reasonable to expect other than great difficulty in enlisting volunteer workers.

Assignment of Prospects

There are so many methods of selecting or assigning prospects that it is impossible to outline all of them. Each method has its adherents as well as its advantages and disadvantages. Perhaps the most efficient method, however, is that of advance requisition. A complete list of all prospects, together with a letter of explanation and instruction, is mailed to every team worker as soon as his acceptance has been reported to headquarters. The worker is asked to study the list carefully and to ask for the cards he believes himself best equipped to handle. For the purpose of facilitating selection it is a good idea to arrange the prospects by lines of business. When the requisitions are returned to campaign headquarters, assignment follows the same procedure as that outlined for the work of the advance subscription committee. In this case, however, requisitions will be received from six or seven times as many men, and that is what makes the task of handling them difficult.

Training the Worker

One of the keys to a successful campaign is an effective training program that will equip the volunteer worker to do an intelligent selling job. Few members know their chamber thoroughly or are acquainted with all its activities. Most members must be told. This can be done by a well-planned instruction meeting and by the distribution of good sales literature—printed or mimeographed.

One of the best means of coaching workers for the job ahead is a sales demonstration presented at a pre-campaign instruction meeting. Such a skit might show how two campaign workers interview a tough prospect. If the skit is to be effective, it is necessary to prepare a complete manuscript and to place it in the hands of a capable cast. It is not necessary that the parts should be memorized. With a copy of a good manuscript in the hands of each "actor" two or three days before the demonstration, it is amazing how well the cues and the gist of the lines will be mastered. With fairly good salesmen as actors, a "finished" performance may be staged with only one or two rehearsals. After the performance—but not before—it is a good idea to hand each campaign worker a mimeographed copy of the entire manuscript because it may be used as a "refresher" manual on the selling arguments of the campaign.

The campaign leaders should do most of the talking at the instruction meeting. The chamber manager should, however, be given the opportunity of outlining the mechanics of the campaign and other details. By so doing it is possible to simplify the program of the subsequent opening breakfast and make it a truly inspirational affair. The pre-campaign instruction meeting serves also the purpose of a "fire drill" in that it may show up possible weaknesses in the campaign organization. A poor attendance by a particular team or division, for example, gives advance warning of probable difficulty and may suggest the necessity of changing leadership or rebuilding before the campaign opens.

The Worker's Kit

One of the last steps in campaign preparation is that of building a worker's kit and assembling the material that goes into it. Whether it is professionally designed and printed or only a mimeographed envelope, the kit should be made of heavy paper stock so that it can withstand days of heavy campaign use. It should be large enough to house comfortably prospect cards, instructions and campaign literature—yet small enough to fit the side pocket of a business suit. If the stock is available, it is a good idea to make the kits of a somewhat flamboyant color so that they stand out and identify the workers. Printing may also be in color, but in that case the stock must be light enough so that the print can be read. The front of the kit should carry the name of the chamber or the slogan of the contest in large letters, and beneath it the name of the worker, his team number and division. The back of the kit is a good place to list, in high-spot fashion, the objectives of the campaign, the chamber's program of work or a roster of services. Volunteer workers cannot be expected to memorize all sales points and it may help them to have a reminder in front of them as they tell the story of the campaign.

The kit should contain the prospect cards assigned to the worker, five or six subscription forms or application blanks, and copies of any sales manual or other promotional materials. Incidentally, by advance arrangement with the police department, the possession of a worker's kit and the display of a windshield sticker might be used to authorize overtime parking for the duration of the campaign.

Kick-Off Meeting

In recent years "early bird" breakfasts have gained increased popularity. Among the advantages of breakfast meetings are: (1) no other meetings or appointments compete for the attendance of business and professional men, (2) food and catering expense is lower than for luncheon and dinner meetings, (3) speakers and audience are not yet burdened with the business worries of the day, and (4) the very fact that breakfast meetings are still the exception marks the event as a "special occasion".

In most cities a breakfast meeting will not secure maximum attendance if it is called for a time earlier than 7:30 A.M. If attendance needs to be promoted, it can be done by mailing a copy of the invitation or meeting announcement to the home so that it will come to the attention of the member's family. Some chambers have successfully conducted a telephone campaign early enough in the morning of the meeting day to get the members up and on their way in time for the breakfast. Such a telephone campaign will usually require a number of operators, however, because all calls must be campleted within a brief period. Moreover, there is always the danger of adverse reaction from members whose families have been unnecessarily disturbed.

The program should call for adjournment not later than 9:00 o'clock. Food should be ready to go on the table promptly when the members arrive. It is a good idea to give the occasion warmth and welcome with music, if only an accordionist is used. Group singing at the breakfast tables, entirely impromptu and undirected, is likely to add a great deal to the spirit of the meeting.

The dining room should be that which is to be used for all other campaign meetings. Shifting around tends to confuse members and to reduce attendance. The workers should be seated by divisions and teams. A long table for each division is better than a series of smaller tables, one for each team. A long table will equalize team attendance, while one or two lonesome and embarrassed men at an otherwise empty team table will merely advertise a campaign failure. All tables should be large enough and there should be sufficient room between tables to enable the men to work comfortably on their reports. Each division table should be clearly identified by a large poster or pennant, and smaller cards should mark the seats of each team. Colorful division and team cards can decorate a meeting room attractively and inexpensively. If the team organization is large, it is advisable to elevate the speakers table slightly. An attractive scoreboard should be erected behind the speakers' table, and should make its appearance at the "early bird" breakfast. It should be lettered to show the designations of divisions and teams as well as the names of commanders and captains. For the purpose of providing a complete record of the progress of each team and division as the campaign proceeds, there should be a separate column for recording the results reported at each report meeting. There should also be a column for "total-to-date" results, but the figures of this column should, of course, be revised at each meeting.

Report Meetings

Report meetings should be held at frequent intervals during the campaign. They are usually most successful when conducted as brief luncheon sessions opening at 12:00 o'clock noon and closing not later than 1:45 p.m. The program of these meetings should be fast-moving and varied. Except for straight announcements, no chamber or campaign official should speak more than once during the campaign. All talks should be short, and needless repetition should be avoided. Discussion from the floor should be encouraged and even prearranged. This might best be done by having the division commanders call on each of their team captains for his report. As each team reports, the results of the day should be recorded on the scoreboard. Individual workers should also be invited to tell about unusual successes and experiences. Such a procedure is likely to kindle division and team rivalry, and to encourage challenges and counter challenges on which the workers will try to make good.

Some campaign workers develop the bad habit of withholding a substantial part of their production from their progress reports. The deception is well intended. The workers may merely try to keep their rivals guessing—or they may wish to be able to report a "thriller" when the campaign draws to a close. Whatever the purpose, if the practice is widespread, the results may be serious. The apparent lack of success during the early part of the campaign may discourage the more timid among the workers—and the feeling of futility may spread to the point where the campaign all but disintegrates. Even if the consequences are not quite that serious, the practice places the campaign leaders under severe handicap. Unless all subscriptions are reported promptly and completely the leaders have no way of knowing whether the campaign is succeeding or failing—or whether the prospects are even being worked. They are therefore in no position to plan intelligently or to take remedial action where needed.

There are several methods of inducing prompt and complete reports at every meeting. Perhaps the best way is to adopt a scoring method that imposes a penalty on the team or worker who thinks that it is good fun to "hold out" on his fellow workers. Such a plan might call for a heavy point bonus for all subscriptions reported at the first meeting, a lesser bonus for those reported at the second meeting, followed eventually by a minimum of points for production reported at the final meeting. The plan is, of course, likely to be most effective if attractive prizes are awarded to the workers who accumulate the largest total number of points. Special recognition may also be given the divisions, teams and individuals who report the largest production at each meeting. Such recognition may take the form of prizes or it may be no more than honorable mention in the campaign bulletin. This bulletin, which should be sent almost daily to the entire campaign organization, should contain complete production records all the way down to the individual worker. If the campaign is centered on new memberships, the bulletin should also publish the names of all new members. A newsy and well-written bulletin will be read and may be one of the most effective means of stirring campaign workers to an all-out effort.

At each meeting a report envelope should be furnished to every worker so that he can complete his report and turn it in to his team captain. The face of the envelope should carry the name of the worker and should provide spaces for reporting the names of the prospects whose subscriptions or applications are enclosed, the amount in cash or check, and the number of production points claimed by the worker. Each captain should be given a similar, although larger, envelope so that he can complete his team report and enclose the sealed report envelopes of his workers. All reports should be audited immediately after the close of the meeting, and the bulletins sent to the campaign workers should list the correct figures. Scoreboard corrections should be made before the organization holds its next report meeting.

Turning the Campaign into Victory

A successful campaign calls for an auspicious conclusion; a celebration that will be *long* remembered—and *well* remembered when the chamber again finds it necessary to call for volunteers to aid in its membership work. This is the time for the chamber to show itself a worthy host by mobilizing all the showmanship and talent at its disposal. The occasion calls for a "victory dinner", special music, perhaps cocktails, speeches, award of prizes and honors, and plenty of stunts. It should emphasize the success gained, and the importance of that success—not only to the chamber, but also to the community as a whole.

With the close of the campaign, the chamber management and the campaign leaders should issue a final bulletin of reports in which they express thanks to the entire campaign organization. It is also important to write personal letters of appreciation to all individuals, business concerns and civic organization deserving special recognition.

SUMMARY

1. Members supply the manpower and the finances for a chamber of commerce and are therefore fundamental to its very existence.

2. Selling chamber memberships is like selling any other type of merchandise—value and advantage to the buyer must be demonstrated.

3. A permanent card file should be maintained for cataloging the solicitation history of every prospect invited to membership.

4. Only firms or individuals engaged in ethical business pursuits should be permitted membership.

5. Membership dues should be continuous—not requiring annual "resale" contact, and membership should constitute a subscription of dollars rather than mere "joining". The membership application agreement should be worded accordingly. "Contributions" less than minimum dues should be discouraged.

6. A dues evaluation committee should determine the amount of support that can reasonably be asked from individual larger concerns.

7. The invoice date for membership dues should in each case be governed by the date of the membership application. This method ensures continuous income and spreads the burden of billing and accounting over the entire year.

8. In order to assimilate new members successfully, definite procedures should be instituted to extend them a hearty welcome and give importance to their affiliation with the chamber.

9. The mailing of membership dues invoices can be made an opportunity for membership conservation by enclosing printed materials reviewing the chamber's current accomplishments.

10. Unpaid dues should be followed up promptly for collection and determination of reasons for delinquency. If suspension is necessary, action taken should be on friendly basis to encourage future reaffiliation.

11. Positive procedures for salvaging resignations should be established; membership committee and board of directors must assume rightful responsibility in this effort.

12. Membership committees and clubs, if developed into groups motivated by friendly interest and stimulated by occasional contests, can be depended upon for continuous production.

13. When it is necessary to conduct a membership campaign, it must be realized that thorough advance preparation and the most detailed organization of every single phase of the entire effort are necessary if the campaign is to be successful. A complete day-to-day chart precisely outlining every step of the campaign should be prepared beforehand and followed without deviation.

14. Men heading up the campaign organization should be selected with great care.

15. Copies of campaign literature and mailing pieces sent to the prospect list should also be mailed to the entire membership for purposes of membership conservation.

16. Local offices of large companies under absentee ownership should not be overlooked when preparing the master prospect list.

17. Difficult prospects should be assigned campaign workers who can exert customer or financial influence, rather than to workers who are on the receiving end of the prospect company's favors.

18. Use should be made of the strategy of pace-setting—accomplished by timely announcements of sizable advance subscriptions.

19. A foolproof system of campaign assignments should be devised to prevent duplication and conflicts in the selection of prospects by the teamworkers.

20. Preparation plans for the campaign must include an effective training program for volunteer personnel. They should be equipped with workers' kits containing complete selling ammunition.

21. During the actual campaign continuous contact with workers should be maintained by frequent report meetings and daily progress bulletins.

22. To prevent teamworkers from "holding out" signed membership applications until the last day of the campaign, a point system which penalizes such delayed reporting can be instituted.

23. All newspaper and radio publicity opportunities of the campaign should be exploited.

24. The campaign should close with a rousing "Victory Dinner" to provide an evening of fun and fellowship and to inspire the teamworkers with lasting pride in their accomplishment.

Appendix to Chapter V

Charting the Membership Campaign

The preceding chapter has stressed the importance of careful preparation as a means of insuring the success of a membership campaign. Each step in the effort must be planned and scheduled in detail. It is the purpose of this appendix to show, by an example, how this may be accomplished.

For this purpose let us assume that the board of directors of the chamber of commerce has come to the conclusion that it is necessary to increase both the membership and the subscriptions of present members. The effort is to be handled by the chamber staff and membership without the aid of professional assistance. It is, therefore, necessary to set up a campaign organization consisting of (1) a speakers' bureau, (2) a publicity committee, (3) an evaluation committee, (4) an advance subscription committee, (5) a national firms committee and (6) a sales organization consisting of divisions and teams. Because the chamber staff is to be responsible for all preparations, ample time must be allowed for planning and organization. We may assume that in this case, seven or eight weeks are believed adequate. It is now September 1. The closing date of the campaign is, therefore, tentatively scheduled for October 21.

Our very first step is to spread a long strip of wrapping paper on a table and draw a day-to-day chart for the period running from Monday, September 4, to Saturday, October 21. Part of such a chart is shown by figure 3. We allow panels of two-inch blocks beneath each day on the chart and we label one panel for each department of the campaign organization so that we have room to pencil in the gridiron of squares the things we are to do in each department each day. The next step is to check every possible agency and the calendar to ascertain all local events as well as all national and religious holidays within that seven-week period. Each is entered immediately under its chart date so that every important community occasion is constantly before us as a warning signal not to schedule campaign meetings in conflict. (See Fig. 3.)

Dinner meetings held on Fridays always involve a dual menu. Furthermore, Friday evenings are becoming increasingly popular for social affairs. Therefore we pick Thursday evening, October 19, for the "victory dinner" and it is entered on the chart. To provide proper spacing between report luncheons we chart the "second report luncheon" for Monday, October 16, and the "first report luncheon" for Thursday, October 12. This automatically charts Monday, October 9, as the logical time for the "opening breakfast" of the campaign. Before proceeding further we now check the manager of the only hotel which has a banquet room large enough to serve the campaign organization, and we make certain that all the dates desired are available. It is injurious to attendance and interest to attempt to move meetings to different hotels, or even from one banquet room to another in the same hotel.

We want our instruction information to be fresh in the minds of the team organization when it starts its work in the public phase of the campaign. Therefore we schedule our "instruction meetings" as close to the time of the opening breakfast as possible—the "clean-up meeting" (for laggards) on October 6, Divisions D, E and F on October 5, and Divisions A, B and C for October 4.

Our instruction meetings are all scheduled for 4:00 p.m. so that only a brief notice will be required. We therefore set October 2 as the deadline for workers to be enrolled. Realizing that we must give team captains almost a week in which to complete enrollment of their workers, we set September 26 as the time of a luncheon meeting with team captains where we will divide a list of desirable workers. This means that we should chart September 22 as a deadline for enrollment of team captains.

To allow sufficient time for division commanders to enroll their team captains we now set September 18 as the date for a luncheon meeting with them to launch the enrollment work. To permit full attendance at this meeting, we now chart September 15 as the deadline for the enrollment of division commanders.

In order to get ready for these meetings, the chairman of the team organization must have the greater part of a week to secure his division commanders, so we now set September 11 as the date when we must have the acceptance of the campaign chairman. In charting the schedule of meetings, and in fact the entire campaign, we find that it will be unwise for us to have any luncheon meetings on Tuesday or Thursday. Rotary and Kiwanis clubs meet on those days; each has an exceptionally large membership, so attendance at our campaign meetings would suffer.

The chart is now filled in with much day-to-day detail between the dates of September 9 and October 21 on the panel scheduling the work of the team organization. We now drop down to the next panel and chart the work of the advance subscriptions committee. Using the same procedure as we did in charting the team organization schedule, we set the date on which the advance subscriptions work should be completed. In fixing this date we must bear in mind that the advance committee should have completed its work and be ready to report on its success to the team organization at the opening breakfast when that organization is about to begin its work. In scheduling all meetings of the advance subscriptions committee we have watched carefully the team organization panel on the chart to make certain that the several luncheons are not in conflict with noon-hour meetings already established. Chamber officers and the manager should certainly attend all of them. The detail and mechanics in connection with the advance subscriptions work are entered on the chart for proper timing. This will include the deadline of enrollment for committee personnel and a much earlier date for the acceptance of the chairman.

The work of the evaluation committee will be confined entirely to the rating of corporations to be solicited by the advance subscriptions committee, so we now chart the appointment of the evaluation committee and its chairman for September 8, and schedule a 5:00 p. m. meeting of that committee for September 14. At its only meeting we will want the evaluation committee to review a classified list of the city's larger firms, so we chart September 9 as the date on which we should have that list ready.

Next, we drop to the national firms panel. We have decided to have an early informational meeting with local branch managers and upon studying the schedule we chart the date of September 21 for that luncheon meeting, and September 14 as the date for mailing our letters of invitation to local managers. This means that we must have our list of national firms prospects charted for completion on September 11; and since we will need the early advice of the national firms chairman, we now chart September 8 as the date when we must have his acceptance. We then fill in other details and mechanics involving the national firms solicitation and our letter-writing campaign.

We now drop down to the next panel which concerns educational meetings and the speakers' bureau. Obviously all speaking engagements on the subject of the chamber's expansion program should be completed before the opening breakfast of the campaign—for we want them to be of the greatest possible help to the early work being done on advance subscriptions and national firms solicitation. Also, they should be concentrated into compact spacing close to the opening of the campaign so as to intensify newspaper publicity and public interest. Therefore we now schedule the period from Monday, September 25, to Saturday, October 7, as the preferred period for speaking engagments.

Before our speakers go forth on their assignments we need a meeting with them to submit a speakers' manual and other material and agree on fundamentals of presentation. We now chart that meeting for September 21 and schedule September 19 as the date when the speakers' manual should be completed. Recalling that especially the large service clubs book their programs far in advance, we chart Tuesday, September 5, for a reminder that the program chairmen of the largest clubs should be contacted for the purpose of setting aside speaking dates.

To interest civic, professional and trade organizations in the chamber's expansion program we now chart September 14 for an informational breakfast to which the presidents, secretaries and program chairmen are to be invited, and schedule September 9 as the date for the invitations to be mailed.

Our first group meeting under the educational program, however, should be with the members of all the chamber's standing committees for a preliminary discussion of the expansion program. This meeting is now charted for September 11; we schedule September 6 as the date to mail the invitational letters and fill in other chart details regarding the educational program.

Leadership requirements for the operation of all the departments of the campaign can now be established as we have charted the scope of activity for each, the period to be covered, and the definite schedule of meetings. Therefore we now chart for September 4 the necessity of preparing a highly briefed outline of leadership requirements for review by the chamber president, and later by the general chairman of the campaign who must now be scheduled for immediate appointment.

We are now ready to chart the publicity and printing program and we first decide on the targets we want to hit by direct mail, the number of impacts advisable and the mailing dates for each printed piece. We can then chart the dates when the manuscript for each publicity piece must be ready for the printer and other details in connection with the direct-mail program.

We have now finished penciling our rough chart on the wrapping paper and must have it typed under date headings starting with September 4 and finishing with October 21. Below each date heading the various panels of campaign department activity will show, under their respective subheads, every detail of all the things which need to be done each day in order to operate the campaign on schedule. This record is typed in multiple copies so that campaign leaders and headquarters staff may have a complete picture of the job ahead. The penciled work chart has now served its purpose and can be discarded. From now on it's important that we adhere religiously to the charted schedule and permit nothing to interfere with it. A well-planned and charted campaign is a prerequisite to success. A loosely-planned campaign which gets off schedule is almost invariably a failure.

Chapter VI

Fiscal Operations

IT HAS BEEN SAID that in an organization such as the chamber of commerce, sound fiscal practices start with the development of a strong program of work. On the one hand, such a program determines to a considerable extent the financial needs of the organization; and on the other, it is the merchandise which the chamber has to sell—the means by which it can secure its financial needs. But it is not enough to have a strong program of work. It is also important that that program should be carried out effectively—that every dollar of income should be so expended as to secure maximum benefits to the organization, its membership and the community at large. This is the only way by which the chamber can make sure of continuous, liberal support from the business community.

Most members of the chamber of commerce are businessmen. Many of them deal with financial problems in their own businesses every day. They know good fiscal practices. They are therefore quick to sense the ability or ineptness of the manager in these respects; and they will invariably establish the quality of financial management as a major criterion for judging the efficiency of the manager and his organization. Fortunately, because of their vast experience, these same men can also be of great help to the manager in developing and carrying out a sound financial plan that will:

(1) Raise enough money on a continuous basis to make possible a sound program of work.
(2) Ensure the expenditure of funds in the best interests of the members and the community.
(3) Establish sound, business-like procedures and records for financial control.

The purpose of this chapter is to outline briefly and simply some basic plans and financial practices that have proved successful. No attempt will be made to set up an ideal, because no pattern will fit every chamber of commerce. Local needs and traditions have established precedents which can—and should—be changed only slowly over time. The important thing is that each chamber should develop a definite plan and adhere to it continuously and systematically.

SOURCES OF REVENUE

Without exception, membership dues constitute by far the most important source of income for all chambers of commerce. Additional revenue may, however, be secured from special subscriptions, service charges, operation of club facilities and dining rooms, publications, directories, as well as from public funds. Each of these sources of income will be considered briefly.

Membership Dues

Because of the importance of membership dues as a source of income, one of the first questions that must be decided is the amount of annual dues. The starting point for that decision is the needs of the chamber. The total income from dues—together with whatever other revenue the chamber may anticipate—must be sufficient to cover all overhead expenses such as salaries, rent, light, heat, telephone, telegraph, repairs and replacements, printing and supplies, as well as the specific cost of all projects included in the current program of work. In addition, there should be sufficient income left over to provide a reasonable reserve fund. Such a need must be established clearly and convincingly. Experience has shown that individual businessmen will readily pay even high dues when they are satisfied that the funds are needed. But they will just as quickly cut their payments when the dues seem excessive in terms of the functions performed and the services rendered by the chamber of commerce.

Need, then, is only the starting point. The chamber must also be able to justify its dues on the basis of a record of accomplishments. Moreover, dues cannot be established in a vacuum. They must take into consideration past precedents as well as the ability of the business community to pay. If the needs of the chamber are such as to require excessive dues, it may be because the organization is overly elaborate and wasteful, because the program of work is too ambitious, or because the chamber has failed to sell itself to a sufficiently broad segment of the community. In the first two cases, retrenchment appears to be the only solution. In the third

BASIC DUES RATES

From the 1950 Survey of Local Chambers by Commercial Organization Department Chamber of Commerce of the United States

Group	A		B		C		D		E		F		G		H		TOTALS	
Population	0-5,000		5-10,000		10-25,000		25-50,000		50-100,000		100-200,000		200-500,000		Over 500,000			
Number of Chambers Surveyed	174		219		255		123		67		47		24		16		925	
	Individual	Firm	Individual	Firm	Individual	Firm	Individual	Firm	Individual	Firm	Individual	Firm	Individual	Firm	Individual	Firm	Individual	Firm
Basic Dues Rates																		
No. of Chambers Having a Basic Dues Rate for Firms and Individuals of:																		
$1 to $5	19	6	13	4	6	—	2	1	—	—	—	—	—	—	—	—	40	11
$6 to $10	14	3	27	6	21	2	4	—	1	1	—	—	—	—	—	—	67	12
$11 to $15	16	5	27	5	42	6	9	—	1	—	—	—	—	—	—	—	95	16
$16 to $20	2	4	3	4	—	2	3	1	—	—	—	—	—	—	1	—	9	11
$21 to $25	7	12	14	30	24	50	15	19	16	10	9	3	2	1	2	—	89	125
More than $25	1	3	1	9	1	4	8	8	3	6	6	7	8	8	5	7	33	52
(No. Reporting)	59	33	85	58	94	64	41	29	21	17	15	10	10	9	8	7	333	227

case, an organized membership campaign—such as that described in the preceding chapter—may provide the answer.

It should be emphasized, however, that experience has demonstrated that minimum dues, even in the smaller communities, should seldom be less than $25 per year. Many an idealist has lured his chamber of commerce into a tragic fiscal position by urging that a low rate of dues—with an even lower bargain rate to ministers, educators and professional men—will foster a wholesome community-wide interest in civic progress and provide substantial funds to give it practical expression. The fact is, however, that such bargain-rate memberships are high in bookkeeping and collection costs; they are precarious, ephemeral and undependable. For the same reasons it is inadvisable to seek—or even to accept—an "annual contribution" of less than minimum dues from the struggling businessman unable to afford a full membership. There are times when it is difficult to refuse such an offer, but it is best to do so.

No chamber of commerce is likely to secure sufficient income merely by selling individual memberships. One of the important problems that faces the management is that of persuading large firms—and others enjoying direct benefits from particular activities—to subscribe plural memberships or liberal sustaining-fund money. These large subscriptions are almost always necessary to provide a firm foundation for the chamber's operations.

Since the late 1920's little has been heard of the sustaining fund plan under which larger companies were asked to make payments over and above their membership dues. These additional subscriptions were usually secured by special campaigns. Commitments were made on a term basis—one to three years, but seldom more. The principal disadvantages of the plan were the necessity of renewal campaigns at the expiration of each term, and the consequent uncertainty and inability to plan ahead.

In recognition of these difficulties most chambers of commerce have in recent years asked larger firms to make a single subscription on a *continuous,* annual basis. Such a subscription usually entitles the company to plural memberships, the number depending on the amount of the payment. Although this plan avoids some of the pitfalls of the old sustaining fund, the problem of arriving at a fair and equitable subscription quota still remains to be solved. Some chambers

EFFECT OF INCREASING BASIC DUES RATES

From the 1950 Survey of Local Chambers by Commercial Organization Department
Chamber of Commerce of the United States

Group	A	B	C	D	E	F	G	H	TOTALS
Population	0-5,000	5-10,000	10-25,000	25-50,000	50-100,000	100-200,000	200-500,000	Over 500,000	
Number of Chambers Surveyed	174	219	255	123	67	47	24	16	925
	Indi-vidual / Firm	Indi-vidual / Firm	Indi-vidual / Firm	Indi-vidual / Firm	Indi-vidual / Firm	Indi-vidual / Firm	Indi-vidual / Firm	Indi-vidual / Firm	Indi-vidual / Firm
Increases in Basic Dues Rates Since 1947									
No. of Chambers Increasing Dues from a Lower Rate to:									
Between $5 - $10	8 / 2	10 / —	6 / 3	2 / 1	— / —	— / —	— / —	— / —	26 / 6
Between $11 - $15	9 / 5	9 / 6	14 / 2	2 / 1	— / —	— / —	— / —	— / —	34 / 13
Between $16 - $20	1 / 2	1 / 1	2 / 7	1 / 1	— / —	— / —	— / —	— / —	5 / 11
Between $21 - $25	1 / 4	15 / 23	9 / 21	4 / 1	3 / —	— / —	— / —	1 / —	33 / 49
More than $25	1 / 8	— / 8	4 / 9	10 / 10	7 / 6	12 / 10	8 / 7	2 / 3	44 / 61
(No. Reporting)	20 / 21	35 / 38	35 / 42	19 / 13	10 / 6	12 / 10	8 / 7	3 / 3	142 / 140
Results of Dues Rate Increases									
No. of Chambers Reporting an:									
Increase in Membership	37	56	44	12	6	7	7	3	172
Decrease in Membership	15	16	19	9	6	5	2	1	73
Increase in Income	40	61	58	22	12	10	9	4	216
Decrease in Income	12	12	5	—	—	2	—	—	31

have tried to develop formulae for determining the amount that should be solicited from each firm, but the results have been only partially successful. Perhaps the best procedure is to have a competent evaluation committee establish the share of the budget that each large firm and beneficiary may fairly be expected to carry. The work of such a committee has already been described in the preceding chapter.

A few of the older chambers of commerce still charge an entrance fee. The practice was started during the early history of the chambers in the belief that such a fee would place a greater value on membership and would help to cover the cost of enrolling the new member. It is now generally regarded as obsolete and is not recommended. Some chambers offer also life memberships against the payment of a substantial fee. Because such payments represent prepaid dues, they should be funded rather than regarded as income available for current expenses.

Income from Special Subscriptions

Many chambers of commerce have found that neither dues nor subscriptions to the general fund yield all the revenue needed. Some of them have, therefore, devised other methods of raising money. In some cases retailers or wholesalers have been asked to contribute additional funds to defray the cost of activities undertaken in their interest. Retail merchants, for example, frequently raise part of the money used to finance the retail activities of the chamber. Wholesalers and processors in the agricultural trades may undertake to defray part of the cost of agricultural activities; and hotels, resorts and other enterprises may make special contributions to tourist and convention promotions.

Special circumstances may also justify a more general solicitation for additional funds. For example, some chambers—sensing that unusual problems would arise during the reconversion period following the war—undertook successfully to raise substantial sums to be spent only for special projects of a post-war nature. Members may, however, easily become weary of frequent solicitations. Most businessmen prefer to make a large subscription once and for all, rather than being dunned repeatedly for small amounts. As a general policy, special drives for funds should, therefore, be held to a minimum. They do not produce permanent income, re-

AMOUNT OF INCOME FOR CHAMBERS OF COMMERCE

From the 1950 Survey of Local Chambers by Commercial Organization Department
Chamber of Commerce of the United States

Group	A	B	C	D	E	F	G	H	TOTALS
Population	0-5,000	5-10,000	10-25,000	25-50,000	50-100,000	100-200,000	200-500,000	Over 500,000	
Number of Chambers Surveyed	174	219	255	123	67	47	24	16	925
1947 Income									
Average Amount	$2,466	$5,928	$11,194	$17,636	$28,625	$49,626	$136,792	$299,257	$25,303
(No. Reporting)	(80)	(142)	(192)	(100)	(59)	(42)	(22)	(16)	(653)
1948 Income									
Average Amount	$3,006	$6,462	$12,203	$19,166	$30,573	$58,542	$143,941	$316,230	$25,224
(No. Reporting)	(112)	(168)	(214)	(110)	(61)	(45)	(22)	(16)	(748)
1949 Income									
Average Amount	$3,044	$6,802	$13,041	$21,713	$34,038	$62,866	$147,720	$323,092	$24,006
(No. Reporting)	(167)	(213)	(252)	(122)	(66)	(46)	(24)	(16)	(906)
1950 Income (Estimated)									
Average Amount	$3,054	$7,199	$13,671	$21,680	$35,544	$63,209	$161,296	$318,561	$25,088
(No. Reporting)	(152)	(193)	(221)	(111)	(60)	(44)	(22)	(15)	(818)

quire a great deal of time and effort, and may cause considerable resentment.

Service Charges and Miscellaneous Income

Some chambers augment their annual income by charging for special services—such as fees for credit reports, foreign language translations, certifying commercial invoices, issuing certificates of origin, furnishing traffic information and the like. Others do a small amount of mimeographing, get out letters or perform miscellaneous services for other organizations. A few chambers in smaller communities act as distributors of automobile and other licenses.

This type of income is usually small. Members and nonmembers who avail themselves of these services, however, are usually glad to pay for them. Moreover, it would hardly be fair to the total membership to render them free of cost. All members have the right to expect that their dues will be spent by the chamber for the good of the membership and the community as a whole, and not for special services that benefit only a few particular members.

Some activities—such as sports events, industrial expositions, festivals and fairs, home shows and auto shows— may actually return a profit over expenses and add to the total income of the chamber. Such activities are, however, generally conducted as a community service and profits are, therefore, usually negligible. The aim should be to make such activities pay for themselves. A profit is always preferable to a loss.

Income from Rents, Club Facilities and Dining Rooms

Chambers of commerce that own their buildings or sublet part of their leased space, add to their income through rentals. As a rule, however, the amount of extra revenue from this source is small. In most cases rents are no more than sufficient to cover operating expenses, interest, taxes and mortgage payments.

Comparatively few chambers provide club facilities. Those that do usually operate them on a fee basis sufficient to pay expenses and return a small profit. They maintain that these facilities are of value in attracting and holding members. A number of chambers that once operated dining rooms have, however, closed them because they showed a loss, took too much of the manager's time, or because they were a source of irritation to hotels and restaurants which complained bitterly about the competition.

A word of caution should be added concerning taxes. A chamber of commerce that sells services, operates a dining room or engages in other activities for profit, may endanger its tax-exempt status. This danger should be carefully evaluated before a chamber decides to buy and operate its own building, serve meals or engage in any activity that might be construed to be in competition with private enterprise. Even though no profit is realized, the accounts of the organization may become subject to scrutiny by the taxing authorities.

Income from Publications and Directories

Some chambers of commerce publish manufacturers' directories and buyers' guides. Others publish rosters of their members, and almost all chambers have some sort of official publication printed or mimeographed. Many of these directories and periodicals carry paid advertisements that produce some additional revenue. In most cases, however, advertising income is not sufficient to cover the cost of publication. The directories and periodicals constitute therefore a net charge against the general budget of the chamber.

Income from Public Funds

Some states have passed laws that permit cities or counties to support certain promotional activities of the chambers of commerce, such as industrial advertising and trade and tourist promotion. In other cases, municipalities and counties have, at their own discretion, appropriated funds for these and other chamber activities.

To the chambers that accept this kind of support, income from public funds may constitute a considerable portion of total revenue. Thus, according to a study of tax supported chambers made by the Commercial Organization Department of the Chamber of Commerce of the United States, revenue from this source ranged from an average of 36 per cent of total income in the case of small-city organizations, to an average of 11 per cent of all income in the case of large chambers of commerce.

The wisdom of accepting support from public funds has been a long-debated question. Those who favor the plan, argue that everyone benefits when new industries and tourists are attracted to the community and that everyone should, therefore, share the cost of maintaining the services necessary to accomplish these results. On the other hand, strong arguments are presented in opposition. The objection usually raised is that the chamber of commerce is a voluntary organization dedicated to community building. When a chamber accepts support from public funds and becomes a tax-supported institution, the very substance and fiber of the organization are destroyed. Moreover, acceptance of public funds may subject the chamber to political pressure and endanger its freedom of action. Its policies and program may be dictated by political expediency rather than by the needs of the community.

Without trying to resolve the controversy, it should be emphasized that the chamber of commerce that looks to public bodies for large appropriations instead of relying on voluntary contributions from private business, may suddenly find itself in serious financial difficulties. A new city administration, for example, may simply decide that it can no longer support the chamber. If tax funds are accepted, they should not constitute a major part of the organization's income. Moreover, it should be definitely agreed, preferably in writing, that such funds are to be administered by the chamber, for appropriate purposes, without interference or restraint by government officials.

THE BUDGET

Every chamber of commerce, whether large or small, should operate under a budget system. The budget is a tool for planning and controlling the chamber's income and expenditures over a stated period of time, usually a year. It is indispensable to efficient and successful operations. Among the major advantages of a budget system are the following:

(1) It compels advance planning and provides a studied estimate of needs and resources.

(2) It forces the chamber to evaluate each proposed activity in terms of its costs.

(3) By making possible ready comparison of anticipated receipts and expenditures with those of preceding years it furnishes a basis for evaluation of the financial soundness of the planned program of work.

(4) It keeps the financial goal for the new year constantly before the manager and officers of the chamber.

Budget Summary
Middletown Chamber of Commerce

Approved by _John Doe, Chm. Executive Committee_   Period from _Sept. 1, '50 to Aug. 31, '51._

TYPE OF INCOME	Income Last Year	Initial Estimate	Comments	Approved Amount
Dues and subscriptions	$20,430.00	$22,000.00	No campaign	$21,000.00
Special Funds	4,375.00	5,000.00	Centennial Pageant	7,000.00
Miscellaneous Income	860.00	1,000.00		750.00
TOTAL	$25,665.00	$28,000.00		$28,750.00

TYPE OF EXPENSE	Expense Last Year	Initial Estimate	Comments	Approved Amount
Administrative	$11,870.60	$12,000.00	Salary increases	$12,500.00
Trade Extension	3,796.41	5,000.00	Centennial	5,000.00
Agriculture	384.05	400.00	No. 4-H Club fair	300.00
Publicity	750.25	1,000.00	Special folder	850.00
Convention	1,286.42	1,400.00	No teachers convention	1,000.00
Industrial	886.86	900.00		800.00
Civic	783.64	800.00		750.00
Membership	427.08	450.00		400.00
Transportation	343.00	350.00		300.00
Rent	2,400.00	2,400.00		2,400.00
Repairs & Replacements	497.83	500.00	New mimeograph	700.00
Contingent Fund	2,238.86	2,800.00		2,750.00
			General reserve fund	1,000.00
TOTAL	$25,665.00	$28,000.00		$28,750.00

(5) It gives control over expenditures, and it enables the chamber to say "no" to appeals for financial help for projects outside its program.

(6) It provides a standard against which actual revenue and expenditures can be measured and evaluated.

Once prepared and approved, the budget should be a source of constant reference. It will be of no value if it is tucked away and forgotten. On the other hand, it should be realized that budgetary control has its limitations. No budget can take the place of sound management. There may be times when it becomes necessary or advisable to engage in activities or undertake expenditures for which no provision has been made in the budget. In such cases the budget should be modified. An undertaking of importance to the community should not be denied merely because it was not anticipated at the time when the budget was prepared. Nor should the budget be permitted to stifle individual initiative or to reduce management to routine operations. It should be regarded as a guide rather than as a tool of inflexible control.

From what has been said it should be obvious that it is impossible to set up a standard or ideal budget. The accompanying form is therefore intended only as an illustration of a summary budget for a small chamber of commerce.

Preparing the Budget

The budget is usually prepared annually for the ensuing fiscal year. Some chambers prefer, however, to set up semi-annual and even quarterly budgets, claiming that budgets covering a shorter period of time offer the advantages of greater flexibility and realism. The best practice is an annual budget revised monthly and modified as conditions may warrant.

The preparation of the budget is fundamentally an administrative matter. Responsibility for its preparation should therefore rest with the manager. In many chambers, however, the manager is assisted by a budget committee. If such a committee is used, its membership should be carefully selected. It is generally conceded that the president, treasurer, and the chairman of the finance committee should be among its members. To these may be added the chairman of the program of work committee and one or two other members who have particular qualifications for this type of work. Whether prepared by the manager alone or by the manager with the assistance of a budget committee, the budget should be subject to approval by the board of directors. The preparation of the budget includes several steps:

1. *Estimate of Income*

In estimating income for the coming year, actual experience during the current and preceding years should be used as a guide. Adjustment should be made for normal growth, for expected results from any planned membership campaign or for the effect of anticipated changes in business conditions. During the depression of the '30's, the budget maker necessarily had to be extremely conservative in his estimates, whereas he had every reason to be optimistic during the war years and for several years thereafter. In general, however, the manager needs to guard against over-optimism At the beginning of a new year it is only too easy to lay plans and entertain expectations that go far beyond the possibility of actual realization.

2. *Estimate of Expenses and Allocation of Funds*

The next step is that of estimating expenses. Many of them—such as rent, light, heat, telephone, insurance, office supplies, contribution to a pension plan and the like—are either contractual or vary little from one year to another. They can, therefore, easily be estimated on the basis of past experience. Although salaries may be included in this group, they should be carefully reviewed for the purpose of determining justifiable increases, if any. Other expenses vary considerably from one year to another, depending on the current and planned activities of the chamber.

In making provisions for the variable expenses two fundamentally different methods of approach are possible. The first method simply calls for a more or less arbitrary allocation of the available funds to different activities and projects. Such allocations may be made on the basis of past experience, or they may represent the amounts that are "reasonable" in the judgment of the manager. At any rate, when an allocation has been made, it constitutes the budget limit within which the particular activity must be conducted. To the extent that the limit is observed, it comes to be an important factor in determining the manner in which the activity is carried out. If the allocation should prove penurious, it may become necessary to trim the activity or to seek short-cuts and savings.

If, on the other hand, the budget appropriation turns out to be generous, that fact alone may invite unnecessarily elaborate or even wasteful activities. This is obviously the lazy man's approach.

The second method approach might be called the "objective and task" method. Under this method the manager attempts to define as accurately as possible the objectives of each activity and the tasks or steps necessary to achieve those objectives. Knowing the tasks, the manager can estimate the cost of each of them. He can, therefore, "build" the necessary appropriation in terms of the jobs to be done. Obviously, this method of approach must also take into consideration the funds available. If the sum of the various appropriations should exceed these funds, adjustments and cut-backs become necessary. With full knowledge of the requirements of each activity, however, such adjustments can be made intelligently and in such a manner as to cause the least possible disturbance.

The budget should also make provisions for contingencies. No manager or budget committee can foresee all needs. Unexpected demands for funds may therefore arise. In such an event—if no provisions had been made for contingencies— it might be necessary to refrain from undertaking a worthwhile service, cut back some planned activity or go to the membership for additionl funds. Each of these alternatives might offer serious difficulties. At any rate, it would be far better to insure against the occurrence of such a situation by making advance plans for contingencies. Finally, the budget should make provision for a reasonable contribution to a general reserve fund. The need for such a fund is dealt with more fully in a subsequent section of this chapter.

Although the manager is ultimately responsible for preparing the budget, it may sometimes be advisable to begin budget preparations by asking the various bureaus and committees to submit their budget requests. This procedure is likely to be most appropriate in the case of the larger chamber of commerce in which the manager cannot be expected to know in detail the plans and needs of every department and committee. When such a procedure is followed, however, it is necessary that each request be detailed and supported by adequate information so that the manager can evaluate its justification. If the manager approves a request for funds, he merely incorporates it in the total budget. If, on the other hand, he believes that an item should be denied or reduced, he should make the necessary adjustment only after conferring with the originator of the request. Although this procedure relieves the manager of a considerable part of the burden of budget preparation, it has also serious disadvantages. Committee chairmen and department heads may attempt to get liberal allotments by padding their estimates, and they may strenuously resist any cuts that the manager might propose. Jealousies may also develop among committee chairmen and even department heads if it is discovered that the requests of some fared better than those of others. Under these conditions a budget committee is a valuable assistance to the manager.

3. *Approval of Budget*

No budget should become final and official until it has been formally approved in the manner prescribed by the by-laws of the particular organization. In most chambers this should be the board of directors.

Many larger chambers place complete control of finances in the executive committee, granting it full authority to approve the budget, authorize unusual expenditures and confirm the appointment and salaries of directors of bureaus and other major assistants. This plan appears to be sound. Not only does it relieve the board of directors of the responsibility for financial details, but the smaller executive committee may be expected to give more careful consideration to the proposed budget than the board which is frequently large and unwieldy. Other large chambers require board approval as well as approval by the executive committee. Still others insist on approvals by a budget committee, the executive committee and then finally the board of directors. Too many "checks and balances" may complicate the procedure without making positive contributions to better budget making. However, having many leaders acquainted with the budget is helpful in financing the chamber.

Regardless of the procedure, it is important that the budget be formally approved. The directors or the members of the executive committee, by the very act of approval, make the budget their own. They may, therefore, be relied upon to be governed by its provisions and to come to the rescue of the manager when "raids" on the chamber treasury are attempted by members with an ax to grind or by other influential groups of the community.

OTHER FINANCIAL POLICIES AND PRACTICES

It has already been emphasized that, in matters of finance, the chamber of commerce should maintain standards as high as those of any well-run business. This means that the chamber must look ahead beyond immediate requirements and make plans for the "rainy days" that are almost certain to come. It means also that it must establish and adhere to definite policies and practices with respect to collection of income, control of expenditures and accounting.

Reserve Fund

There was a time when most chambers of commerce put nothing aside for a rainy day. Even today, there are those who contend that a chamber has no right to build up a surplus. They maintain that the member who pays his dues has a right to expect performance and that the chamber is, therefore, under a moral obligation to spend all funds received each year. This idea is, however, no longer generally held.

There are cycles in business. There are also cycles in chamber of commerce support; the more prosperous business is, the greater is the chamber revenue. The depression of the '30's emphasized the value of a reserve fund. Since then, many chambers have accumulated a surplus. The amount varies, depending on the particular community and the judgment of the manager and his board of directors. There is no uniform practice. Perhaps a happy medium is a reserve fund equal to the annual budget. At any event, some surplus should be accumulated. In the absence of such a surplus the chamber may not be able to function effectively during the very period when its services are most needed: when the community is down and out and looking for ways and means of rebuilding itself.

Collection of Income

Dues should be collected promptly when they fall due. Timely mailing of statements, tactful follow-up letters that sell the organization, and personal calls by a paid official or a volunteer committeeman help keep payments on a current basis. The by-laws of most organizations make specific provisions for handling delinquents. These provisions should be strictly observed unless circumstances justify exception.

Delinquent accounts should be charged off promptly as soon as their collectibility becomes doubtful. Failure to do so results merely in a misstatement of the financial condition of the chamber and tends to lull the manager and the board of directors into a false sense of security and accomplishment. Efforts to secure reinstatement of the delinquent member should, however, continue until the case is deemed hopeless.

Income from other sources should also be collected promptly and in a business-like manner. Service charges should either be collected at the time when the service is rendered, or billed monthly. All moneys received, whether in cash or by check, should be promptly deposited with the chamber's bank, and no payment should be made directly from cash so collected.

Control of Expenditures

Control of expenditures rests with the board of directors or the executive committee, which should authorize the manager to act in its behalf under prescribed procedures and safeguards. Some of these safeguards may be spelled out by the by-laws, others should be set out in the operating manual of the organization. Among the more important are the following:

(1) No expenditure shall be made and no debt or obligation shall be incurred in behalf of the chamber by any officer, employee or agent of the organization, unless such expenditure or obligation has been authorized in the budget or by special action of the board of directors or the executive committee, whichever body has the power to authorize expenditures.

(2) No committee, other than the executive committee, shall contract any financial obligation in behalf of the chamber.

(3) No transfer shall be made from a general to a special fund except upon authorization of the board of directors or the executive committee.

(4) When an approved special fund is to be raised, no obligation shall be incurred for the use of such fund until it has actually been collected.

(5) All payments, except payments out of the petty cash fund, shall be made by check.

Under the budget system there is no need for the manager to take every expenditure to the board of directors or the executive committee. Presumably, he has been appointed chief executive of his organization because the members have confidence in his ability to handle the job in all its ramifications. As long as he keeps within the budget the board of directors is not concerned and should not be bothered with the minute details of spending. If the approved budget exceeds income, the wise manager will hold expenditures within the income.

Because the manager is the one immediately responsible for sound financial operations, he should have direct control over all purchases and other expenditures, handling them personally or through an authorized member of the staff. Although all purchases should be made at the lowest possible price, taking quality and service into consideration, it is of course no more than fair that as many orders as possible should be placed with chamber members. When several members are in a position to furnish the wanted article, the business should be awarded as equitably as possible. Competitive bids should be requested on all major purchases. Centralized purchasing is recommended because it eliminates haphazard methods of buying and facilitates record keeping.

Payment of Bills

A chamber of commerce should pay its bills promptly when they are due, discounting them whenever possible. Prompt payment accomplishes several things. Not only does it preserve the credit standing of the chamber and its reputation as a well-run business organization, but it may also encourage suppliers to quote lower prices and give better service. Prompt payment reduces the cost of purchases by enabling the chamber to deduct cash discounts. In the course of a year, such discounts may add up to a considerable amount.

All invoices should be carefully checked to see that prices and extensions are right, and that the goods and services billed for have actually been received. Payment should be made by check, for a check serves as a receipt and facilitates accurate record keeping. Most organizations require two signatures on checks. Some require two signatures only when the amount exceeds $100. The signatures may be those of two authorized staff members, but are usually those of an officer and a staff member. All employees handling the funds of the organization should be bonded.

TOTAL PAYROLLS — SALARIES — RENT

From the 1950 Survey of Local Chambers by Commercial Organization Department
Chamber of Commerce of the United States

Group	A	B	C	D	E	F	G	H	TOTALS
Population	0-5,000	5-10,000	10-25,000	25-50,000	50-100,000	100-200,000	200-500,000	Over 500,000	
Number of Chambers Surveyed	174	219	255	123	67	47	24	16	925
Amount of 1949 Payroll									
Average Amount	$1,497	$3,366	$6,310	$9,395	$16,441	$30,687	$85,922	$175,678	$12,978
(No. Reporting)	(114)	(187)	(233)	(114)	(65)	(46)	(24)	(14)	(797)
Per Cent of 1949 Income Expended For:									
Staff Salaries (incl. Mgr.)	32.7%	48.3%	51.1%	48.5%	53.4%	50.5%	59.9%	58.3%	48.4%
(No. Reporting)	(80)	(155)	(192)	(104)	(56)	(39)	(23)	(14)	(663)
Salary of Chief Executive	43.6%	42.6%	35.5%	29.9%	25.7%	17.3%	10.0%	6.6%	32.3%
(No. Reporting)	(26)	(108)	(172)	(95)	(58)	(39)	(21)	(12)	(531)
Amount of 1949 Salary of Chief Paid Executive									
Average Amount	$3,052	$3,439	$4,456	$5,494	$6,891	$9,132	$12,484	$17,000	$5,409
(No. Reporting)	(37)	(133)	(210)	(109)	(65)	(45)	(21)	(11)	(631)
Per Cent of 1949 Income Expended for Rent									
Average Per Cent	7.3%	6.9%	6.4%	6.4%	7.3%	7.0%	5.3%	6.2%	6.6%
(No. Reporting)	(27)	(79)	(135)	(76)	(41)	(33)	(15)	(13)	(419)

RECORDS AND REPORTS

If a manager is to do his job intelligently and effectively, it is essential that he should keep himself constantly informed about the operating results and financial status of his organization. In a small chamber the manager is likely to be in such intimate touch with daily activities that he will feel no need for frequent formal reports. In a larger organization, however, the manager should be supplied with monthly, semimonthly or even weekly reports on income, expenditures, bank balances, new members, delinquents, resignations and similar pertinent facts.

The manager, in turn, is responsible for keeping the board of directors and the executive committee fully informed about the financial and membership affairs of the organization. For this purpose he should prepare a financial operating report at regular intervals. Such a report should show budgeted as well as actual income and expenditures, and should give full information about membership turnover. The amount of detail shown by these reports should be governed by the preferences of the board or the executive committee. Some boards require detailed information with all sorts of comparisons, but the typical board of directors does not care to be bothered with excessive details. It wants merely a summary report to determine whether or not the chamber of commerce is operating within the budget plan and whether the income is equal to the budget.

Accounting Records

The source of practically all information that should be included in the reports to the manager, the board of directors and the executive committee, is the accounting records of the organization. A good system of accounts is an indispensable tool of management—and a must for every chamber of commerce. Yet, surveys reveal that a shockingly large number of chambers attempt to operate without adequate accounting records. There is no excuse for this. No matter how small the community, there are accountants who could be called upon to assist the manager in establishing an adequate and efficient system of records.

The accounting system of a chamber of commerce need not be elaborate or complex. Fundamentally, it should be no different from the systems used by any well-run business.

It should, however, be so designed as to make available readily and accurately the facts in which the manager and the board are especially interested. For example, the usual account receivable records of most accounting systems should be supplemented—or even replaced—by a comprehensive accounting record on memberships. Such a record should provide full and detailed information on the dues, billing dates, payment and arrears of every member. For most chambers a visible card record with a separate card for each member is likely to prove most serviceable, although smaller chambers may find the use of a loose-leaf binder system or 3" x 5" cards, properly indexed, quite satisfactory. It is desirable, however, that the accounting membership record should be distinct and separate from the working membership records used by the staff and volunteer workers in their membership contacts. The maintenance of two sets of membership records not only increases efficiency, but makes it also possible to safeguard vital information.

It is not enough, however, that the chamber has a good *system* of accounts. It is equally important that the books should be kept up-to-date, and that all entries should be made correctly and accurately so that the exact financial condition of the chamber can be determined at all times. Usually the manager himself should not operate the system, but should be fully acquainted with all its details. His time should not be consumed with clerical work. The small chamber with only one girl in the office should have a person capable of keeping the books with supervision.

Audits and Reports

The books of every chamber of commerce should be audited at least annually. The large chamber should employ the services of a certified public accountant for this purpose, whereas a smaller organization may find it sufficient to rely upon an audit made by an outside bookkeeper or a competent auditing committee. Complete operating and financial statements should be prepared at the time of the audit or even more frequently. The wise manager will insist upon an adequate audit.

Some chambers of commerce follow the practice of furnishing all members with annual financial and operating statements. Others do not. They maintain that the average member is interested only in the accomplishments of the organization, and not in the details of its finances. It would seem, however, that all members are entitled to a full accounting of the way in which their dues have been expended as well as to complete information about the current financial condition of their organization. Information of this type constitutes part of the knowledge of the organization that is necessary to keep members sold on the chamber of commerce and its work. If members are disinterested, it may merely reflect the fact that the manager has failed to present the financial and operating data in an interesting and compelling manner. To do so requires the exercise of some effort, ingenuity and originality.

SUMMARY

1. Adequate finances and capable financial management are essential in the operation of a chamber of commerce.

2. Membership dues and subscriptions constitute by far the most important source of revenue. Other sources are of little consequence to most chambers of commerce.

3. The amount of dues should, in each case, be determined on the basis of the financial needs of the chamber, the value of the chamber's services to its membership and the community at large, and the ability of members to pay. Minimum dues should, however, rarely be less than $25 annually. Large business firms should be asked to purchase multiple memberships or to subscribe additional funds on a continuous basis.

4. The collection of dues is not a perfunctory thing. It requires tact, ingenuity and persistence. Delinquent accounts should be charged off as soon as their collectibility appears doubtful. Efforts to secure reinstatement of the delinquent member should, however, continue.

5. A budget system should be adopted by every chamber of commerce, whether large or small, because it serves as an indispensable tool of planning and control.

6. Business-like methods of authorizing and handling expenditures should be adopted. Safeguards should be established to prevent unauthorized expenditures.

7. A simple, yet satisfactory system of accounts is a must for every chamber of commerce.

8. Chamber of commerce accounts should be audited at least annually by a competent accountant or auditing committee.

9. Complete financial reports should be prepared periodically for the board of directors and executive committee, and at least annually for the membership at large.

Chapter VII

Publicity

PUBLICITY is essential to successful chamber of commerce operations. It helps make things happen.

The chamber of commerce is a quasi-public institution, dependent on public support and engaged in public activity. The public has therefore every right to share the confidence of the organization. It is entitled to know what the chamber is doing, what it hopes to do, and why. A successful publicity effort encourages membership growth and interest. It contributes to financial strength, fosters public confidence and support, and promotes community progress and prosperity.

Publicity is a valuable tool. But like every other tool, it has its limitations as well as its uses. Publicity alone does not produce success. Publicity is not a substitute for a program of work and a record of achievement. On the contrary, these things are the basis for meaningful publicity. The manager who seeks to build support for his organization and good will for his community by merely gushing empty claims and unrealized dreams, soon finds himself shouting into an unechoing void.

Publicity that is not supported by substantial accomplishments must inevitably lead to membership indifference, financial loss, and public suspicion and antagonism. Continued publicity failure is almost certain to lead to the organization of competitive agencies to perform functions that are rightly those of the chamber.

PURPOSES OF PUBLICITY

Chamber of commerce publicity is broadly of two types. The first of these seeks to interpret the work of the chamber to the public. Its aim is to create acceptance of the *organization* and its program so as to secure widespread participation in its activities and enlist adequate financial support. The second type is concerned with the *community*. It seeks to cultivate community pride and to sell the community to its market area, to prospective investors, to tourists, and to conventions.

Publicity may be addressed to the membership, to the general public of the community, to the world at large or to all three. The purposes, in the order of importance to most organizations, are:

1. To inform the membership
2. To interest prospective members
3. To influence public opinion
4. To advertise the community

Merchandising the Program

The fundamental purpose of the chamber of commerce is to promote constructive endeavor that will lead to achievements of value to the community. Publicity is important to every process in this enterprise. In this day and age, when so many interests clamor for attention, publicity has become a requisite to success. It needs no apology.

The effective chamber of commerce starts with a well-planned and well-adapted program of work. To achieve its goals, however, the chamber must have the support of its membership and, in many cases, that of the public. It must sell its program. Publicity is essential for this purpose. Helpful publicity:

1. Inspires personal activity on the part of members and progressive citizens.
2. Performs the useful function of circulating constructive ideas and interesting information.
3. Dispels suspicion, promotes understanding, encourages cooperation, and creates public confidence in the chamber's program.
4. Contributes to the growth, influence and achievement of the organization that is sound and effective.

To be effective, publicity must be soundly built. The first requirement is that the program itself must be worthy. Publicity cannot materially or permanently strengthen a cause that is fundamentally weak. It may fail to sell an idea simply because the plan or project cannot survive critical consideration by intelligent people. The fault is not with publicity, but with the cause it represents.

Effective publicity is restrained, factual and purposeful. Publicity that has no purpose other than that of keeping the name of the chamber before the public, cannot succeed. Vain boasting is never acceptable and soon becomes very offensive. The public has little patience with mere promises. Premature announcements are, therefore, dangerous. They are likely to be interpreted as promises that must be fulfilled if public confidence is to be preserved.

Keeping the Membership Sold

In dealing with the membership, publicity becomes a duty. Members have a right to know what the chamber is doing. The average member has little opportunity to observe at first hand the broad scope of the activities of the chamber. Publicity is the only means by which he can be fully and continuously informed.

If an individual member is working on an important project in which he is deeply interested, he may be sold on the worth of the chamber of commerce on the basis of that one function alone. In order to build and retain the interest of a broad membership, however, there must be a continuous and regular flow of information. In the absence of such continuous promotion, membership interest, financial support and personal activity must inevitably falter.

Promoting Specific Projects

It is frequently necessary or desirable to employ publicity for the purpose of promoting specific projects. The chamber of commerce may, for example, initiate bond elections, charter revisions or taxation programs. The success of these projects, however, must depend on public acceptance and support. It is therefore necessary to find some means of reaching the voters of the community with factual information and sound reasoning. Publicity, in its various forms, affords such a means.

The promotion of specific projects is important also for another reason. Chambers of commerce must of necessity engage in many activities that are continuous and do not lend themselves to effective publicity. Important as these activities may be, they come to be taken for granted. They add little to the stature or public esteem of the organization. Other projects, however, are spectacular. Their publicity value may therefore be exploited to fill the void. Completed projects are, of course, particularly valuable for this purpose.

Definite accomplishments have meaning to the membership and the public. They stand as mile posts to measure the progress of the chamber. It is therefore important that the program each year should include some projects that can be brought to successful completion during the year.

Advertising the Community

Chambers of commerce employ publicity for the purpose of selling the community. The form which this effort takes, varies greatly from one community to another. In some cases the objective is to foster a spirit of loyalty to the city. In other cases, publicity is used as a means of creating a favorable opinion of the city throughout its trading area. Publicity for this purpose may, for example, emphasize the marketing facilities offered by the city, its fine retail stores, or the quality of the products manufactured and sold by the city. Chambers of commerce in some vacation and resort centers may exist primarily for the purpose of advertising the tourist attractions of the community. Others use publicity as a means of attracting new industries and payrolls.

FUNDAMENTALS OF GOOD PUBLICITY

No publicity can be expected to be effective unless it has a purpose and a plan. The first task of the chamber of commerce is therefore to define the goals of its publicity efforts. In planning such goals, it is helpful to distinguish between long-run objectives and immediate tasks. The former provides a basis for long-range planning, while the latter determines the publicity program for the specific project, the particular purpose or the current period.

Once objectives and tasks have been clearly defined, it becomes possible to plan strategy by determining the audience to be reached, the media to be used and the appeals to be employed. Obviously, publicity planning must also take into consideration the costs involved and the funds available. Costs must be carefully calculated and weighed against possible benefits. In this respect, chamber of commerce publicity is like all other advertising and publicity effort. The returns must justify the cost. It is generally accepted, however, that effective planning starts with the objectives and expresses the plans in terms of those objectives. If costs are too high or funds are insufficient, the plans may have to be modified or the effort abandoned altogether.

Plans that are evolved primarily in terms of trying to operate within an arbitrary and limited publicity budget, are likely to result in wasteful expenditure of funds. Too many chambers of commerce, for example, set aside some money for publicity on the general principle that publicity is desirable. There is no clearly defined objective, and certainly no clear recognition of the requirements and the costs of the task to be performed. Hence, money is fritted away aimlessly and ineffectively, with complete disregard for the fact that effective publicity must be purposeful, persistent and consistent.

Selection of Audience

Publicity can be effective only to the extent that it reaches and influences the proper audience. Unless that audience is carefully defined and identified, wasted circulation and sterile efforts are inevitable. In many cases, correct identification of the audience is a relatively simple matter. That is true, for example, when the purpose of the chamber's publicity is to keep the membership sold on the organization, or even to attract new members. In other cases, correct definition and identification of the audience are as difficult as they are crucial to success. Thus, it is inconceivable that publicity intended to attract new industries to the city can be effective if it is merely broadcast indiscriminately through mass media. Publicity of this sort must seek out the prospective investor. There is no infallible formula for doing so, however, other than ingenuity, inventiveness and just plain, hard work.

Selection of Appeals

Once the purpose of the publicity effort has been defined and the audience identified, the next step is to decide upon the appeals to be used. It is a principle of good publicity that it should be written from the point of view of those to whom it is addressed. It should present the facts in which the reader is interested, and present them in a manner that appeals to him. Empty generalizations and vain boasting has no place in good publicity.

It is unnecessary to point out that this fundamental principle is violated every day. For example, most tourist

148 CHAMBER OF COMMERCE ADMINISTRATION

literature describes in glowing terms the scenic wonders, the historic shrines and the incomparable recreational opportunities of the area. But it says nothing specific about the available tourist accommodations, the rates they charge, and the attractions offered by each. Yet, those are the things in which the prospective tourist is interested. They are the considerations that determine whether or not he will visit the community. Chambers of commerce, in common with other organizations, could vastly improve the quality and effectiveness of their publicity effort if they would keep in mind that publicity is good or bad as it serves the needs, convinces or plays upon the emotions of the reader to whom it is addressed.

Selecting Media

The list of possible media is almost unlimited. One large chamber of commerce offers the following as a typical list of the various forms of publicity employed during a period of twelve months:

Newspapers	Magazines	Radio
Moving pictures	Billboards	Exhibits
Highway signs	House organs	Badges
Booklets	Folders	Souvenirs
Maps	Reports	Paper matches
Charts	Posters	Floats
Postcards	Civic lectures	Speakers
Window-displays	Bulletins	Sports events
Meetings	Information offices	Tours
Bus and car cards	Letterheads	Convention stunts
Membership cards	Membership plaques	Photographs
Windshield stickers	Automobile plates	Correspondence
Hat bands	Envelopes	

The selection of the most effective medium becomes an important problem. It must be based upon considerations of the purpose of the publicity effort, the audience to be addressed and the appeals to be used. It must take into account the size and quality of the circulation of the medium, its editorial policy, its versatility and flexibility, and the cost of reaching each reader to whom the appeal is addressed.

General Principles

There are some general principles that should be observed in all chamber of commerce publicity. In addition to those already discussed, the following may be suggested:

   1. Tell the simple truth. Misleading statements, exaggeration, pretense or untruthfulness never pays.

2. Tell about things done. A simple story about *current* achievements is far more impressive than flowery recitals of past glories or future dreams. Anticipation should be confined to announcements of programs and definitely planned events.
3. Feature the organization or the community rather than the manager's name. If the mention of names is appropriate, they should be those of the president, chairmen and other leaders of the chamber or the community.
4. Maintain friendly, courteous and cooperative relations with publicity media. Obvious attempts to cultivate and seek favor, however, are as undesirable as being secretive, flippant, neglectful or untruthful.
5. Prepare publicity copy early, whether it be for newspapers, bulletins or reports. Allow time for careful preparation and painstaking analysis.
6. Have something to say. Know what it is. Tell it in the most effective manner to the proper audience. Stop when it is said.

INTERNAL PUBLICITY

Every chamber of commerce uses internal media to carry publicity to the membership. These media range all the way from elaborate house organs and printed reports to modest direct-mail pieces and postcards. A few of the largest organizations publish periodicals that have considerable circulation outside the membership.

House Organs

Almost without exception, chambers of commerce have some type of house organ. It may be a single mimeographed sheet issued whenever the manager of a one-man organization finds time to dash off a few paragraphs of news; or it may be a well-printed and well-illustrated monthly magazine. In either case, its primary function is to keep the membership informed about plans, activities and achievements.

1. *Printed publications.* Most of the larger chambers of commerce have a printed house organ of one form or another. Some of them are issued monthly; others are published weekly. The organizations that have weekly membership meetings, commonly publish weekly bulletins featuring the coming programs. A few printed periodicals are issued on a quarterly basis.

Popular sizes for printed publications are 5½ x 8½ inches, 8½ x 11 inches, and 9 x 12 inches. The number of pages vary from four to sixty. About half of these house organs carry paid advertisements. The principal advantage of this practice is that advertising revenues may cover a considerable portion of the cost of publication. There is some danger, however, that regular membership income from the advertising firms may be jeopardized. In some communities the practice may also be criticized by other local publications.

Although all house organs carry organization news, some of them may attempt to broaden their appeal by stressing other features. Some publish national, regional and local statistics. Others feature extensive articles on local industries, civic problems, the outlook for business or other topics of interest to members.

2. *Mimeographed and multigraphed bulletins.* This type of publication may be issued either weekly or monthly. Some managers believe that mimeographed bulletins are more thoroughly read than are printed periodicals. They are, therefore, a favorite medium for publishing information intended for members.

In their capacity of news bulletins, the editorial content of these publications should be brief, compact and to the point. Bare information should be given, although no important fact should be omitted. Official statements should be crisp and terse. Each issue should carry date, city and state.

The obvious disadvantage of this type of publication is that it is less attractive and less impressive than the printed house organ. But this need not be a serious handicap. Modern equipment combined with care in preparation are capable of producing a publication that should measure up to all reasonable standards.

There is no hard and fast rule by which an organization can determine which type of publication is more advantagous. Available funds, advertising support, editorial skill, purpose, as well as the temperament of the organization and the community are factors that bear on such a decision. The general rule can be laid down, however, that a good bulletin is worth much more than a poor magazine. Unless a chamber of commerce can afford a worth-while magazine type of house organ, well prepared and printed, it is far better to devote time and effort to a snappy news bulletin.

Special Bulletins

In addition to their regular house organs, a number of chambers publish special bulletins devoted to topics of particular interest to special groups within the membership. For example, the retail trade division may mimeograph a bulletin that is sent to all retailers. It may contain news about the activities of the retail committee, special events sponsored by retailers, market news of interest to retailers and the like. The traffic department may issue a regular or special bulletin to all shippers, giving them the latest traffic news. Such special bulletins may be issued by practically any department.

Direct Mail to Members

The necessity of keeping the membership sold requires the exercise of ingenuity in developing new types of membership contacts. Envelope stuffers and other forms of direct mail advertising may be effective. Many organizations never send out a bill for dues without including a printed insert telling about some recent achievement or some current activity in which many members are likely to be interested. Special events, such as the annual banquet or an outstanding public affairs luncheon, may also be brought to the attention of members by means of direct mail.

Direct mail may be used effectively to call the attention of the membership to some particularly significant activity, to a city-wide drive to put over some important civic project, or to a membership campaign. Originality of design, quality of paper stock and typography, and the way in which the message is written combine to determine the worth of this type of publicity.

Reports

Correctly prepared and used, reports serve as one of the important media of information and publicity. Two types of reports are of particular significance for this purpose: reports of officers and creative reports.

Reports of officers include all reports that are customarily required of the officials of an organization, such as annual reports of the president and the chairmen of committees, reports of the treasurer on finances, reports of the manager on membership, and the like. All of these reports have publicity value.

Some of them, such as the report on finances, may be intended only for circulation among members. They constitute, however, one of the foremost means of informing the membership about the condition and progress of the organization. They are, therefore, an indispensable element in the effort to keep the membership sold. Other reports, such as the annual report of the president, may be of considerable interest also to community at large. They may afford one of the most effective media of selling the chamber of commerce to the community.

Creative reports are reports on the investigations, recommendations and actions of the chamber of commerce. They are most frequently the result of committee activities. Some of these reports may be confidential or intended only for a restricted leadership. An example might be a report by a committee to the board of directors. Others may, however, be addressed to a larger audience, such as the entire membership or the community at large. Because they present the findings of investigations, offer recommendations, or announce decisions, policies or actions, these reports constitute, in a sense, the core of the chamber's publicity effort. The acceptance of the chamber or the success of particular projects may be significantly affected by the quality of these reports.

The recognition of the importance of reports as an effective medium of publicity, both within the organization and in its external relationships, has led to a constant search for new ideas and new ways of presenting the facts. The annual report, for example, may be a simple recital of the work of the year. Or it may be an elaborate presentation, supported by effective diagrams, charts and pictures. It may be in the form of a booklet, a brochure or a broadside. It may be written by the manager or a staff member, or it may be a compilation of reports of various departments, committees and officers. However written and presented, it should be a clear, honest and forceful account of the outstanding activities of the year.

Because of the range of problems covered by creative reports and the diversity of the audience to which they are addressed, there can be no magic formula that will always produce success. Each report must be prepared and written so as to meet the requirements of the topic which it covers and the purpose for which it is intended. Certain general comments on effective report writing may, nevertheless, be helpful.

It ought to be unnecessary to observe that no report can be better than the quality of the work on which it is based. Effective presentation is no substitute for complete facts, careful analysis and sound judgment. But effective presentation can be used to show relationships, lend emphasis and add convictions.

The first requirement of a good report is that it should clearly and precisely define the problem or issue. Failure to do so almost inevitably leads to aimless discussion of irrelevant facts. Furthermore, it places the reader under an unfair handicap. If he does not know the exact issue, he can hardly be expected to understand the argument. Failure to define the issue militates, therefore, against agreement or conviction.

It is generally agreed that a report should be as short as is consistent with the nature of the issue. This does not mean, however, that it should omit important facts, arguments or objections. A report can be convincing only by being complete and thorough.

The text should be clear, concise and brief. But brevity should not be gained at the sacrifice of clarity. In their idolation of brevity many businessmen tend to telescope their language to such an extent that reading becomes difficult and understanding well-nigh impossible. A few additional words may not only make reading easier, but add immeasurably to the effectiveness of the argument. If well done, the use of colorful phrases may add spice to the report; but superlatives and exaggerations have no place in chamber reports.

If the nature of the issue necessitates a fairly long report, it is advisable to provide a summary of facts and conclusions. Such a summary is likely to be most effective when it is placed at the beginning of the report.

If tables of figures are used in the text, they should be simplified as much as possible. In order to facilitate reading, understanding and comparison, a uniform plan of construction should be used for all tables. Such a plan should be designed to bring out and highlight important relationships.

Charts, diagrams and drawings are frequently valuable. They may enable a reader to visualize a problem or a relationship far more clearly and easily than mere description or cold figures. Furthermore, they help to dress up the report. But the use of these devices can easily be overdone. A report that looks more like a child's picture book than a serious piece of work, is not apt to be very effective. It should not be forgotten that charts, unsupported by figures, tell only an inexact story. For that reason they are likely to irritate, rather than assist, the reader who is interested in details or exact relationships.

A report of the chamber of commerce to the public should clearly convey the fact that the activities reported on are those of the organization and not of individuals. It should avoid emphasis on the personality of the manager or any officer of the chamber. On the other hand, it should give credit where credit is due. This is, of course, of particular importance when organizations other than the chamber or individuals who are not members of the chamber of commerce, have participated in the work on which the report is based.

THE NEWSPAPER

Without question the local press is the greatest publicity ally of the chamber of commerce. Stories of happenings within the organization are news, just as much as any other daily happening chronicled in the public press. There is rarely a day when even the smallest organization does not develop a news story, if only the manager or publicity secretary has the news sense required to recognize it. Anything in which the public is interested, has news value. The actions of the board, the establishment of policy, the report of a committee, the receipt of significant information, the delegation of new responsibilities to a committee—all of these facts are news. Many newspapers recognize this and assign reporters to make daily calls on the chamber of commerce.

Value of Support

The newspaper is usually one of the most constructive community forces. It is, therefore, a valuable ally of the chamber of commerce. The local newspaper reaches a majority of the homes of the community, going to non-members as well as to members. Its services are available free of cost to the chamber, as long as its requirements are met. The importance of building the right kind of relationship between the newspapers and the chamber of commerce, therefore, cannot be over-emphasized.

Values in News

News is current, truthful and interesting information. News value depends upon such factors as timeliness, proximity, prominence, consequence and human interest. If it is to accomplish its purpose, publicity released by the chamber of commerce to newspapers must be kept above the level of "free advertising". It must be given a definite news slant. It must be about something in which the public is interested and written in such a way that it is read.

The newspapers will generally print any information of special or general interest. They will print the facts. They will print some detail, the amount depending on their own measures of news value. They will print reports, the substance of speeches, statistics, significant pronouncements, and every item possessing genuine human interest. What the newspapers are really looking for, however, is the unusual. Nothing has greater power of attracting attention—and thus greater news and publicity value—than the unusual. In a straight news story, the newspapers want facts, not opinion. Opinion may appear as an interview statement, but the good newspaper rarely permits editorial comments in its news columns. Personal publicity and common propaganda are especially repugnant to news writers, editors and the reading public.

News is highly perishable. A real news story should not be kept under wraps to get a Sunday spread. On the other hand, the manager or his publicity secretary should observe news trends. If several important stories are crowding the newspapers columns, it may be advisable to postpone the release of a news story. It is important to learn the art of smothering bad publicity with good. When the "heat is on", the manager should be ready with a good constructive story to offset the organization's bad publicity.

Writing the Copy

A "story" is the written form in which news is prepared and presented to the public. The construction of news stories may vary greatly, but the purpose is always to present the most important facts in the most interesting manner. The "lead", or beginning of the story, usually tells who, when, where, what, why and how. The details that follow the lead may be brief or voluminous, depending upon news values and space available. In general, following the lead, the facts are presented in the order of their decreasing importance.

News is ordinarily given to the press in one of two ways— in stories prepared by the chamber of commerce or in interviews, the reporter writing his own story on the basis of information given him. When the story is prepared by a member of the staff it should be written in accordance with the style book of the newspaper for which it is prepared. In addition, it should follow the principles of good news writing. Some of the general rules are:

1. A skeleton outline of the story should be given in the opening paragraph, and somewhat elaborated or explained in the paragraphs following the lead.
2. All the facts should be available, even though some are not considered sufficiently important to use. Accuracy is of great importance not only in facts, but also in names, initials, addresses, and titles.
3. News stories should be brief and simple, unless their importance calls for further details to satisfy the demand of readers for complete information. Opinion should be left out of news stories.
4. Stories should not be overplayed. Superlatives, laudatory adjectives and self-commendation should be studiously avoided.
5. The feature of the story—that is, the most interesting fact—should be emphasized in the opening paragraph.

A news story should be more than just information. It should be interestingly written. It should be dressed up. Statistics, for example, may be livened up with charts and diagrams. Pictures have news value. They may be self-sufficient and tell their own stories with the aid of brief cut-lines; or they may be illustrations of news stories. They need not be limited to photographs, but may include drawings, sketches, maps and graphs. Photos intended for newspaper use should, as far as possible, have "action". Large groups should be avoided in news pictures.

Relations with the Press

In order to enjoy full support of the newspapers, the chamber of commerce must be fair, frank and honest with the representatives of the local press. In a "two-paper" town, for example, each paper has the right to expect "protection" up to press time, or up to the established "deadline" for copy that is to appear in the final edition. There is no surer way of making enemies among newspaper men than playing favorites. No attempt should ever be made to hoax the newspapers. There is a place for created publicity, but the newspapers should be taken into confidence on such stories.

Premature declaration of policy or announcement of decisions is dangerous. There are therefore times during the consideration of important issues—while the matter is in an evolutionary stage—when it is not advisable to give out either complete or even partial information. This fact may frequently give rise to misunderstanding. In such circumstances a simple, tactful statement may be sufficient to appease curiosity and restore public confidence. At other times, the issue may be so confidential that it is inadvisable even to admit that it is under consideration. In such a situation, it is necessary to deal with the reporter as one "good fellow" with another. Most newspaper men can be depended on to "play fair". They will keep a secret if the confidence is honorably imposed. But they demand fair play in return.

Chambers of commerce should, in the main, confine their dealings to reporters. They should resist the temptation of attempting to go over the heads of reporters to pull wires with the editors. When the organization gets the worst of a news story, it should not rush into the news with furious denials. That may merely double the damage. If a denial seems absolutely essential, it should be good humored and courteous.

Good press relations can be encouraged by having advance copies or digests of important speeches and statements, by remembering the press with complimentary tickets for dinners and special events, and by being reasonable in requests made of the newspapers. Frank Fogarty, whose administrative position in chamber of commerce work was preceded by a wealth of experience in the publicity field, compiled "fifteen rules for making an enemy of a reporter". They are apropos of the discussion of newspaper relations:

1. Lie to him.
2. Try to conceal facts which are certain to come out anyhow.
3. Threaten to get the reporter's job.
4. Tell him what to print.
5. Tell him what not to print.
6. Call the managing editor and complain about what has been printed.

7. Be a publicity hound. Seek publicity for yourself, your wife, your pals.
8. Tell only one reporter, thereby scooping his opposition.
9. Be a turnquote. Say thus-and-so, and then, after it appears in print, issue a denial.
10. Try to get in the back door of the paper, i. e., through the business office.
11. Promise to protect a reporter on a story—then forget about it.
12. Shoo him away from visiting big shots when he is trying to interview them.
13. Go direct to the city editor with advance tip on a story which the reporter normally would pick up on the run.
14. Be a smart-aleck. Take the attitude that "newspapers never get a story straight anyhow".
15. Try to cram your story into the paper on a day when half a dozen big stories break.

RADIO PUBLICITY

Radio has become an important auxiliary medium of publicity for the chamber of commerce. In most communities radio reaches a larger audience than newspapers and magazines combined. It offers a flexible medium. By careful selection of station, time and program it is possible to beam the message to the audience for which it is intended. Radio publicity has human appeal. It can be made alive, animated and dramatic. And because of the expressiveness of the human voice, it can be made compelling, friendly and warm. On the other hand, radio publicity is extremely perishable. There is one, and only one, chance to deliver the message, and unless it is spoken simply and forcefully it is quickly forgotten.

Most listeners regard radio as a medium of entertainment. A program that does not appeal to them, is quickly tuned out for a better program. The first principle of good radio publicity is, therefore, that the program be tailored to fit the audience for which it is intended. Few businessmen listen to soap operas. 'Teenagers won't tune in on a weighty forum. But most listeners—whether businessmen, housewives or 'teenagers—want variety. They want *some* entertainment, *some* music, *some* information, and *some* local news. They are interested in those things that affect their welfare, their family, their future, their pocketbook and their communitty. These are some of the appeals around which the chamber of commerce may build a successful radio program.

Radio speeches have only limited appeal. Some chambers of commerce have attempted to present programs of their annual meetings or addresses before weekly or monthly forums. Experience indicates, however, that unless the speaker is very outstanding, few listeners will stay tuned in for more than a few minutes. An interview or a dialogue seems to have greater radio value. Business summaries can be made interesting to listeners. Special programs of from five to fifteen minutes, including entertainment and very brief statements on chamber of commerce activities, have proved effective. So have weekly broadcasts or events of the coming week. The best publicity opportunity for radio, however, is a short announcement or a place in the regular news broadcast.

Radio news style is almost the opposite of that of the press. The newspaper aims to pack the whole story into the opening sentence, while the radio news story is allowed to unfold. The facts are fed one by one, allowing the story to build up to a climax and then to taper off before the newscaster turns to his next story. Radio copy must be written to be *heard* and not to be *seen*.

The policies of featuring accomplishments and keeping the manager in the background should be observed as fully in radio as in other forms of publicity. If the manager is asked to speak on a radio program, he should speak of and for the organization. He should use simple language, with sentences of average length and construction that is not involved. The style should be conversational, and strict attention should be given to punctuation.

Although still in its infancy, television appears destined to become another publicity medium of considerable importance to the chamber of commerce. To some extent it may replace the radio, but to an even greater extent it is likely to afford new opportunities for publicity. Television may, for example, prove an effective medium for dramatizing civic activities and for disseminating community publicity.

PUBLIC RELATIONS

The success of a chamber of commerce depends not only on its program, its activities, its achievements and its publicity. It depends on the *acceptance* of these things by the membership, the public and the employees of the organization. It depends on its public relations.

The editor of a business weekly has summed up the modern concept of public relations in these words: "Public relations is not something you *say;* it isn't something you *do;* it is something you *are.*" Public relations is to the chamber of commerce what good manners, good morals and a winning personality are to an individual. A public relations program is the business of making friends for the chamber of commerce. It is the business of creating goodwill and establishing harmonious relationships not only with members, but with employees of the organization and the general public as well.

A constructive public relations program involves two essentials: First, an alert and objective evaluation of policies and actions as they may be construed by the public; and secondly, a conscious effort to guide and influence such reactions. Good publicity is obviously an important part of such an effort. But it is by no means its only element. Equally important are the impressions that are established by the officers of the chamber of commerce, its directors, its staff and its members in their daily contact with the public, other civic groups, public officials, business and industry. It is these contacts and impressions that, as much as anything else, clothe the chamber of commerce with personality and make it what it is.

A sound public relations program must build on certain fundamental requirements. They include: a soundly conceived philosophy and objective; a well-rounded program of work, shaped to the needs of the community; a net-work of committees under the leadership of competent chairmen; and a result-getting executive and staff, with a flair for interpreting and reporting. With this foundation, public relations becomes the practice of doing the right thing in the right way at the right time and place, and then explaining it in the right words to the right people. The success of the public relations program is measured by the standing and reputation of the chamber of commerce among its own members and staff, in business and industry, among people in the city hall, the court houses and the state capital, among other civic groups, and among the citizenry of the community.

COMMUNITY PUBLICITY

There is a clearly defined distinction between publicity whose aim it is to build the chamber of commerce, and that whose purpose it is to advertise the community. The former seeks to sell the chamber of commerce as an institution; the latter attempts to make the world aware of the assets and attractions of the community.

It has become evident that communities must make themselves known in order to hold their place in the world of affairs. Communities compete among themselves. They compete for business, industry and prestige. Furthermore, by drawing communities closer together, improved transportation and communications have tended to make this sort of competition progressively keener. Proximity increases competition.

Competition among communities is wholesome. It stimulates progress. It forces communities to subject themselves to critical self-examination; and it encourages them to supply the needs and correct the weaknesses they may uncover. They attempt to reshape themselves, and to develop strength and influence. Community publicity is an important element in these efforts. It pays business to advertise. Likewise it pays communities to advertise their amenities, assets and attractions. By so doing they succeed in attracting capital and industry, promoting business, achieving a better balanced economy, and enticing tourists and conventions.

The Product

Before a community can launch an effective publicity campaign, it must have something to advertise. Chambers of commerce are therefore doing that which is statesmanlike when they promote community-building programs. The responsibility of the organization is first to see to it that the community is headed in the right direction. Only then can it tell the world about it.

Scope of Campaign

A community publicity campaign may take the form of an intensive drive of relatively short duration, or it may be a continuous effort on a somewhat less spectacular scale. One community may profit most from the former, while another may harvest the greatest yield from the latter. The purpose in mind, local conditions and circumstances of the times are factors to be weighed in planning the campaign. So are costs. The expected returns must justify the costs.

There are three methods of raising necessary funds: from tax money collected by state, municipal or county governments; by private subscription; or by a combination of these methods. It is submitted that those individuals and institutions that benefit most from the campaign should assume the greatest financial burden. By following this plan the chamber of commerce is at least consistent with its stand against higher taxes. Financing out of tax revenue may, however, be justified in the case of a community which depends mainly on tourists for its income. When planning the budget, provision should be made for follow-up work, stenographic help, postage and the like. In other words, know all the costs and control them.

Tourist Promotion

Publicity designed to attract tourists is a field of specialization. Travel is big business, and every community should analyze the attraction it has to offer tourists and those on vacation. It cannot be gainsaid, however, that some communities and some states have tourist assets far superior to those of others. Publicity in this field, as in all others, should therefore be on a scale proportionate to possible benefits. Full development of those attractions of the community in which visitors may be interested, should precede any large-scale tourist publicity.

Tourist promotion involves four problems:

1. How to reach the prospective visitor in his home.
2. How to attract the visitor to the community.
3. How to extend the period of time he spends in the community.
4. How to change the casual tourist into a regular visitor or permanent resident.

The answer to the first two questions is publicity and advertising. The problem of reaching and attracting tourists resolves itself into the necessity of spending money wisely in order to make money. Paid advertising, illustrated literature, displays, moving pictures, personal solicitations, and effective follow-up to answer inquires for specific information may be phases of the campaign. Next, there is a vast opportunity in most communities for improving the reception and service accorded the visitor. The hundreds of proprietors and employees who contact visitors, must be courteous and informed. These things, as much as the recreational facilities of the community, determine the time visitors will spend there. When visitors are made to feel at home in the community, progress is made on the fourth point mentioned above.

Convention Activities

Convention promotion is another phase of chamber of commerce promotion closely related to community publicity. Conventions afford one of the best cash crops of the community. In addition, they are themselves an important medium of publicity and a means of selling the city to visiting delegates. They serve to stimulate the desire for self-improvement and progress, and they encourage the community to make itself more attractive and livable.

Most convention work is carried on either by a division of the chamber of commerce or by an organization closely affiliated with the chamber through some inter-locking arrangement. Few cities can afford the luxury of both an adequately equipped chamber of commerce and an independent convention bureau. Some chambers of commerce employ a convention specialist, others operate through a committee.

Although successful convention promotion requires skill and persistence, the technique is simple in outline. The first step is to build a file of prospects. Obviously, the list must give consideration to the size of the community, its location and its facilities for entertaining conventions of various sizes and types. The file should include only those organizations that can be adequately served and may reasonably be expected to be interested in the community as a convention city. For each such organization the prospect card should give correct name and address, names and addresses of national and local officers, date and size of convention, facilities required, method of selecting convention city, and any other information that will ensure an intelligent and effective campaign.

The next step is to contact local officers and leaders of the organization for the purpose of securing their cooperation in extending an invitation. In most cases, the details of the campaign should be worked out with them. Tentative plans should be made for housing the convention and delegates, for entertainment, and for financing the gathering. These plans should be incorporated into a formal invitation. The convention invitation should be an attractive document, representing an investment reasonably commensurate with the size and importance of the gathering.

If the convention city is selected by the officers of the organization or by a convention committee, this may be as far as the campaign need to go. If, on the other hand, the delegates to one convention select the next convention city, the campaign may barely be started. There are a thousand and one gadgets and lures that convention bureau managers use to interest delegates. Management of the local delegation, hospitality rooms, lobby banners and other forms of advertising may all have a part in the campaign.

Securing a convention is only the beginning of convention promotion. Equally important is the service to conventions once they assemble in the community. Discretion should be used in making promises, but once made they should be lived up to in every detail. Among the proper services to a convention, the following may be suggested:

1. Registration. Registration clerks from the convention bureau staff are usually furnished gratis, with extra help being paid for out of the convention fund.
2. Housing. Where hotel facilities are inadequate, the chamber of commerce should be prepared to furnish a list of available tourist rooms, Y. M. C. A. rooms, etc.
3. Publicity. Requisite contacts should be made with local papers, and other arrangements provided to insure adequate publicity.
4. Meeting place. Practice differs on the matter of furnishing free meeting places. Auditoriums are customarily rented by the association assembling there; hotels furnish their facilities gratis.
5. Badges. Practice also differs greatly in the matter of furnishing badges. The trend is away from free badges. When they are furnished free, it is usually a standard badge rather than one designed specifically for the particular group.
6. Entertainment. Complimentary dinners are largely practices of the past. Only occasionally is free entertainment justified. The rule is a little more liberal with respect to ladies' entertainment.
7. Attendance building. This is a legitimate activity of the convention bureau, since every additional delegate means additional income to the community.
8. Program. Services in this field are more limited. The chamber of commerce can be of assistance, but seldom pays for speakers or entertainment.
9. Program advertising. Although it is not always easy, groups should be dissuaded from selling advertising in their programs to defray expenses.

10. Tour of city. When possible, the host group should be encouraged to furnish cars for local tours.
11. Stenographic service. Expense of the reporter taking convention proceedings, as well as incidental stenographic expenses, should come out of the convention fund.
12. Police escort, parade, floats, etc. These should be arranged by the local host group.
13. Decorations. Some chambers furnish window cards. A cooperative venture may be arranged on street decorations, with the chamber serving as a cooperative rather than as the sponsoring agency.
14. Cash contributions. Buying conventions is likely to prove an expensive luxury.

Free hotel rooms for officers of a convention are still given in some instances, but the trend is away from this practice. A pitfall to be avoided by the chamber of commerce is the selection of a headquarters hotel. It should refuse absolutely to participate in this decision.

SUMMARY

1. Publicity is not a substitute for a program of work or a record of achievements. But publicity helps make things happen. It is a tool used by the chamber of commerce to merchandise its program, to build and maintain its membership, to promote specific projects, and to advertise the community.

2. Effective publicity has a purpose and a plan. It is directed at a selected audience, through proper media, and it uses appropriate appeals.

3. Most chambers of commerce use various internal media. They include house organs, special bulletins, direct mail and reports.

4. The chamber of commerce needs the support of local newspapers, and should seek to cooperate as fully as possible with them. It should be fair and honest with reporters.

5. Radio offers many publicity opportunities. Programs should be adapted to the objectives of the organization and to the audience to be reached. Television promises to become another important medium.

6. In its publicity program, the chamber of commerce should also explore the possibilities of movies, bill-boards, exhibits, contacts with civic clubs, correspondence and other publicity opportunities that present themselves daily.

7. The best way for a chamber of commerce to obtain favorable publicity is to carry on worth while projects so successfully that the public as well as the membership will be interested in knowing about them.

8. Good publicity is only a part of a sound, well-planned program of public relations.

9. Community publicity should be based upon the major assets of the city and should be directed as definitely as possible to those who may be interested in taking advantage of those assets and, in so doing, benefit the city.

Chapter VIII

Office Administration

THE RESULTS of competent office administration are reflected in greater efficiency and effectiveness of every phase of chamber of commerce work. The office of the chamber of commerce is analogous to the production department of an industrial concern. Both are responsible for producing a product and the degree of success or failure of the undertaking is dependent upon the manner in which various factors are utilized in making it as well as the quality of the product itself. In a manufacturing company, material goes through a series of processes until a finished product has been made. The department manager must exercise care in planning and controlling the various factors which affect the economy and effectiveness of the operations of the department. Even before the processing starts, the company executives must decide upon the product, the quality desired, the equipment to be used, and the rate and methods of manufacture. Every phase of the manufacturing process has to be worked out in such a way as to produce a finished product with the maximum of value at the least possible cost.

The chamber of commerce office also produces a product. Its product consists of the services which it renders to its membership and to the community. Administration of the office therefore involves the responsibility of providing sufficient space, equipment and personnel to perform the work, and of using methods and procedures which will ensure completion of the work in an efficient and effective manner. To accomplish this, the chamber of commerce office manager must apply sound principles to the organization and operation of his office.

ELEMENTS OF OFFICE MANAGEMENT

The principles of office management as applied to the internal operations of a chamber of commerce are essentially the same whether the office is small and has a limited staff or is large with a correspondingly large office personnel. Their application will differ, however. In a small office each person may be performing a wide variety of duties; whereas in a larger office the work will be more specialized and each person may be performing only one or a limited number of duties.

The many values which competent office management contributes to the success of the undertaking result from the proper execution of the functions of planning, organizing and controlling office work. These values are accomplished chiefly by means of efficient and economical communication, computing, and recording devices that insure that the required clerical work will be of the proper quantity and quality. The principal objectives of the office manager may be summarized as follows:

1. To provide and maintain office conditions that are conducive to the maximum economy and effectiveness in work.
2. Efficient internal and external communication service.
3. Effective and economic utilization of the office force in such clerical work as computing, recording, classifying and filing.
4. Development and application of correct office rules and procedures.

In order to present this subject in its complete form, it is assumed that the office manager is dealing with a reasonably large organization. Reference is made, therefore, to various office assistants whose functions in many offices may be combined with other positions. The application of basic principles to a larger office will indicate the corresponding application to the conditions of a smaller office.

An Example of Efficiency

The organization of the chamber of commerce office should be as nearly as possible a model machine for the performance of its many activities. This is true because it is a focal point for every line of business activity and most of its financial support comes from the business and professional men and women of the community. These people look upon the chamber as a business organization and compare or contrast its operation with that of their own organizations.

This does not mean that the office manager should become a slave to system. Neither does it mean that the organization should devote most of its time and energy to operating the system and neglect the fundamental product—service. It does mean, however, that no manager should attempt to justify slipshod methods on the grounds that he and his staff "do not have time for red tape", if by that term he means more systematic methods. It should be the goal of every manager to justify the claim that the chamber of commerce is the most efficiently operated office in his town.

CONDITIONS FOR ECONOMY AND EFFECTIVENESS OF OFFICE WORK

If a chamber of commerce office is to be administered well, and if it is to furnish the services for which it was created, it must necessarily have adequate quarters. For good operation, for pride and morale of local members and other citizens, and by all means for impressions created upon visitors, chambers of commerce quarters should be adequate in space and attractive in appearance. It is not too high a standard to say that they should be in keeping with, or even better than, the average office or place of business in the community.

Adequacy of quarters means more than just space. It means, also, the location of the chamber in the business community, the type of building it is in, the location of the office within the building, the amount of space available, the accessibility of this space to the public, the way in which the space is adapted to the use of the organization, and the general appearance of the quarters. No arbitrary rules can be established for deciding any of these questions but the following is a good principle to apply. The quarters should be of sufficient size and should be located in such a way that the local situation and the size and type of the organization are best served.

Office Arrangement

The arrangement of the chamber of commerce office is important, especially if there are a large number of departments in the organization. Departments should be placed in such relationship to each other that procedures and routines can be developed and maintained with efficiency. Some practical suggestions for layout in the office are:

1. The receptionist, or whoever contacts the public first, should be near the entrance and near the facilities for giving quick and accurate information.
2. In smaller organizations if a stenographer or the telephone operator serves as the receptionist, her desk should be readily accessible to the public.
3. The general manager usually has his office farther from the main entrance so as to be somewhat removed from the noise and commotion of the outer office. The staff man or men who have the greatest amount of daily contact with the chief administrative officer should also be located in close proximity to him.
4. Office service units, such as the central files, the library and the bookkeeping department should be accessible to those who make use of their services.

The old adage "Money saved is money made" is just as applicable to office procedure as it is to factory. Some chamber of commerce executives watch meticulously stamps, pencils, paper clips, stationery, etc., but at the same time allow dollars to be wasted in poorly planned office arrangement. Wasted or unnecessary motion in an office is as bad as wasted or unnecessary motion on an assembly line. In the chamber of commerce office inefficiency is especially bad because many of the members have developed efficiency in their own operations and will expect the same from their chamber.

Equipment and Supplies

Desks, files and other office furniture should be arranged in an orderly manner. This condition not only enhances the office appearance but also contributes to greater efficiency and happiness. All furniture and equipment should be kept in good repair. Typewriters in particular should be kept clean, oiled and properly adjusted so as to provide the greatest ease and speed of operation. Specialized equipment such as mimeographs or other modern printing and duplicating machines call for specialized maintenance and well trained operators.

Unless supplies are controlled carefully, much waste can take place. Whenever possible the job of exercising control over supplies should be delegated to one employee. This will result in keeping costs down and will make it convenient to order additional quantities before the supply of a given item is exhausted. In some large organizations, supplies are kept in a central storeroom and departments check out limited amounts as needed. Cabinets in the various offices harmonizing with other woodwork or furniture, furnish a convenient storage for such supplies without detracting from the appearance of the office.

General Appearance

The general appearance of the office should be in keeping with the impression which the total of the facilities of the chambers of commerce is expected to make upon its employees and its members. The office should be orderly and clean, and it should have an air of business. Employees will work better and will enjoy their work more if it is done in cheerful, clean and pleasant surroundings. The impression which visitors to the chamber of commerce office receive will determine not only their opinion of the caliber of the chamber manager; but also their confidence in the quality and standard of the entire office operation. Because the chamber may be the first place they visit in a town or city, these impressions may influence their opinion of the city as a whole.

The chamber of commerce manager should, therefore, strive to maintain high standards of good housekeeping in his office. He should indoctrinate all employees in the philosophy of keeping the office a neat and orderly place of business. Some suggestions for maintaining high standards of office appearance are:

1. Window shades should be kept as uniform as possible without interfering with light and ventilation.
2. The tops of tables, files, bookcases and the like, should be kept cleared of all material which is not actually in use.
3. Desks and table tops should be cleared at closing time and all material should be placed inside or filed.
4. Confusion caused by unnecessary noise and loud talking, as well as that brought about by visiting between members of the staff during working hours should be discouraged.

COMMUNICATIONS

The intercourse of the chamber of commerce through letters, interviews, and other forms of direct contact with members and the public is a direct channel of public relations. It is one that should be cultivated and its results should be evaluated in terms of the objectives of the organization. The media of office communications are: personal contacts inside and outside the office, telephone contacts, and letters and other written forms of intercourse.

Personal Contacts

The personal contact is the most important form of communication for the organization. Personal contacts in the chamber of commerce include:

1. Contacts with members of the chamber, contacts with non-members, and contacts between members of the staff of the office.
2. Contacts with operations relative to the subjects, principles and policies being considered or acted upon by the chamber of commerce.

Principles, rules and methods of procedure should, therefore, properly relate to the conduct of the members of the office staff, first, in contact with persons, and, second, in contact with impersonal subjects and operations. Personal contact on the part of members of the staff takes place either within the office or outside the office.

Contacts Within the Office. Because the staff members make most of the contacts within the office, each should be well trained in the essentials of meeting and serving those who make use of the chamber of commerce services. At least the following essentials should be included in any method or procedure used to guide the conduct of the members of the staff in making personal contacts within the office:

1. Promptness in receiving and serving callers builds confidence in and respect for the organization. This should be the aim of each person in the office.
2. Provisions should be made to ensure that a caller will be referred to and see the proper person in relation to the subject the caller has in mind.
3. Politeness and courtesy pay off in any organization. These attributes should always govern a staff member's actions.
4. Tact is the ability to get people to do willingly what you want them to do. It may be employed effectively in a chamber of commerce office.
5. Concentration of attention upon the subject which the caller came to discuss should be the rule. This demonstrates an interest in his problem and will save time for both the caller and the staff member.
6. The effort to serve and to do things and to do them promptly should become a habit.

First impressions are as lasting in an office as they are throughout life. A chamber of commerce should strive to make these first impressions beneficial to it, to its members and to its community. One of the key personnel in these impressions is the receptionist in the office. The receptionist should be carefully chosen and should be trained to greet visitors courteously, interview them tactfully and intelligently, and serve them efficiently.

The receptionist should be alert and should recognize the presence of a caller as quickly as possible. If the person who is sought by the visitor is out of the office, or otherwise temporarily inaccessible, the receptionist should determine if some other staff member can serve the request. If this is not feasible, the visitor should be handled courteously and carefully. His waiting should be made as painless as possible.

When a caller has been announced to a staff member, and the word given back that he will see him shortly, the receptionist should follow up as necessary to see that such promises are fulfilled. Unexpected delays or changes in plans should be explained to the waiting caller and he should be allowed to decide what course of action such changes necessitate in his plans. Wherever possible the receptionist should make sure that no caller leaves the office without having seen the person whom he came to see, has seen a substitute, or has made arrangements for a return at a later time.

Contacts Outside the Office. Each member of the staff is a personal representative of the chamber of commerce in all contacts outside the office. The character and standing of the organization is likely to be a reflection of the impressions gained from the appearance, manner, attitude, tactfulness and ability of the personnel. For that reason, employees of the chamber are virtually on duty seven days a week whether they realize it or not. If their conduct is good, it makes for good public relations. If bad, it results in bad public relations. Although an employee may try to separate his public from his private position by saying, "These are my personal views and in no way represent the chamber of commerce," the public will nevertheless associate him and his remarks with the office of which he is officially a part.

Telephone Contacts and Practices

One of the principal advantages of a personal contact is the opportunity for each of the participants to watch the expression and to study the inflection of the other. This opportunity is not equally present in a telephone conversation. The voice carries the entire responsibility for influencing the hearer. Thus, every time a staff member speaks over the telephone he helps either to build up the reputation of the organization or to tear it down. There is considerable difference between the effect of a pleasing, warm, friendly, helpful and convincing voice and a lifeless, mechanical, impersonal and indifferent one.

Because of the importance of the telephone contact, the office telephone operator should be carefully trained in telephone usage. Such training can be secured through professional training courses or the local telephone company will frequently make its services available. Some rules of telephone usage which the operator as well as all other staff members should follow are:

1. Have a prompt and pleasant greeting for every telephone caller.
2. Be easily and accurately understood.
3. Identify yourself or your organization, instead of saying, "Hello".
4. Be sure pencil and pad for taking notes are near the telephone.
5. Transfer a call to someone else only when you cannot handle it satisfactorily yourself.
6. When answering a call for someone who is not available, offer to take any message or to be of service to the one calling.
7. When placing a telephone call, be sure to be on the line when the called person answers.
8. Place calls by number whenever possible to save the operator's time.
9. Be sure to wait long enough for an answer before hanging up.
10. Close a telephone conversation in a friendly manner and to sure to replace the receiver gently so that the caller will not get the impression you hung up abruptly.

Correspondence

The third medium of office communication is the letter or other form of correspondence. Proper handling of this means of communication, both in its substance and in its mechanics, is a prime necessity both from the standpoint of the chamber of commerce and from the standpoint of the manager.

In discussing this phase of the general subject of office administration, the objective shall be to point out certain principles of importance to the organization and to the manager rather than to attempt to elaborate the techniques and procedures of letter writing. These general principles should govern all correspondence:

1. **Promptness.** Every letter received is entitled to as prompt a reply as possible. If immediate response is not possible, it should be acknowledged and responded to as soon as possible.
2. **Neatness.** Neatness is a valuable attribute in all correspondence. The appearance of letters and documents creates an impression of the character and standing of organization.
3. **Brevity.** A chamber of commerce is a business organization made up of business men. Because time is important, the observance of appropriate brevity will increase their respect for the organization. On the other hand, each letter should give all the information necessary to accomplish its purpose, and brevity should not be gained by the sacrifice of clarity and ease of reading.
4. **Clarity.** The language used in a letter should be adapted to the vocabulary of the addressee. All information, opinions or thoughts expressed in the letter should be so clear that the recipient will understand the intent of the writer.
5. **Certainty or Planning.** Each letter should be planned so that the writer will be sure of what he wishes to say. Not only will this save the stenographer's time: it will also ensure an orderly sequence of thought.
6. **Arrangement.** The arrangement and order in which thoughts are expressed is important in effective writing. The first paragraph should gain attention. The middle paragraphs should hold it, and the final paragraph should clinch the idea.

Letter Writing Principles. The quality of letters written by a chamber of commerce determines the respect they create and the attention they receive. The competent manager sees to it that all letters sent from the office have an attractive mechanical set-up. The arrangement on the page, the width of the margins, and the position of the date, inside address, salutation and the complimentary close should follow recognized principles of good usage. The following are minimum rules to follow:

1. Appropriate salutations and signatures should be developed for each type of letter.
2. There should be a simple system of designating on each letter the person dictating as well as the stenographer transcribing.
3. All copy work should be carefully checked for comparison.
4. A copy of each letter or document sent out of the office should be maintained in the files.
5. When enclosures are to be included in a letter, a method should be developed to ensure their inclusion.
6. Provision should be made for having all stenographically prepared documents dated and initialed by the stenographer who originates the material.

Form Letters. Form letters are used frequently in chamber of commerce operations. Such letters can be worth-while salesmen for the organization, and they can be used to good advantage in the administration of the office. Form letters should be carefully planned and written because they go to groups rather than to individuals. Since it is more difficult to write a letter to a group than to an individual, the group and its interests should be carefully analyzed so as to make the appeal as applicable as possible.

Whether the form letter is used in collection efforts, in advising of committee matters or for any one of a number of other reasons, it should gain and hold attention. It should indicate the main reason for the letter, relate this to the interests of the reader, get him to react as desired, and close with essential information on what to do and how to do it.

Telegrams. Telegrams are used for two main reasons: speed in sending the messages to their destination, and for attention and effectiveness. Definite procedures should be established for using them, however. A waste of a few cents here and a few cents there in the use of telegrams when other, and cheaper, means of communication would accomplish the objective, can cost the chamber of commerce a considerable amount of money each year. This waste may occur from improper use of the telegraphic service or from use of the service when it is not justified. It is a bad practice to allow members to charge messages to the chamber unless authorized by the proper person in that organization. A good way to control their use is to have an executive order requiring copies of all telegrams to be filed with the manager at the time of sending.

FILES AND FILING METHODS

Files constitute the key to the successful physical operation of a chamber of commerce office. They are the repository in which are placed all the papers, documents and material of various types which must furnish the basis for consideration and action by members of the staff, committees and the board of directors.

In any approach to the problem of filing, several things should be kept in mind.

1. It is difficult to describe a filing system that will fit all chambers of commerce, large and small. General instructions, therefore, must be adapted to the needs of the individual office.
2. Large offices with voluminous files require the full-time services of employees to operate them, while small offices have some members of the staff operate the file in connection with other duties.
3. There should be a central informational file in each chamber of commerce office. Departmental files may be centralized or decentralized depending upon the circumstances.

Requisite Principles

The following general principles are equally important in the creation and use of a filing system for correspondence alone, or to a system designed to include also the filing of other papers, documents, statistical reports or pamphlets. They are applicable regardless of the size of the organization.

1. It should be a "finding" system; it should not only put the papers out of sight, but also produce them instantly when required.
2. It should be as simple in plan of construction as possible.
3. It should not require an efficiency expert to operate it.
4. It should be elastic; that is, capable of expanding with the growth of the organization with the least possible alteration or rearrangement of material and space.
5. It should serve and not dominate or revolutionize the office organization and operation.
6. It should be thoroughly understood by members of the staff who are going to use it.
7. It should be definitely placed under the authority of persons who have been given responsibility for the operation of the files.

8. It should be protected against depredations; that is, control must be maintained over materials taken out of the files and a charge-out record should be inserted in the place of every item taken out.

Bases for Filing Systems

There are two fundamental bases upon which the mechanical construction of an efficient filing system may be built. These are:

1. Subjects
2. Names

The filing system is a very essential tool in the conduct of the chamber of commerce business. It is highly important, therefore, that the nature of that business should be considered carefully in order to determine the exact type of filing tool adapted to serve the requirements of that business. Because a chamber of commerce deals primarily with principles, that is, subjects, the filing system should be constructed upon the basis of subjects rather than of names.

A commercial organization differs radically from most industrial concerns in this respect. Industrial establishments deal in many cases with only one subject, such as "steel", or, at most with a relatively few subjects descriptive of their respective stocks in trade. With such a business establishment, the name is the important thing. Experience and necessity have evolved the conviction that the subject basis, with the most elastic plan of operation, serves the purposes of a chamber of commerce best.

Methods of Filing

Two methods of filing material are recognized: One, the direct alphabetic method, and the other, a numerical method.

Alphabetic Method. Subject filing by the direct alphabetic method consists of arranging, in alphabetical order, individual folders upon which are written the subject titles. Where subjects are divided, the sub-divisions are placed in separate folders and filed immediately behind the principal folders, with subject title and their divisions both shown on the tabs of the subject folders.

Equipment for this method usually consists of compressed

board guides for the alphabetical divisions behind which the individual names of subject folders are placed. Miscellaneous folders—one for each alphabetical guide—are often used to hold correspondence of a strictly miscellaneous character, or relative to an active subject until the matter has become sufficiently important or voluminous to require an individual folder. This system is preferred by most small organizations.

Numerical Method. Some organizations, especially the larger ones, prefer the numerical method. Under this system consecutive numbers are assigned to the principal subjects. These subjects are then divided into as many groupings as seem necessary by the use of an auxiliary number separated from the principal number by a decimal point or hyphen. This method provides unlimited elasticity with a minimum of disarrangement of the existing files.

Whenever a division of a dependent subject becomes advisable, additional digits may be added to the auxiliary number, after decimals. To illustrate: the subject of *Public Relations* may be given numbers 200-299; a dependent subject, *Newspapers*, may be given number 210; divisions of the dependent subject, Dailies, Weeklies, Daily and Sunday, Farm, etc., may be given numbers as follows: Dailies 210.1, Weeklies 210.2, Daily and Sunday 210.3, Farm 210.4. Divisions of any of these sub-dependent subjects may be given numbers which are derived by merely adding additional digits after the decimal. For instance, The News, a daily, may be given the number 210.11.

To facilitate the finding of papers in the files relating to any one of these numerically arranged subjects, there should be (a) a list of subjects arranged numerically on suitable sheets of paper, or in a folio book, and (b) a card index of subjects and sub-subjects arranged alphabetically.

Operating the Filing System

A number of rules which are essential in the operation of large offices, but which are not as applicable to smaller organizations are summarized below. These are summarized because they will be helpful to the new members of a large staff and supply suggestions to the manager of a smaller office.

All material sent to the files should show that it has received proper attention. Correspondence should be checked to indicate that it received the attention of the one to whom it was referred. If an answer was given in person or by telephone, this fact should be noted on the letter. The person, or persons, in charge of the files should not accept any material for filing unless certain it has had proper attention.

Some organizations make two carbon copies of all outgoing correspondence. One is filed in the subject file, and the other serves as a name index and is filed alphabetically. Two copies of circular or form letters are similarly filed. For each document or letter taken out of the files, a charge sheet (Letters Taken Out) is made in substitution and is filed in the folder from which the correspondence was taken. All correspondence, reports, papers or documents, which will ultimately reach the files should be sent to them promptly. This is the only way in which the files may be kept complete.

Orderliness and neatness of the files are important for securing efficiency, accuracy and speed in handling the material. General routine correspondence should either be destroyed or transferred at appropriate intervals. Current, active correspondence should be kept in the active file. Inactive material may be kept in a transfer file, following exactly the same procedure as is followed in the general active file. Some correspondence can be transferred at the end of a stated period and, after a subsequent period of inactivity, be destroyed.

Many chambers of commerce which operate through several closely related departments have found it advisable to create one central filing department. This system is most efficient in some large offices because no matter how many different departments there are, each will need common material from time to time. This system has two additional advantages:

1. It makes all files and documents readily available to the chief executive of the organization.
2. It places the full responsibility for effectively operating the filing system upon one individual.

In smaller organizations, as well as in a number in larger cities, some advantage is gained by decentralizing the files and making the stenographer in each department responsible for the filing of material pertaining to that department. When this practice is followed, there should be as much uniformity as possible in the filing systems of the several departments. This makes it possible for anyone in the office to locate material in any one of the files.

General Rules of Filing

The successful use of any filing system implies willing and effective cooperation among all users of the files. The following rules should be observed if this is to be secured:

1. All outgoing letters and office memoranda should have sufficient copies to fill filing requirements, in addition to copies to others directly involved in the correspondence.
2. Every letter, memorandum, report, etc., should be dated.
3. Correspondence should not be held on desks awaiting attention. The follow-up system should provide slips to be used on correspondence which will be required at a later date.
4. Correspondence, when sent to the files, should bear some notation to indicate the action taken on it.
5. If a letter refers to more than one subject, cross-reference should indicate where the material may be found.
6. Only those who have responsibility for the files should have direct access to them.
7. Correspondence taken from the files should be replaced by "charge-out"sheets. These are removed from the file when the correspondence is returned.
8. Each morning the person in charge of the files should remove from the files all correspondence entered in the tickler file for that day, and submit it to the individual or department whose signature appears on the return slip. The slip should remain attached and when the correspondence is returned to the filing department it should show what action was taken and what disposition to make of it.

It is becoming general practice for many chamber of commerce managers to require that a carbon copy of every letter that is written in the office be supplied him daily, or at other stated intervals. By this procedure, the manager is informed of what is going on in each department and he can exercise more effective supervision. Care should be observed, however, to make sure that this practice does not result in stifling the initiative of the staff members.

OFFICE ORGANIZATION, RULES AND PROCEDURES

If the office staff of a chamber of commerce is to maintain a high degree of efficiency and effectiveness in its work, the staff must be properly organized and suitable rules and procedures must be developed and maintained.

Organization of the Office Staff

The staff of a chamber of commerce may consist of a manager and one stenographer-assistant, or it may consist of a manager and many subordinates. In either case, certain principles of organization apply and unless they are observed, confusion and waste will result.

1. A clear definition of the responsibilities, relationships and authority of each member of the organization should be made. Responsibility should always be coupled with corresponding authority.
2. Each member should have a clear understanding of the scope and nature of his duties. Changes should be made only after their effect on other employees is considered.
3. The various members of the staff should have a comprehension of the inter-relations existing between the duties and responsibilities of each. This ensures better coordination of effort and teamwork. No staff member should be subject to direct orders from more than one person.
4. A spirit of loyalty to the chamber of commerce and to each other should be encouraged at all times both inside and outside the office. To ensure this: (1) criticism should be made privately; (2) no difference between employees should be considered too trivial for prompt attention; (3) no employee should be expected to be both an assistant to and a critic of another at the same time.

Some of these features of organization lend themselves to definition in rules or charts; others do not. Nevertheless, they are all essential to a proper staff organization and form the basis for effective work in the office.

Personnel Relations

The chamber of commerce manager must be vitally interested in all phases of personnel relations. It is not sufficient to provide a well equipped office and a well organized office staff. The personnel of the office must be well chosen in terms of the jobs which they are expected to perform and they must be adequately trained in the skills and knowledges of the job. In addition to this the morale of each individual and of the group must be maintained at a high level. To accomplish this the manager should have frequent consultation with the other employees. These consultations should include the objectives of acquainting all members of the organization with the general purposes and activities of a chamber of commerce, and of discussing new activities that arise and interpreting the meaning of the work of each unit of the office.

Practical rules and methods of procedure should be established in every chamber of commerce, regardless of size, for guidance of the staff. Such regulations should be designed to promote unity and efficiency and should be observed in letter and spirit.

Courtesy. Among the many courtesies that contribute to the happiness and efficiency of an office organization are:

1. Consideration of other staff members. For example, when a member is interviewing the manager, no other member has a right to interrupt until the conversation has been finished.
2. Although the manager should be readily available to members of the staff, this privilege should not be abused by too frequent or trivial reasons.
3. When visitors are admitted to the office of the manager, or that of department heads, other employees present should be introduced.
4. Although first names of staff members may be appropriate for inter-office routine, in the presence of visitors a more formal atmosphere should be maintained.
5. Since chamber of commerce work requires a high degree of cooperation, it is necessary when work piles up in any department, the rest of the organization must be available to help out in the rush.
6. Orderly conduct and courtesy toward the public and fellow workers should be observed at all times. The chamber is a quasi-public institution. Because of this, the conduct and service of its employees should be of such high character as to command the greatest respect.

Interviews. No member of the staff should have any hesitation in consulting freely with the manager on either business or personal problems. Although, in general, personal problems should be separate and apart from business relations, if these problems are of such a nature as to influence the effectiveness of the employee, they are matters which should be discussed with the manager.

Absences. Staff members who leave the office during office hours, should leave word where they can be reached and should indicate the time they will be back. Members of the secretarial staff should leave the office only with permission of the manager or someone in authority. Should it be necessary for a staff member to be absent due to sickness, or any other reason, the office should be notified promptly.

Suggestions. Suggestions should always be welcomed from all employees. This is true not only of suggestions for improvement in their own activities but also of suggestions for the general good of the organization as well.

Miscellaneous Rules and Regulations

In the efficient administration of any chamber of commerce there are numerous other matters worthy of consideration. Some of these are more or less general with all such organizations, and some are applicable only in specific instances. Brief mention is made of some of the former.

1. **Insurance.** There are many hazards to be considered and consideration should be given to the insurance needs of the office. Public liability, casualty, group life and accident insurance, and fire insurance should be investigated and where desirable should be incorporated into other office procedures.
2. **Confidential matters.** Because a chamber of commerce is an institution to which affairs of a confidential nature are entrusted, each employee should keep whatever information he acquires in strict confidence.
3. **Endorsements.** A chamber of commerce manager should be very careful about giving letters of recommendation and endorsements. When a chamber gives its endorsement to an individual enterprise it has really become a part of it.
4. **Accidents.** Accidents and injuries should be reported promptly. All employees should be instructed in the proper procedure to follow in reporting an accident and the manager should have a well worked out policy ready for handling such cases.

Efficiency engineers are often employed in factories to check the output of men and machines, to study factory layout, movement of materials, to detect lost motion, measure the lighting and see that the ventilation is conducive to good health and good work. After the engineer has made his study he formulates a plan to eliminate the unsatisfactory condition and to bring about more efficiency.

In the chamber of commerce organization and operations the manager must frequently be his own efficiency engineer. He, with whatever help is available, should plan wisely the office and its work and should operate in such a manner as to produce the greatest results, regardless of the size of the organization.

SUMMARY

1. The chamber of commerce should be a model of efficiency. Its offices should be well located and carefully arranged. Its program of work should be tailored to fit the needs of the community and there should be well trained personnel to produce the desired results.

2. Personal contacts inside and outside the office, proper handling of correspondence, and first rate telephone practices are forms of communication which build good will for the chamber of commerce.

3. The organization and operation of the chamber of commerce office should be planned as carefully as the steps in a manufacturing process.

4. The best filing system for a chamber of commerce is the one which makes all letters, reports and documents quickly available, is as simple in its plan of construction as possible, has enough elasticity to take care of new material, and does not require an efficiency expert to operate it.

5. Office rules, policies and procedures of a chamber of commerce should be clearly defined and well understood by every member of the staff.

Chapter IX

Commercial Activities

THE MAIN function of the first American chambers of commerce was to protect and promote the interests of those engaged in trade. They gathered and disseminated information, provided a forum for the discussion of trade problems, and made rules governing the market place. Some of them even operated trading floors. Although the early emphasis on trade has given way to a far broader program of community building, commercial activities continue to occupy an important place in the program of work of the modern chamber of commerce.

The commercial activities of the chambers of commerce fall into three groups:

1. *Retail trade activities.*
2. *Wholesale trade activities.*
3. *Foreign trade activities.*

Some chambers of commerce are actively engaged in promoting all three types of projects, while others limit their efforts to but a single field. In the smaller communities, the chamber of commerce ordinarily finds its first interest in the problems of the retailer; in the larger city the welfare of the wholesaler and exporter may be given as much attention as that of the retailer.

RETAIL TRADE ACTIVITIES

The ability of a community to develop as a retail trade center depends on a host of factors. Some of these, such as the natural resources of the region in which the community is located, are more or less immutable and must be accepted as given. Others—such as the degree to which the agricultural and industrial resources of the region are exploited—can be modified and developed over time. Chambers of commerce take an active part in such a development through their agricultural, industrial and civic activities. Still other factors are under the control of the merchants themselves. They include such things as the quality of the services offered by the retailers, the attractiveness of their merchandise and prices, the extent and effectiveness of their sales and advertising efforts, and the appearence of the business district. Through its retail trade activities, the chamber of commerce seeks to organize and channel the efforts of all merchants so as to bring about a community-wide improvement in retailing practices and a fuller exploitation of the opportunities available to the merchants.

Organizing for Retail Trade Activities

Many chambers of commerce in larger cities have separate retail divisions, staffed with personnel that devotes its entire time to the problems of the retail merchants. In smaller communities, however, all retail trade activities are generally conducted by one or more committees. The size and elaborateness of the committee structure should, of course, depend upon the program of work. Most chambers have a retail executive committee whose function it is to coordinate all retail activities. Some chambers have tried, with success, to give representation on the committee to all retail trade groups. Under this plan, the merchants in each line—such as dry goods, shoes and jewelry—select one of their number to represent their interests. Although the retail executive committee is ultimately responsible to the board of directors, it is sometimes given more authority than other committees. It may have its own budget and be a self-governing body in all matters pertaining exclusively to its own affairs. All questions affecting the chamber of commerce as a whole are, however, referred to the board of directors for approval.

If the retail trade program is large, additional committees may be needed. Some chambers have a committee for each important retail project, and the plan works well. It is important, however, that the committee structure should not be overbuilt. It is far better to have a few active committees than to have a large number that merely meets and produces a lot of minutes. It is therefore a good rule to start with a general or executive committee, and then add others as the need develops.

Determining the Retail Trading Area

In order to develop an effective program of retail trade promotion it is necessary to have full knowledge of the retail market. Such knowledge should include not only information about the boundaries of the retail trade area, but also facts about the people living and working in that area.

Information of this sort is needed for a variety of purposes. It provides a basis for estimating the total market potential of the area as well as for judging the sales possibilities of specific lines of merchandise. It serves as an aid to more intelligent buying and to more effective merchandising, advertising and sale promotion. It is needed by retailers to secure dealerships, to obtain advertising support, to evaluate quotas, and otherwise to strengthen their relations with supplies.

The first step in an analysis of the retail trading area is the attempt to delimit the market from which the merchants of the community can reasonably expect to attract business. This is a problem that cannot be solved merely by drawing a circle on a map. Such a circle may look nice and symmetrical, but it does not usually mean a thing—except that someone has preferred the use of a compass to the task of digging out the facts.

Obviously, the extent of the trade area varies by lines of merchandise. Few consumers find it necessary or advantageous to go far out of their way to buy such "convenience goods" as foods, tobacco or gasoline. They buy these things from the nearest retail store or filling station. Hence, it is difficult to speak about the trading area for such commodities. On the other hand, people will travel considerable distances to purchase men's and women's wear, furniture and amusements. It is merchandise of this sort we have in mind when we measure the trading area of a city.

Communities vary in their ability to attract business from the countryside and from other towns. Some centers draw trade from a large area, while others may actually lose more business than they attract. A number of factors bear on the size of the retail trading area. Some of the more important are:

1. The population of the trade center relative to those of competing centers.

2. The distances to competing trade centers.
3. Accessibility of the trade center (roads, bus, trains, parking facilities).
4. Normal flow of freight, mail and passenger traffic.
5. Quality of retail stores in the trade center (quality and variety of merchandise, service and prices).
6. Availability of amusements, banking and other services.
7. Coverage by local newspapers and radio stations.

A number of careful studies suggest that the two first factors in the list are by far the most important. In fact, they are so important that a fairly accurate determination of trading areas is possible by the use of a formula which gives consideration only to them.[1]

Although the use of such a formula affords a short cut and may give fairly accurate information about the boundaries of a retail trade area, it must be remembered that it gives expression only to average relationships. The formula does not take into consideration any peculiar conditions that may affect the trade area of a particular community. Furthermore, the formula can tell only what the retail trading area ought to be, and not what it really is. Hence, other methods should be used to supplement and check the results obtained by the use of the formula.

Many chambers of commerce have sought to outline the boundaries of the retail trade area on the basis of information obtained directly from retailers. In its simplest form

---

[1] The formula was first developed by William J. Reilly in 1931, and has become widely known as "Reilly's law of retail gravitation". It has since been improved upon, and has been successfully used by a number of research organizations interested in the problem of retail trade areas. In its most useful form, the formula states that the distance, measured in miles, from a retail center (city A) to the boundary of its trading area toward a competing center (city B) is equal to:

$$\frac{\text{Distance from A to B}}{1 + \sqrt{\dfrac{\text{Population of B}}{\text{Population of A}}}}$$

For a discussion of the formula and its use see: Paul D. Converse, **A Study of Retail Trade Areas in Eastern Illinois.** Bureau of Economic and Business Research, Business Studies No. 2, College of Commerce and Business Administration, (Urbana, University of Illinois, 1943). See also an article by the same author, "New Laws of Retail Gravitation," **Journal of Marketing,** XIV: 3, (October 1949) pp. 379-84.

such an attempt may call for a meeting of all retailers at which each of them is asked to outline the territory in which he does business. The information so obtained may then be recorded on a large-scale map by the use of colored push-pins. Although this method appears disarmingly simple, it suffers from serious shortcomings. First, if the number of retailers is large, the meeting is likely to become unwieldy. Secondly, few retailers have accurate knowledge of the residence of their customers. Moreover, the mere fact that a retailer happens to have a few customers in a distant town does not necessarily mean that his trade area extends to that town. The density of business must be taken into consideration. Consequently, no retailer is likely to be able to supply significant information about his trade territory except on the basis of a careful analysis of his customer roster. And finally, such a meeting may well kindle the spirit of competition to such an extent that each retailer will try to outdo his competitors by reporting a larger trade territory than he really has.

The conclusion is inescapable that there is no short-cut to a reasonably accurate delimitation of trading areas. The facts must be dug out. Several methods are available. On the assumption that most out-of-town shoppers come by car, it is possible to list the license numbers of cars parked in and around the business district. In order to secure a representative sample it would probably be necessary to do this over a period of several typical shopping days. The addresses of the owners can be obtained from the state motor-vehicle records. When they are plotted on a map, they show the geographical origin of trade.

A more direct method is that of plotting the addresses of cash and credit customers of representative stores. If the stores have a great many charge accounts, a sample check may have to suffice. The addresses of cash customers must be obtained by sales people at the time of sales.

Closely related to the preceding methods is the use of questionnaire and interview among consumers in an ever-widening area around the trade center. The purpose of such a survey is to determine where the respondents purchase particular goods, their reasons for buying where they do, frequency of shopping trips and the like. On the basis of such information it is possible to determine the "breaking points" at which the particular trading center ceases to attract a substantial proportion of the retail trade. These breaking points constitute the limits of the retail trade area. A questionnaire survey of this sort is, however, likely to prove expensive and time consuming. Furthermore, the design of a significant sample, the construction of a good questionaire and the conduct of interviews that will elicit complete and unbiased answers, require a high degree of technical competence.

Although these several methods provide facts, judgment is still required to define the trade area. For example, a map showing the geographical origin of trade will almost certainly bring out that the density of trade decreases gradually as the distance from the city increases. In the absence of a river or some other natural barrier, there may be no clear-cut line at which the trade territory ends. Hence, the decision as to where to draw the boundary is a difficult one. By comparing the results of several methods or by determining the "typical" experience of several stores in a particular line of retail trade, however, it may be possible to arrive at some reasonable compromise for each line of trade and for all shopping goods trades combined.

By comparing the trade areas secured by these methods with the "ideal" or, "average" trade area obtained by the use of formula, it may also be possible to exercise some judgment about the efficiency of the local merchants. If the actual trade area falls short of the ideal, it may be because the retailers have neglected the trade possibilities of parts of the area. Such a comparison may therefore suggest the directions in which trade could and should be expanded.

Analyzing the Retail Market

Once the boundaries of the retail trade area have been determined it is possible to analyze the characteristics of the market. Merchants need information about the total number of consumers living and working in the trade territory, their age and sex distribution, their income and the sources of that income. They need to know how many customers live on farms, how many own their homes, and how many homes are wired for electricity or connected with gas mains. They need to know how many people have automobiles and how many of them subscribe to the local newspaper and listen to the local radio stations. Information of this sort provides the background against which merchants can plan their operations.

Much of this information is readily available. The censuses of population, housing, agriculture, manufacture and business are invaluable sources of data. So are periodic or special reports issued by the Departments of Commerce, Agriculture and Labor, the Treasury, the Federal Reserve Board, and other national agencies. State offices and university bureaus of business research may also publish helpful information. One difficulty may arise. Most official statistics are compiled on the basis of political units, such as states and counties. A trade area, on the other hand, is an economic unit. It does not recognize political boundaries. Hence, a trade area may overlap several counties and cover only parts of them. When this happens resort must be had to adjustments and estimates.

The analysis of the market should not stop with a description of its characteristics in terms of published statistics. The merchants need information about the buying habits of the people in the trade area. They need to know their likes and dislikes, as well as their evaluation of the local retail establishments. Information of this sort is invaluable in uncovering weaknesses that may be corrected, and directions in which improvements should be made. The information can be obtained only from the consumers themselves by a carefully planned and painstakingly conducted questionnaire survey.

Certain segments of the market—such as the farm market for agricultural supplies, the institutional market, the student market in university towns or even the industrial market—are frequently overlooked or neglected by local merchants. A special analysis of these market segments may reveal unsuspected possibilities of additional sales, if the local merchants would only take advantage of them. Chambers of commerce should be on the lookout for such opportunities.

In recent years, many chambers of commerce have successfully made use of the "community inventory" services offered by the bureaus of business research of some state universities. These agencies undertake a complete survey of the retail and other service establishments of the community. They examine critically the appearance and layout of the retail stores, the selection and completeness of their stock, the selling ability of their sales people, their advertising and sales promotional efforts, and their accounting and stock control records. On the basis of such an examination they make recommendations for improvement. Some of these recommendations apply to individual retailers. Others suggest general improvements—things that need to be done by all retailers acting in concert.

Retail Trade Promotion

The facts and conclusions made available by quantitative and qualitative analyses of the retail trade area may be used by individual merchants, or they may form the basis for a cooperative program of retail trade promotion. An analysis of consumer reactions may show, for example, that many people in the trading area fail to come to the city because of parking difficulties, or because store hours do not meet their convenience. Or again, an analysis of the farm market may bring out that considerable business is lost because farmers prefer to go to another town where there is a wider selection of farm supplies. Problems of this sort, if they are to be solved at all, must be attacked by cooperative action. They might well become parts of a program of retail promotion sponsored by the chamber of commerce.

Such a program should, in each case, reflect the conditions and needs of the particular community. No two chambers of commerce are therefore likely to have the same program. Some suggestions as to the content of a program may, however, prove helpful.

1. *Transportation.* The retail business of many communities suffers because train and bus schedules to and from towns in their trade areas are far from ideal. In other cases intracity transportation may be inadequate. By working with the proper officials, chambers of commerce may do much to improve situations of this sort.

2. *Parking facilities.* Congestion and inadequate parking facilities have become a serious handicap to the development of retail trade in most communities. It is a problem that requires continuous attention. Chambers of commerce may take the lead in promoting better traffic control and in developing off-street parking facilities. Serious consideration might be given to the possibility of financing such facilities, at least in part, by parking-meter collections.

3. *Store hours.* Merchants have come to realize that store hours must be set so as to serve the convenience of the customers to whom they cater. As a result, shopping nights have become increasingly popular. At the same time, however, store hours must be reasonable from the point of view of employees. The problem of developing a satisfactory schedule is therefore an important one, and one that can be adequately solved only by cooperative action.

4. *Store modernization.* The problem of retail store modernization is one that must generally be solved by the individual merchants. In some communities, however, cooperative activities in this field has brought excellent results. A cooperative plan of store-front modernization may, for example, bring about adherence to a common architectural treatment that makes for a striking and pleasing appearance of the retail section.

5. *Improved merchandise selection.* Numerous surveys of consumer reactions to the retail facilities of smaller communities suggest that one of the most important factors in driving business to competing centers is the lack of adequate merchandise selection. It is obvious that no small-city merchant can duplicate the selections offered by the large-city stores. Nevertheless, much can be accomplished by careful planning—by the individual retailer as well as by the whole trading community acting in cooperation. The merchants might, for example, set up a master plan into which the activities of the existing stores are meshed. And through cooperation with real estate owners, it might be possible to direct the future development of the shopping district in such a manner as to create a really efficient retail center. The purpose of such a plan should be that of achieving balanced merchandising so that the needs of all consumer groups are adequately served. The plan would probably call for a greater degree of specialization than that currently practiced by retailers. Such specialization should make it possible to eliminate much wasteful duplication of basic stock, and to increase the selection of "assortment" merchandise. It is, of course, the assortment or variety—and not the basic stock—which the consumer has in mind when he speaks of merchandise selection.

6. *Retail training.* Merchants are becoming increasingly aware of the need for employee training. Large stores provide such training within their own organizations, but the chamber of commerce might well assist in organizing a retail training program for the employees of smaller stores. As a part of such a program it might sponsor a "courtesy in stores" campaign.

7. *Returned goods.* The return privilege has become an accepted part of our free enterprise system. From the point of view of the merchant it is an important tool for increasing sales by building consumer confidence and good will. Nevertheless, retailers in many communities are plagued with excessive returns. The blame lies frequently with the individual merchant and may be ascribed to faulty selling or poor store systems. When such is the case, corrective action must, of course, be taken by the retailer himself. In other cases excessive returns may be the result of overliberal policies fostered by competition. Consumers may have come to consider returns an absolute right, rather than a privilege. Once such an attitude is established, abuses are almost certain to follow, and may become a communitywide problem. To correct the situation, group action may be necessary.

Any such group action should be broadly conceived. It should call for uniform policy and procedure on returned goods. It should include a campaign among consumers to inform them about the new policy and to call their attention to the costs and disadvantages of excessive returns. But, even more important, it should call for an educational campaign among retailers and their employees to eliminate or minimize the causes of returns for which they alone are responsible. Experience has shown that where such a program has been carefully planned and faithfully followed, drastic reductions in returns have resulted.

8. *Solicitations.* Requests for "donations" or for "program advertising" of questionable value have become so prevalent as to constitute a problem of considerable magnitude. Individual retailers find it difficult to refuse these requests for fear that refusal may adversely affect consumer good will. An effective method of handling the problem is for retailers to pay to the chamber of commerce a certain amount of

money to be used for contributions. The fund so accumulated is administered by the chamber, thereby enabling the individual retailer to refer all requests for donations and program advertising to that organization.

9. *Special retail events.* Merchants—particularly those in smaller cities and towns—have found that community-wide promotions may be far more effective than those staged by individual retailers. Such promotions may be of almost infinite variety. In some cases they may be directed to particular consumer groups, such as farmers, people living in the suburbs or visitors brought to the city by a convention. A "farmers' day", an "auction sale", a "suburban day" and an "Elks' day" are examples of this type of sales events. Others may have more general appeal, such as Christmas promotions or July clearance sales. In some cases the promotion may be designed to emphasize the quality and variety of merchandise available in the local stores; in other cases its purpose may be to dramatize the low prices and bargains offered by the retailers. Some promotions may call for participation by all merchants, while others may be limited to particular types of stores. A spring or fall fashion revue is an example of the latter type of event.

A program may be worked out for a full year, with special events staged at reasonable intervals. A calendar of sales dates should be arranged, each event planned in detail, and a budget established. In order for such a program to succeed, it is necessary to have the full and enthusiastic support of the majority of the important retailers. Each event must have a definite purpose and must be built around a "theme" selected with that purpose in mind. Common policies must be adopted with respect to the types of merchandise to be featured, the price ranges to be emphasized and the appeals to be used, and these policies must be adhered to by all participating retailers. In addition, cooperative advertising, street decorations, parades or other appropriate attractions must be planned and financed.

10. *Special retail services.* As a clearing house for all types of community problems, the chamber of commerce may find it advisable either to provide a number of more or less specialized services or to see that they are provided. A number of these—such as statistical and research service in connection with market analysis, regulation of store hours

and provision for retail training—have already been mentioned. Others might include such projects as the establishment of a retail credit bureau or a better business bureau. In the past many chambers of commerce have interested themselves in the organization of cooperative delivery systems for retail merchants. In most communities today, however, this service has been taken over by privately operated companies or by the stores themselves. "Where-to-buy" information, advertising and merchandising counsel, retailers' bulletins, mailing lists and mailing services, and meetings and social functions are some other specialized services that may be provided by the chamber of commerce through its retail trade committee.

Meeting Retail Competition

Except for the largest cities, there is hardly a community which does not complain that a considerable amount of "its" retail business is lost to some competing metropolitan center. Much of this loss is probably inevitable. It grows out of the inherent competitive advantages of the metropolitan store, the lure of the big city, and the fact that people like to move about—to shop and to enjoy themselves in new places. Even so, however, it is probably true that almost every town and city can recapture a considerable amount of the business now lost by an intelligent program of community merchandising. Some of the elements of such a program have already been suggested. A few words of caution should be added, however.

To be effective, such a program must be truly constructive. It is useless to start a mere "buy-at-home" movement. Hundreds of campaigns of this sort have been tried, and they have all failed. People go out of town to buy for good reasons. They seek wider selections, better quality, lower prices, or more intelligent and courteous service. Unless the local merchants are able to provide the things that the consumer wants, it will do no good to implore him to buy at home or to play on his local patriotism. The only way to make a loyal customer is to serve him as he wants to be served. That is a fundamental tenet of the free enterprise system.

Financing Retail Activities

As business men and members of the community, retailers benefit—directly or indirectly—from *all* activities of the chamber of commerce. The retail trade program is in the nature of an additional and specialized service organized and carried on by the chamber for the merchants. The retailers should, therefore, shoulder the major burden of financing this program. No large appropriations should be made from the general budget of the chamber for retail trade activities.

In accordance with this principle many chambers of commerce raise separate funds for retail trade promotion. Such funds may be secured by an annual subscription plan, or by voluntary contributions or special assessments to finance particular projects. Special assessments may be made on the basis of store frontage, volume of business, number of employees, or according to a scale determined by an assessment committee. The funds so collected should be expended on the retail program exclusively, under the direction of the retail executive committee.

Even though the retail program is separately financed, it is a good rule that all retailers who participate in that program, should first have a membership in the chamber of commerce at its prescribed rates of dues. The subscription to the retail trade promotion fund should be an additional subscription. There are chambers of commerce which find themselves in a situation where some retailers contribute to the retail fund without being members of the chamber itself. This is an unhealthy situation which should be corrected by a policy declaration by the board of directors.

WHOLESALE TRADE ACTIVITIES

The wholesale trade of the United States is highly concentrated in a relatively few metropolitan areas. It is estimated that the ten largest market cities do about one-half of the total wholesale business of the country, and that another 52 major trading centers account for an additional one-third of all wholesale activity. Even so, wholesaling is of considerable importance also to many smaller communities. Moreover, during recent decades there has been an apparent trend toward greater decentralization of the wholesale trade. This trend, brought about by improved transportation facilities and changes in relative freight rates as well as by new industrial and agricultural growth, suggests that many communities might well profit from an organized and planned program of wholesale trade promotion.

The need for cooperative action is emphasized by the fact that, contrary to popular opinion, most wholesale firms are comparatively small. It has been estimated that in 1948 there were approximately 240,000 establishments engaged in all phases of wholesale trade, doing an average volume of business of less than 800 thousand dollars. Obviously, no firm of this size can singly undertake an effective program of market promotion. By mobilizing the support of all wholesalers in the community, however, a chamber of commerce may well take the lead in launching such a program.

Organizing and Financing Wholesale Trade Activities

Most chamber of commerce carry on their wholesale trade activities through a committee structure similar to that developed for retail trade promotion. A wholesale executive committee may be responsible for planning and coordinating the program. This committee is, of course, ultimately responsible to the board of directors, but—as in the case of the retail executive committee—it may be given considerable autonomy and may be virtually self-governing in all matters pertaining to wholesale trade promotion. Other committees may be added as the program of work creates the need.

Because the wholesale trade program is designed to serve the interest of a particular group, the main burden of financing it should fall upon the wholesalers themselves. The chamber of commerce may reasonably be expected to provide some staff assistance and to carry some general expenses, but funds necessary for any major project should not be a charge against the general budget of the chamber. They should be raised by an additional subscription or a special assessment against wholesalers.

Wholesale Trade Areas

The character of the wholesale trade varies greatly from one community to another. Some trade centers function primarily as markets for the products of agriculture. These markets, which range from the modest country assembly point to the vast central or terminal markets, may be characterized as "buying" markets. They serve as focal points for the concentration and redistribution of farm produce. Other markets serve mainly as distribution centers for manufactured goods. They may be termed "selling" or "jobbing" markets.

The wholesale trade area of any buying or selling market may be defined as the area in which commodities are bought and sold in competition with buyers and sellers in other wholesale centers. The size and shape of these areas are determined, first, by the products handled. The buying areas for cattle, for example, are generally much more extensive than those for hogs, and somewhat less extensive than those for sheep. Similarly, the wholesale selling areas for drugs are much larger than those for groceries, but smaller than those for dry goods. These variations can be explained in terms of differences in product and demand characteristics—such as bulk and weight in relation to value, perishability, degree of standardization, insistency of demand and rate of consumption. The relatively small size of the wholesale trade territories for groceries may, for example, be explained by the fact that the wholesale grocer is selling convenience goods for daily consumption. In order to serve his retail customers adequately he must be available to them on virtually a daily basis. The dry goods wholesaler, on the other hand, distributes shopping goods that are consumed over a longer period of time and replenished less frequently. Consequently, nearness of the dry-goods wholesalers to his retailer customers is not nearly as essential.

The wholesale trade areas of a particular market center are affected not only by the types of commodities handled, but also by a host of other factors. Among these, the distance to competing centers and the availability of adequate transportation, communication and financial services at low cost are important. So are price and price policies, size and variety of stocks, as well as the aggressiveness and enterprise of wholesale merchants and manufacturers. Many of these factors are subject to change through time. Consequently, the boundaries of competing trade centers are never clearly defined, but in constant flux. New methods of transportation or a mere change in relative freight rates or in relative prices may bring about radical changes in existing market areas. The improvement of financial services or the development of new processing or trading facilities may serve to enlarge the market areas of a particular wholesale center.

It is useful to distinguish between actual and potential trade areas. The former are the areas actually exploited by the merchants and manufacturers of the community. They may be defined by securing data on the territories in which wholesalers sell and buy and by plotting these data on maps. The potential trade areas, on the other hand, must be ascertained by analyses of relative prices and freight costs to and from competing trade centers. Such analyses will show the lines or zones of indifference that separate market areas. A comparison between actual and potential trade areas may reveal that wholesalers are neglecting certain market segments, or that they are expending too much effort in territories in which they are under severe competitive handicaps.

Wholesale Trade Promotion

It is probably safe to lay down the generalization that buyers and sellers in the wholesale market are influenced more by rational considerations and less by emotional factors than buyers in the retail market. Furthermore, they have more precise knowledge of market opportunities. It follows that any attempt to promote the wholesale business of a trade center must be firmly based upon the provision of real advantages and solid attractions. Mere "puffing of the wares" of the market is not enough. Within these limitations, however, there are a number of things that a chamber of commerce may do to foster the wholesale trade of the community. A few suggestions are as follows:

1. *Freight rates and transportation facilities.* Because freight rates are an important factor in determining the area in which the wholesalers of a community can effectively compete, the chamber of commerce should keep constant vigil to make sure that freight rate parity with rival markets is established and maintained. Although sweeping rate revisions are apparently a thing of the past, the competitive position of a trade center may be improved by rate changes or reclassification of individual commodities. The demand for such revisions must, however, be supported by convincing arguments based upon facts. It may also be necessary to exercise considerable pressure. The aid and support of the chamber of commerce may, therefore, be essential to success.

The breadth and variety of transportation services, speed of delivery and convenience of schedules are other factors that affect the efficiency and, therefore, the competitive position of a trade center. Modern terminal facilities and adequate storage capacity are also important. The chamber of commerce may well subject these factors to critical scrutiny, and take the lead in urging improvements wherever necessary.

2. *Improved trading and processing facilities.* The competitive position of a wholesale market may be strengthened by the provision of improved trading and processing facilities. A modern farmers' wholesale market may, for example, attract additional business. New processing facilities to enable conversion of a raw material into a product of higher value and less bulk has been a traditional method of expanding trade and enlarging the area of distribution from producing centers. Although it is hardly the function of a chamber of commerce to participate directly in the establishment of such enterprises, it may well be on the look-out for opportunities of this sort and lend its support to their realization.

3. *Featuring market seasons.* Many lines of trade have distinctive buying seasons. These have been fixed by seasonal demand for goods and the general experience of the trade. There are shoe buying seasons, ready-to-wear seasons, furniture seasons, and so on through many lines.

Effective work may be done by featuring each of these periods. Special invitations in the name of the chamber of commerce may be sent to the buyers in the particular line. Trade or style shows may be arranged, and merchants' meetings may be staged for the discussion of problems of the trade. The event may be climaxed by some special attraction at which the hospitality of the community is extended to the visiting buyers. There is room for almost infinite variation, but the common requisite is that all events should be of interest and benefit to the market visitor whose patronage and good will are sought.

4. *Advertising the wholesale market.* Market publicity may take various forms. Direct mail pieces—such as folders, announcements or invitations—may be sent to a list of merchants in the trade territory. Such a list may be supplied by jobbers, secured from commercial rating agencies or prepared from the classified section of telephone directories. Envelope inserts, prepared by the chamber of commerce, may also be turned over to wholesalers for use in their regular mailings. Paid advertising in trade and other periodicals is sometimes

used to advertise some special event, such as a market week. Some chambers publish, "buyer's guides" listing goods and services available in the market.

5. *Good will building.* "Good-will trips" into the market area have been conducted successfully by chambers of commerce for many years. Such trips should be carefully planned and the program should be arranged in cooperation with business organizations in each community to be visited. Good will may also be cultivated by having delegates attend county fairs, reunions and other festivals in communities throughout the market area.

6. *Educational activities.* Wholesalers as a group have sometimes been accused of lethargy and backwardness. Such a charge is hardly justified today. During the last decade or two wholesaling has undergone vast changes. Modern warehouses and mechanical devices have radically reduced the cost of physical handling of goods. Improved methods of stock control have brought about cleaner stocks and more rapid stock turns; and planned selling has greatly increased the efficiency of the sales work of wholesalers. These rapid changes have, however, emphasized the need for continuous educational activities to keep individual wholesalers abreast of what is going on. The chamber of commerce might well sponsor such an educational program.

FOREIGN TRADE ACTIVITIES

Chambers of commerce in many communities have for years maintained foreign trade bureaus or have otherwise been equipped to render specific services to exporters and importers. In the past the demand for these services has come mainly from manufacturers and merchants eager to increase sales by expanding markets abroad. The foreign trade work of the chambers of commerce has therefore been concerned largely with the problems of the exporter. With the growing realization that foreign trade cannot be a one-way affair, however, chambers of commerce have in recent years placed increasing emphasis on import business and have sought to render assistance to merchants and manufacturers who are interested in securing goods from abroad.

Sources of Foreign Trade Information

The problems of foreign trade are much too complex for adequate discussion in this book. As a matter of fact, no chamber of commerce can reasonably be expected to have ready answers to the variety of questions, some of them highly technical, that arise in connection with the export and import business. What may be expected, however, is that the chamber—even in a community that does not have a diversity of export or import trade—should be able to place its members in touch with the principal sources of foreign trade information. The purpose of this section is, therefore, to discuss briefly some of the major sources of assistance available to exporters and importers.

The Chamber of Commerce of the United States is not only concerned with questions of international trade policy, but stands ready to assist local chambers in the solution of specific foreign trade problems. Its Foreign Commerce Department maintains a complete file of sources of information and serves as a clearing house for foreign trade intelligence. It engages in research and publishes special reports on important problems. It keeps members informed about pending legislation that affects international commerce, and it publishes a trade opportunity bulletin. Each year since 1935, the Chamber of Commerce of the United States has sponsored the "National Foreign Trade Week". It works in close cooperation with the Office of International Trade (Bureau of Foreign and Domestic Commerce) of the U. S. Department of Commerce, as well as with other organizations interested in foreign trade.

The main source of information on export and import problems is, however, the Office of International Trade of the U. S. Department of Commerce. The Commerce Department maintains field offices in the principal cities throughout the United States where staff members are on call to answer specific questions raised by exporters and importers. In addition, the Department publishes periodicals and special reports of paramount interest to the foreign trader. Most imporant among the periodicals is the *Foreign Commerce Weekly*. Its two main sections are usually "News by Countries" and "News by Commodities", but it contains also such sections as "New World Trade Leads", "Foreign Exchange Rates", "Trade Mark Applications" and the like. Two other publications are the *Industrial Reference Service* and the *Interna-*

tional Reference Service. The former is a series of looseleaf reports, issued as completed, presenting data on important commodity and industrial developments at home and abroad. The latter—also published in looseleaf report form—offers surveys of foreign market areas; appraisal of transportation problems; basic export and import data; analyses of foreign commercial laws; studies of foreign tariffs, quotas, documentations, restrictions and regulations; and much other material of value.

The Office of International Trade maintains also the *World Trade Directory* which contains information on nearly one million firms and individuals engaged in international trade. World Trade Directory Reports may be obtained at nominal cost. Each report gives data on the firm's methods of operation, its reputation, capital volume of business, number of employees, and management. The *Trade Lists* published by the Office provides such information as sources of foreign supply, principal processors and service organizations, and usual channels of distribution. Listings are classified under 100 major commodity groups for almost every trading area.

Although the services mentioned suggest the range of assistance available from the Department of Commerce through its Office of International Trade, the list is by no means exhaustive. The Office stands ready to assist exporters and importers in their everyday problems. It is staffed with individuals well versed in foreign affairs. In recent years the Office has considerably expanded its services to importers. In a real sense, this represents a new departure in United States trade promotion. It reflects official recognition of the fact that foreign trade is a two-way street.

The Department of State works very closely with the Department of Commerce in providing information and services to American foreign traders. A great deal of the information that is disseminated by the Office of International Trade is actually secured by the State Department through American Foreign Service officials. Nevertheless, exporters and importers should generally direct their requests for information and assistance to the Department of Commerce.

A number of other Federal agencies are concerned with foreign trade and are in a position to supply information and render assistance. The Department of Agriculture has assumed increasing responsibility for international trade in agricultural commodities. Its Office of Foreign Agricultural

Relations secures foreign crop information, conducts investigations into foreign commercial policy and cooperates in the reciprocal trade agreements program. The U. S. Tariff Commission is largely a research and advisory body. It performs invaluable service to the formulation and administration of tariff laws, negotiation of trade agreements and formulation of commercial policy. Its bulletins, monographs and special studies are important additions to our foreign trade literature. The Treasury Department is in charge of the administration of the tariff law through its Bureau of Customs. It publishes the *Customs Regulations* and the *Treasury Decisions*, both of which are invaluable to importers.

In addition to the official sources of information and assistance, there are a great many quasi-public and private organizations that stand ready to aid the experienced as well as the neophyte foreign trader. The National Foreign Trade Council is unique among these organizations. Its membership includes manufacturers, banks, steamship lines, export and import houses, trade associations, and practically every type of private organization interested in foreign trade. In addition to trade services to its members, the Council is actively interested in matters of national policy and legislation. Its annual convention attracts delegates from all sections of the United States and from many foreign countries. Another national organization, The National Council of American Importers, renders valuable assistance to importers. Its activities includes tariff and customs questions, transportation and insurance problems, and the like. It maintain a bulletin service through which it supplies its members with prompt and accurate information about major developments affecting the import trade.

In addition to the national associations, there are a great many local organizations interested in foreign trade. In almost every large community there is an "export managers' club". Some of them are sponsored by or cooperate closely with the local chambers of commerce. All of these clubs function in the interest of their members. They hold regular meetings and attempt to promote good fellowship among the members of the foreign trade fraternity. They provide the machinery for interchange of experience in such matters as sales and credit terms, sales representation, packing and shipping. Membership in these clubs is of particular value to the inexperienced exporter or importer.

Perhaps most important among the private organizations interested in foreign trade are the export and import publications. In addition to general promotional services, many of these journals supply lists of customers, possible agents, distributors and importers. In fact, some of the best lists of foreign prospects may be secured from this general source. Some of the journals also furnish credit information.

Many transportation companies, both rail and ocean, maintain offices and representatives in the principal industrial centers abroad. They are frequently a valuable source of information. So are export freight forwarders and customs brokers. American banks, both large and small, are often able to supply general as well as specific information and assistance. Many experienced exporters and importers are eager to share their experience and technical know-how with the beginner.

Helping Exporters and Importers

The chamber of commerce that wishes to do more than merely guide its members to appropriate sources of foreign trade information, has a great many different opportunities to render service. Many chambers have organized foreign trade advisory committees whose members are experienced exporters and importers. These committees stand ready to advise and to assist. They have been found extremely valuable. A variation of the same idea is the sponsorship of an "export managers' club" or a "foreign trade round table". The purpose of these organizations is to provide the machinery for discussion of foreign trade problems and for the interchange of experience.

Other chambers have compiled lists of manufacturers and distributors who are interested in exporting or importing. Copies of the lists, containing information about the products which the firms buy and sell, are furnished to the Department of Commerce for incorporation in the Department's *Trade Lists*. They are also sent to American chambers of commerce abroad.

Chambers of commerce that maintain foreign trade bureaus may perform a number of additional services. Some of them are as follows:

1. Analyses of foreign trade opportunities.

2. Information on sailing dates, shipping rates, routing of shipments, packing requirements, customs rates and import regulations.
3. Aid to members in working out problems of foreign trade financing, exchange, marine and other insurance, as well as other technical problems.
4. Assistance in filling out required documents, and certification of documents when a foreign country requires such certification by the local chamber of commerce.
5. Translation service, and assistance in coding and decoding cablegrams.

Some foreign trade bureaus go even farther. They seek actively to promote the export and import business of the community by bringing specific trade opportunities to the attention of manufacturers and merchants. They compile export catalogs, put them in the hands of all U. S. trade promotion agencies abroad, and circulate them elsewhere overseas and in the United States. They send delegates to foreign trade conventions and may organize trade tours to foreign countries. They seek to awaken the community to the possibilities and advantages of foreign trade.

In all these activities, the chamber of commerce should work closely with other agencies engaged in foreign trade promotion. It should avoid duplication of any services already provided by other organizations.

SUMMARY

1. Commercial activities of a chamber of commerce may include retail trade, wholesale trade, and foreign trade promotion.

2. More chambers of commerce are interested in retail trade promotion than in any other type of commercial activities.

3. The first step in a planned program of retail promotion is delimitation and analysis of the retail trade area. Such an analysis, if comprehensive and carefully done, will suggest the elements of an effective program of retail trade promotion.

4. Wholesale trade extension is a matter of importance to some chambers of commerce and of major concern to others.

5. Because retail and wholesale activities are designed to benefit particular groups, their cost should be borne largely by these groups.

6. The possibilities of foreign trade should be investigated by chambers of commerce, and foreign trade promotion should become a part of the chamber's program whenever foreign trade opportunities warrant such a project.

Chapter X

Industrial Activities

THE GROWTH and prosperity of a majority of our great cities have been closely identified with industrial development. That identification has led many agencies—public, quasi-public and private—to launch more or less elaborate programs of local industrial promotion. As a matter of fact, such activities have frequently been regarded as a panacea and as an Open sesame! to success and a more abundant life for the community.

Perhaps it may be said that in no field of endeavor have the chambers of commerce achieved more outstanding successes—and suffered more disheartening failures—than in the field of industrial promotion. Experience has clearly demonstrated that when the essential factors of industrial growth are present in a community, a carefully planned and effectively executed program of industrial activities can achieve remarkable results. But it has no less clearly demonstrated that in the absence of growth factors, even the most ambitious program must fail. Moreover, successful industrial promotion requires know-how and persistence. Wishful thinking, temporary enthusiasm, slip-shod planning or amateur efforts can lead nowhere but to failure.

The nature and the extent of the industrial activities of chambers of commerce vary widely. As a matter of fact, the most successful programs are those that are tailored to fit the resources, needs and aspirations of the particular community. They are long-range programs designed to achieve carefully defined goals. In spite of such diversity, however, three major types of activity may be recognized and differentiated. They are:

1. Service to existing industry.
2. Activities designed to stimulate and facilitate the development of locally-sponsored industry.
3. Activities designed to attract industry from without the community.

These activities are not clearly set apart, but tend to shade into one another and to overlap. Service to existing manufacturers, for example, may be an important factor in encouraging the establishment of new local industry or in attracting branch plants or relocations to the community. Similarly, many of the activities designed to stimulate local initiative may serve as an inducement to "foreign" manufacturers to locate plants in the city. In spite of such overlap, however, the purpose and, to a lesser extent, the methods of each type of activity are rather sharply differentiated. The classification is, therefore, useful both as a device of exposition and as a tool to a clearer understanding of the purposes, problems and methods of industrial promotion.

The relative possibilities of each of the three types of industrial promotion presumably vary greatly from one community to another, as well as from time to time. In recent years, for example, there seems to have been a trend toward industrial decentralization, suggesting that growth by the attraction of new enterprise to the community may have gained importance. Nevertheless, there seems to be little doubt that most cities owe a considerable part of their industrial development to the expansion of existing plants. Moreover, a recent survey indicates that the establishment of new local industry is a more important factor in industrial expansion than the acquisition of plants and factories from the outside. The results of the survey are summarized in Table I. They suggest that, in most cases, a program of industrial activities that seeks to promote local industry and to render service to established manufacturers, may be more effective than one that seeks to entice "foreign" companies to the community.

TABLE I

ORIGINS OF NEW INDUSTRY

	Percent of No. of Plants	No. of Employees
Total new industry	100.0	100.0
Relocations	9.4	18.7
Branch plants	8.8	25.0
New industry started within the community	81.8	56.3

LOCATION FACTORS

The first requisite of a successful industrial promotion program is an understanding of the fundamental fact that industrial growth does not "just happen". Industry tends to gravitate to and expand in those communities in which location factors are favorable. Stated in its simplest and most rational terms, this means that industry seeks to locate where profits promise to be maximum, now and in the future. The factors that go into such profit calculations, however, are many and diverse; and the exact importance that is attached to each of them must vary not only from one industry to another, but also from time to time and from one case to another, depending on the individual circumstances of the particular firm seeking a location. Moreover, it would be a mistake to assume that economic factors are the only determinants. In the case of a new firm starting within the community, for example, purely personal considerations may be the controlling factor in the choice of location.

The diversity of location factors emphasizes both the possibilities and the complexities of industrial promotion. Because no two industries and no two companies look for exactly the same inducements, almost every community is apt to have at least some attraction that appeals to some industry. On the other hand, few communities possess all the requirements of an ideal industrial location. Each chamber of commerce must, therefore, tailor its industrial activities to the circumstances of its own location. To do so, it must not only have complete knowledge of the assets and limitations of the community, but also sufficient understanding of the requirements of industry in general—and each industry in particular—so that it can effectively exploit the appeals at its disposal.

Location Factors Can Be Developed

Many location factors—such as climate, availability of raw materials and nearness to markets—are more or less completely outside the control of the community and the chamber of commerce. Others may, however, be developed or modified over time. They include such factors as adequate transportation facilities, reasonable freight rates, abundant water, skilled labor supply, available buildings and building sites, and satisfactory financial and other services to industry. Although no chamber of commerce could reasonably be expected to assume direct responsibility for the provision or development of all of these facilities and services, they are factors that might well be included in a comprehensive program of industrial activities. Merely by calling attention to the needs of the community and by planning and working for their fulfillment, the chamber can contribute greatly to industrial growth.

Community Attidude Important

The attitude of the community toward new enterprise is an important element in industrial growth. No manufacturer can afford to locate in an unfriendly town and few, if any, will do so. Vested interests, factions or public officials who are cold to industrial expansion, must inevitably impose a serious handicap on any program of industrial activities. One of the first jobs of the chamber of commerce is, therefore, that of developing an appreciation of the value of industry and a genuinely friendly and cooperative attitude toward new enterprise.

Most businessmen in the service and distribution trades are eager to support any activity that promises to bring about industrial growth. They look forward to new payrolls, larger markets and greater prosperity for their businesses. The attitude of the established manufacturers, however, may not be nearly as favorable. Even if the newcomer is not in direct competition with them, they frequently look upon him as an intruder and as a competitor for labor, sites and services. They fear that industrial expansion will bring in its wake higher wages, increased unionization, greater costs and problems of all kinds. They prefer, therefore, to preserve the *status quo*. Although they may not oppose the efforts of the chamber, they may refuse to take an active part in the development program or to give it more than pious lip service.

Experience has clearly demonstrated that the fears and unfriendly attitude of established manufacturers are hardly justified in fact. On the contrary, they stand to gain as much as anybody from industrial growth. In the absence of growing job opportunities, the character and quality of the labor force is likely to deteriorate because the younger and more able workers seek employment elsewhere. Expanding payrolls, on the other hand, tend to build morale, keep the skilled and ambitious at home, and attract labor from elsewhere. As a result, the labor force is improved in quality as well as in quantity. Moreover, the potential benefits of industrial growth are not limited to an improved labor force. Industrial expansion, almost inevitably, brings in its wake improved transportation facilities, better banking services, and more adequate market organization. As the scope of local industry is broadened, established manufacturers are likely to experience the advantages of proximity of related processes and to find their procurement problems greatly simplified.

Once local manufacturers become aware of these advantages, they may be expected to become the greatest boosters of the industrial expansion program. Moreover, their active support is likely to be invaluable to the chamber of commerce. They possess the technical insight and know-how that are indispensable to effective industrial promotion, and their word carries weight among other manufacturers.

Zoning and Planning for Industry

There are many types of urban communities—residential, church and school towns, state capitals and county seats, trade centers and market towns—but the fact remains that a great many of our important cities are primarily industrial and derive at least a substantial part of their livelihood from manufacturing activities. For this reason, industrial areas are entitled to top consideration in planning the city.

The number of sites where manufacturers can secure adequate railroad, highway and utility services along with workers conveniently near, is not as plentiful as it is generally supposed. Lack of planning in the past has cluttered up prime factory locations with residential and other structures that might better have been placed elsewhere. Once such mistakes have been made, they become difficult to correct. New factories are looked upon as nuisances and intruders by adjacent residents, and vociferous attempts are made to block their establishment.

It has been said that city planners are generally prejudiced against industry. They prefer to develop cities that are beautiful, clean and unsullied by the grime of the factory. If it is recognized, however, that the city is primarily an economic phenomenon and that industry is the heart of urban economy, such an attitude becomes untenable. Except in rare cases, no city can hope to grow and prosper unless it plans realistically and adequately for industry. No matter how beautiful a city may be, life in it cannot be wholly satisfactory unless community income is reasonably high. Good jobs are just as important as good houses and fine parks.

PLANNING INDUSTRIAL ACTIVITIES

No chamber manager should attempt to launch an industrial development program on his own initiative. Such a program involves policies and problems of community-wide significance. It should, therefore, be the responsibility of a broadly representative committee, sufficiently strong and influential to exercise real leadership. Many chambers have found it advantageous to separate the service aspects of the program from the more strictly promotional activities, and to assign each function to a special committee. Experience has demonstrated that established manufacturers do not always make the best members of the committee on new industry. They are, however, indispensable as members of the committee on service to industry.

The principal functions of the committees are to decide policy, establish the broad outlines of the program, and lend moral support to the activities of the chamber. Responsibility for the day-to-day work of service and promotion must devolve on the manager and his staff. As a matter of fact, if the promotional efforts are to be successful, much of the work must be accomplished quickly and on a confidential basis. Names of prospects must be kept secret and preliminary negotiations must be conducted in strict confidence. Only when negotiations have reached the stage where there is no danger of embarrassment to the prospect or the chamber, should the manager seek the active support of the committee. At such a point the assistance of individual members or the committee as a whole may spell the difference between success and failure.

The Industrial Survey

An effective program of industrial activities must be built upon facts. The truth of this statement is obvious in the case of industrial promotion. No chamber of commerce can hope to attract manufacturing plants or develop local industry merely by spouting glittering generalities and engaging in empty boasting. But the statement is no less true for the development of a program of service to industry. If such a program is to be effective, it must be based on a full knowledge of the assets, limitations and the needs of the community. Its very purpose is that of counteracting the limitations and supplying the needs in order to facilitate industrial expansion.

The survey should, first of all, be an accurate inventory of community facilities that bear directly or indirectly on the operation of industry in general. It should show advantages and shortcomings. If, in addition, the survey includes studies revealing assets and limitations as they apply to particular branches of industry, its usefulness is, of course, greatly enhanced. A typical outline of the topics that should be covered by an industrial survey, is printed as an appendix to this chapter. It may be expanded or contracted to meet the needs of the local situation. Other outlines have been published by such organizations as the Chamber of Commerce of the United States, the American Industrial Development Council, the U. S. Department of Commerce, the departments of commerce or the development agencies of many states, and the industrial development departments of some railroads and public utility companies. They are readily available to any interested chamber of commerce.

Making the Survey

The compilation of an industrial survey is no easy matter. It requires time and effort. Moreover, if the survey is to be complete and accurate, it presupposes an extensive knowledge of sources of data and a complete understanding of their significance and limitations. Even the most experienced manager will, therefore, need assistance. He may secure such help from the development agencies of the state, the industrial departments of railroads and public utility companies, the bureaus of business and economic research maintained by some universities, and from professional people available in the community and elsewhere. If the chamber has no personnel qualified to undertake the survey, it may find it advisable to turn over the task to a reliable firm of industrial engineers.

The sources of data are almost legion. Among the more important, however, are the U. S. Departments of Commerce, Agriculture and Labor; state and local government departments and development agencies; utility and transportation companies; regional Federal Reserve Banks; universities; engineering firms and established manufacturers. The chambers of commerce in the metropolitan centers have frequently assembled data about smaller cities and towns in their general trading area. They are, therefore, in a position to be of assistance to the chambers in these communities.

Although data available in published form are likely to supply all the information needed for a general industrial survey of the city and its trading area, the chamber of commerce will almost certainly be called upon to answer specific questions of highly technical nature. In order to answer these queries the manager will need the counsel and advice of people with special knowledge and information. It is, therefore, important that he should build up a wide circle of contacts in the city and state, and even further afield.

The survey data should be reproduced in the most flexible form possible. The loose-leaf, mimeographed form is popular and practical. Subjects should be separated so that any combination of them can be assembled to meet the requirements. Maps, charts and photographs add much to the attractiveness of the materials. They should, insofar as possible, be reproduced in such a form as to fit the 8½ x 11 inches basic size. A ring binder in the form of a briefcase or otherwise is a useful device for assembling the materials.

Using the Survey

The assembly of the data and the compilation of the survey are merely a first step. The survey is valuable only to the extent that it is used. Its first function should be that of supplying the basis for the development of a sound and well-balanced program of industrial activities. Accordingly, it should be carefully studied by the best qualified persons available—by men who understand industry and its needs. These men should be thoroughly in sympathy with the idea that the chamber should, if practicable, undertake a long-range program of industrial promotion; but they should also be ready to advise against such a program if, in their opinion, the survey shows that the community lacks essential requisites for industrial growth. The purpose of the study is to supply answers to questions such as the following:

1. Does the city now possess the requisite factors for industrial development?

a. What are the major assets of the community? How do these assets compare with those of competing centers?

b. What are the limitations of the community? How serious are they? To what extent and by what methods can they be counteracted, modified or eliminated?

2. In view of the existing conditions, should the chamber of commerce undertake a program of industrial promotion? If so, should it call for:

  a. Service to existing industry?
  b. Promotion of new local industry?
  c. Attraction of industry from outside the community?
  d. A combination of these?

3. To what area should the program extend? Should the chamber seek to develop industry only within the immediate community or are there factors of economic interdependence that make it desirable to extend the program to a wider area?

4. If the program should call for service to established industry, what services should be rendered?

  a. What are the needs of the community?
  b. How can the chamber contribute to the fulfillment of these needs?

5. If the program should call for promotion of local industry, how can this be accomplished?

  a. Can present enterprises be expanded? Can they take on new products or allied lines?
  b. Is there management, money, men, materials and markets available for launching new local industry? What kind of industry?
  c. Can local aid be arranged to finance new buildings or otherwise assist the establishment of new industry?

6. If the program is to call for the attraction of industry from outside the community, what types of industry are the most logical prospects?

  a. To what industries do the assets of the community appeal? To what industries are its shortcomings least objectionable?
  b. To what extent are these industries already established within the general area?
  c. To what extent are related industries established within the community?

The preceding outline is intended to be no more than suggestive of an approach. The exact questions to be asked and answered must, of course, vary from one case to another. The important thing is that the chamber make full use of the survey in constructing its program of industrial activities.

Moreover, once the broad outlines of such a program have been decided upon, the survey should continue to serve not only to give the program specific direction, but also as a working tool for accomplishing concrete results.

The Time Element

Industrial growth is rarely rapid or spectacular. It is more often a process of slow accretion. Moreover, the need for new industry never stops. If the community is to hold its own in this day of change and growth, it must continue to expand. The industrial development program should, therefore, be planned as a truly long-term program.

There is another reason why continuity and persistence are imperative. New industries and new enterprises are not created over night; nor are decisions to relocate or to construct new plants made lightly. Months and even years may elapse between the first cautious inquiries and the final realization of a project. If the chamber of commerce does not consistently follow developments and lend its assistance, the prospective manufacturers may lose interest in the community.

Like all promotional effort, industrial activities tend to be cumulative. At the outset, there may be few concrete accomplishments. Once the chamber succeeds in bringing some industry to the community, however, its efforts are likely to be more productive. The mere presence of related industries, the growth of a labor force and the development of industrial facilities tend to encourage and attract new enterprise. In short, industry tends to beget industry. This is another reason why the industrial promotion program needs to be a long-range program.

Coordination with Other Agencies and Programs

A number of agencies, other than the chamber of commerce, engage in industrial promotion activities. They include public agencies of the state, some state chambers of commerce, railroads and public utility companies. Some of them limit their activities to publicity and advertising; others undertake research and render advisory service to industry.

Although the interests of these agencies do not necessarily coincide with those of the chambers of commerce, most chambers have found that they have much to gain by maintaining close and cordial relations with them. In this as in other fields of activity, the chamber of commerce should avoid the waste of duplication of work that is already capably handled by other organizations. The chamber is also likely to find that the effectiveness of its own program is enhanced when that program is coordinated so as to mesh into and complement the activities of other agencies.

Industrial promotion is not a thing apart. Many other activities in which the chamber of commerce engages, have a direct bearing on the ability of the community to attract and develop industry. More highly developed markets and market organization, better living conditions, improved transportation facilities, lower taxes, more adequate public services, and more efficient government all contribute to industrial growth. The industrial activities program should, therefore, be coordinated also with the civic, commercial and agricultural projects of the chamber.

SERVICE TO ESTABLISHED INDUSTRY

Service to established enterprise occupies an important place in the industrial activities program of most chambers of commerce. There are good and sufficient reasons for this emphasis. Chambers of commerce have found that a carefully planned program of service can contribute significantly to the expansion of existing enterprise. Such expansion means increased payrolls and may afford a more stable form of community growth than that resulting from the acquisition of new and untried industry. There also is another consideration that should not be overlooked. In the long run, there is only one method by which the chamber can attract and hold the support of its members: by rendering worth-while services to business and industry.

In spite of these advantages, some chambers give little emphasis to service activities. Such lack of attention is sometimes fully justified. Specialized agencies may already provide most of the services for which there is need, or there may be no significant industry to serve. In most cases, however, justification does not come so readily. Rather, the explanation must be found in the fact that service activities are neither as spectacular nor as attractive as promotional activities, that community leadership has succumbed to the gilded lure of brand new industries, or that established manufacturers have been reluctant to admit that the chamber of commerce can be of assistance to them. Whatever the explanation, the result is failure to exploit one of the most effective and least expensive methods of industrial development.

Planning Service Activities

The service program should be carefully planned to meet the needs of the community. The opportunities to serve are legion. They include such possibilities as manufacturers' directories and exhibits; market analysis and advice on markets and products; sales promotion; promotion of healthy community attitudes; participation in a program to develop better employer-employee relations; development of adequate municipal services; safety campaigns; vocational training in schools; provision of risk capital; and many others. The problem is, therefore, not one of finding opportunities to serve, but rather that of selecting and emphasizing the services that are of the greatest benefit to the industrial community.

The mechanics of planning vary widely from one chamber to another. Some chambers take the attitude that they will consider only services for which there are specific requests from industry. They believe that by so doing they avoid the possibility of waste that may come from the development of expensive services for which there is no real demand. Other chambers take a more aggressive attitude. A New England chamber of commerce, for example, concentrates all its industrial activities on building the town from within through expansion of existing industry. The program started with four young engineer consultants who visited local plants to see whether they could be of assistance to the manufacturers of the community. In a recent year they made 2,153 calls resulting in more than 1,000 requests for specific services. The chamber believes that its activity contributed substantially not only to expanded operations of existing plants but also, as a by-product, to the establishment of no less than 84 new local manufacturing enterprises.

Most chambers should probably adopt some compromise between patient waiting and extreme aggressiveness. They might, for example, set up local manufacturing councils to sponsor such general activities as foremens' clubs, employer-employee relations programs, job and incentive studies, and formulate common policies for action on problems confronting industry. In the case of more specific services, however, they might await the development and expression of demand.

Industrial Relations

With the growing industrialization of city and town there has been a tendency for chambers of commerce to become more active in the field of industrial relations. Employer-employee relations programs, foremen's clubs, and industrial safety programs are some of the activities engaged in. Sometimes a chamber can be effective in a situation of labor strife, bringing about amicable settlement of differences without loss of production. The very process of bringing management and labor together with public representatives of unquestioned ability and integrity tends to minimize differences and to emphasize the public interest.

Taxation and Industry

Tax rates, systems of taxation and efficiency of state and local government have an important bearing on the success of established enterprise as well as on the attractiveness of the community to new industry. Many chambers of commerce are, therefore, taking an increasingly active interest in state and local government affairs. Their interest extends also to national problems. Because these activities are of concern not only to manufacturers but to all economic enterprise, however, they are more appropriately dealt with in the chapter on Civic and Governmental Activities.

Sales Promotion

Although the chamber of commerce is not maintained as a selling agency for local manufacturers, it may profitably engage in several activities designed to increase sales and broaden markets. Among such activities are the publication of a complete manufacturer's directory, sponsorship of industrial exhibits, public tours through industrial establishments, and other programs designed to call attention to the breadth and quality of locally manufactured product lines. Some of these activities may be addressed to people of the community; others may have a far wider appeal.

Some chambers engage in more specific promotional activities. In cooperation with other chambers of commerce they may seek agents, distributors and dealers for local manufacturers. They may also render assistance in facilitating contacts with government procurement agencies.

Aid to Marginal Industry

In almost every community there are industries and enterprises that operate as near failures. In some cases, fundamental conditions are so unfavorable that there is little or no possibility of salvaging them. More often, however, lack of success is brought about by no inherent conditions, but by such factors as undercapitalization, obsolescent equipment, faulty product or ineffective management. If these causes were identified and eliminated, many a marginal firm or industry might develop and contribute significantly to the industrial growth of the community.

By making available expert assistance, the chamber of commerce can play an important part in such salvage operations. It should do so, however, only upon invitation; and it must exercise caution and discretion in order to make sure that it does not become involved with special interests. It should, of course, avoid direct competition with financial agencies, industrial consultants and others interested in this field of endeavor.

Aid to Small Business

Similar opportunities to serve offer themselves in connection with small business. In this age of large, powerful and expertly run corporations, small firms frequently find themselves at a competitive disadvantage. They do not command the expert management, the technological skills or the financial resources necessary to effective competition. To a considerable extent, however, these handicaps can be removed by cooperative action.

The chamber of commerce can help to solve the problems of small manufacturers by serving as a clearing-house for experienced and tested management ideas. It can also set up panels of lawyers, accountants, engineers, marketing consultants and other experts who are willing to lend assistance at reasonable cost. Because small manufacturers, in the aggregate, occupy an important place in the economy of almost every city and town, services designed to meet their special needs deserve a place in the industrial activities of most chambers of commerce.

Traffic Bureau Service

Freight rates—on raw materials and supplies as well as on finished products—are an important factor in industrial growth. They determine in part the delivered price and, hence, the limits of the market area in which local manufacturers can effectively compete. Many chambers of commerce have, therefore, found it desirable to include traffic service as part of their program. This is, however, a specialized field of activity in which technical training and competence are imperative. As a rule the traffic bureau is, therefore, organized as a separate department.

Such a bureau seeks to secure the most equitable freight rates possible, both for old and new industries. It may negotiate with carriers, argue freight-rate cases before the regulatory bodies and otherwise work for the best possible rates and service. In addition, it may be of assistance to individual manufacturers by advising on rates and classifications, routing and tracing shipments, auditing freight bills and filing claims for overcharges.

Miscellaneous Services

The preceding discussion does by no means cover all the services that a chamber of commerce may render to established industry. The limits are defined only by the needs of the community and the ability of the organization to meet them. The chamber should, however, guard against the danger of spreading its efforts too thinly. It is far better to render a few, important services expertly than to offer a large number in such slipshod manner that they meet the needs of no one. The manager should remember that it matters little whether the chamber itself offers a particular service. The important thing is to make sure that the job is done, and done well.

DEVELOPING LOCAL INDUSTRY

It has already been pointed out that the development of new, local industry is one of the most important sources of industrial growth. Most new manufacturing firms are established as a result of individual, private initiative without the aid or encouragement of outsiders. Even in such cases, however, development is stimulated and facilitated by favorable conditions. Hence, any service that the chamber renders to established industry is also likely to promote new enterprise.

Industrial Financing Plans

The chamber of commerce may also play a more direct role in promotion of new manufacturing establishments. In a number of cities the chamber has, for example, taken the lead in organizing separately incorporated industrial "foundations" to provide capital or credit with which to encourage increased industrial activity. These foundations have been successful in providing risk capital when funds were not obtainable by regular methods of financing.

Incubator Buildings

A related method of encouraging new enterprise is that of providing so called incubator buildings which offer convenient factory space at low cost. Although this method has been explored only in a few of our larger centers, it has already proved its worth. It is likely to be especially successful when such a building is instrumental in bringing together small manufacturers in related-process industries.

Technical Assistance

The new manufacturer always encounters a large number of unexpected problems. He feels himself badly in need of advice and assistance; and if there are no sources to which he can turn for help, he may decide to give up his venture. The chamber of commerce can, therefore, render invaluable service by making available the technical skills and experience of its staff and members. Such aid may prevent costly mistakes and change a situation of failure into one of success.

Direct Sponsorship

A few chambers of commerce have, at one time or another, undertaken direct sponsorship of a new enterprise. The purpose has always been that of creating new industry for the community. This type of activity involves a great deal of risk and responsibility, however, and should be attempted only in rare cases. Extreme care must be exercised to ensure that the project is thoroughly sound and that the industry is one that not only meets the needs of the city for additional payrolls, but also has every chance of success under the conditions of the community. These things should be investigated and ascertained with the aid of thoroughly competent technical, financial and marketing advice.

If it is decided to launch the enterprise, it should be started on as small a scale as consistent with economy. The underwriting group should be small and should include only men who can afford to speculate. At the same time, undercapitalization should be avoided. The cost of launching and establishing a new firm is always high, and during the postwar years it has almost invariably exceeded even the most liberal estimates. The management should be the best obtainable, and the working directors should be experienced men who can and will give the enterprise all the time it needs.

The risk of locally-sponsored enterprise is always increased by the fact that decisions may be swayed by personal considerations and community pride. Inexperience, insufficient capital and unqualified management are serious hazards that may easily be overlooked by the unwary. On the other hand, the advantages of successful local industry are many and important. Not only does it provide payrolls and profits, but its very success promotes an atmosphere of "industrial-mindedness" which, in turn, may stimulate further initiative.

ATTRACTING NEW INDUSTRY TO THE COMMUNITY

There is a third source of industrial growth: attraction of industry to the community. One caution should be repeated at the outset, however. It takes more than an urge and wishful thinking to induce manufacturers to locate in the city. It takes long, persistent and well-directed effort. Moreover, the community must have tangible advantages to offer. It may be difficult for a chamber of commerce to admit that the community lacks elemental requirements for successful industrial growth, but manufacturers in search for a location will have no difficulty in recognizing that fact. Successful enterprise gained success because it acted deliberately and objectively on the basis of fact. No campaign to attract industry, however ambitious and well planned, can therefore be effective unless it is backed up by much more than a mere desire for industry.

Finding Prospects

The first problem of an industrial promotion campaign is that of determining the prospects to whom it should be addressed. The industrial survey, and the analysis of it, should be invaluable in approaching the solution of this problem. By knowing the assets and limitations of the community, the chamber of commerce can also know the broad lines of industry to which its location may have particular appeals. Even such knowledge, however, does not provide a complete solution of the problem. There still remains the task of uncovering active prospects.

Almost every chamber of commerce secures some prospects unsolicited and without effort. Nearly all our cities have some attractions that result in occasional inquiries. Moreover, a manufacturer in search of a new location may first determine upon the general area in which he is interested. Having made that determination, he may contact several chambers of commerce in the area for the purpose of obtaining information about specific locations. Such inquiries constitute live leads. They should always be followed up, carefully and intelligently.

The chamber of commerce that depends on unsolicited inquiries, however, is not likely to get far in its quest for new industry. The chamber must undertake active prospecting. It has been said that there are only three approaches to industrial development: economics, kinfolks and business politics. All of them should be used.

First, the members of the chamber can be an important source of leads. The manager should, therefore, make every effort to enlist their active interest in the promotion campaign. He should solicit their ideas and suggestions, and attempt to get them into the habit of looking out for prospects. Other and perhaps more important sources are the industrial agents of railroads and public utility companies, engineering firms, state chambers, and development agencies. The manager should keep in close touch with these organizations and cooperate freely and promptly with them.

Prospects may also be uncovered by watching news items in trade papers and newspapers. Technological developments, research activities and new products often mean new plants. The alert manager watches these developments and evaluates them in terms of "is there anything in this situation that looks like possible new business for my town?" Personal contacts with logical prospects may also produce other leads. The manager should, therefore, get around as much as possible—to establish new contacts as well as to cultivate those which he has already made.

Advertising may produce leads; but unless the campaign is carefully planned, it may become extremely expensive in terms of results. Two kinds of advertising is used—direct mail and advertising in general and trade periodicals. Direct-mail advertising has the advantage of great flexibility. It can be beamed at the exact industries and companies that are the most likely prospects; and the message can be tailor-made to meet the requirements of each situation. Advertising in either general or trade periodicals involves considerable waste circulation. On the other hand, it may reach unsuspected prospects; and the cost per reader is much lower than in the case of direct-mail advertising.

For both types of advertising one important principle holds. Advertising can be effective only to the extent that it is specific and meaningful. It does no good merely to advertise the name of the town or to proclaim that it is a good factory location. On the other hand, when the advertisement offers and describes a market, a labor pool, a source of materials, an available building or a development corporation which can assist industry, it is selling something tangible that may be of interest to a manufacturer. Advertising, to be effective, must also be sustained. The total cost is likely to be high. Consequently, no chamber ought to launch a campaign unless the thing it has to sell is really big and worth while.

Dealing with Prospects

To the manufacturer in search of a location, correct selection is an important matter. Location studies are, therefore, usually handled by a top officer of the company or his chief assistant. Moreover, most manufacturers wish to keep their interest as quiet as possible. They prefer not to stir up their employees; and they want to avoid disclosure of their plans to competitors and to escape premature and useless solicitation by real estate brokers, contractors and the thousand and one salesmen who descend on every new plant.

These attitudes are important. They emphasize the need for confidential treatment of all inquiries and for prompt, efficient and intelligent service. Obviously, the chamber that enjoys the confidence of its community as well as that of manufacturers with whom it has dealt, will have a decided advantage over a chamber that has a reputation for slip-shod and dilatory attention to inquiries.

A manufacturer wants facts, not generalities. He wants complete and accurate facts, but he does not want to be loaded down with information that has no bearing on his problem. The facts supplied to each prospect should, therefore, be carefully selected with his requirements in mind. They should be assembled and organized to form an attractive, concise and informative presentation. The manager who cannot resist the temptation of giving every prospect every bit of information available in his files, gains nothing. On the contrary, by so doing he merely creates the impression that either he has failed to understand the requirements of the manufacturer or he does not care.

Few firms will decide upon a location merely on the basis of briefs supplied by the chamber of commerce. They want to make their own investigations, confer with bankers and industrialists, and investigate available sites. The chamber can, of course, be of great assistance in these activities. And ultimate success depends to a very large degree upon how well this part of the campaign is handled.

One caution should be introduced at this point. An active industrial development program involves all sorts of prospects. Many of them are well-established firms or individuals with a record of profitable operations and successful experience. But there are also the incompetent and unscrupulous. The chamber should, therefore, investigate every prospect—secure dependable company and personal histories, financial statements, and any other information that prudence suggests. Such investigations should be conducted before obligations are incurred by the chamber or by any firm or individual in the community.

Appealing to Prospects

Most out-of-town prospects have the capital necessary to branch out or relocate. Even so, some of them may prefer some local participation in order to ensure local interest and support. Most manufacturers are, however, looking for other advantages—nearness to markets, ample labor supply, adequate public services, low taxes or any number of other things. In recent years, the availability of suitable buildings has determined more locations than any other factor. Whatever the situation, it is the responsibility of the manager to determine as accurately as possible the requirements of each prospect—and the order of their importance—and then plan his appeals accordingly.

Whenever a prospect requires capital support as a condition of locating his plant in the community, extreme caution becomes necessary. This is by no means the same as saying that every such request should be summarily rejected. Under some circumstances, reasonable capital support may be fully justified. Moreover, some forms of support are far less objectionable than others.

Aid in the construction of new buildings may work out to the mutual advantage of city and industry. A going and successful concern cannot always afford a new building at the same time as it incurs the costs of relocation. To the city, such a building may represent a sound investment. Even so, however, caution is necessary. The country is full of empty, community-owned factory buildings that testify eloquently to the folly of some over-optimistic citizen group.

In some cases, communities succeed in attracting industry by tax exemptions. They may work out satisfactorily when the industry is non-competitive in the local field and when it brings compensating values to the community. But tax exemptions establish a dangerous precedent that may lead to internal bickering and dissatisfaction.

Straight loans and stock subscriptions are at the same time the cleanest and the most dangerous form of capital support. Many an enterprise that seeks this kind of aid has no background of successful experience. It may plan to produce new products which have not yet been tested in the market, or with which the management is unfamiliar. If this form of aid is attempted, all the cautions already emphasized in the discussion of locally-sponsored industry, should be exercised.

Gratuities and bonuses are rapidly becoming a thing of the past. Nevertheless, there may still be instances when this form of aid is justified. In more rural areas where the community offers no particular advantage, a gratuity or bonus may be the only inducement that will attract industry. In general, however, there is no reason why the community should not get equities for any contribution. Capital support, if it is to be given at all, should be temporary and carry the obligation of eventual repayment.

SUMMARY

1. There is wide variation in the pattern of the program of industrial activities in our chambers of commerce. The emphasis may be on seeking relocating plants, branch plants or new and expanded manufacture within the community. Equally or even more important is the service rendered to the concerns already in operation in the community. Caution in avoiding ill-advised and fallacious planning in this field of work is extremely important.

2. More care is being exercised in the location of manufacturing plants today than in the past. Industrial operations are becoming more and more complicated. Hence an adequate fund of up-to-the-minute and accurate facts bearing on plant location and the establishment of new enterprise is a prime requisite.

3. Good working relationships with persons and organizations that can contribute to the successful operation of a program are obviously important. Such contacts both within and without the community should be kept active and are invaluable when information or assistance, beyond the knowledge and capacity of the staff, is needed.

4. Continuity of effort is essential to success. Impatience and discouragement come easy. There are many time-consuming steps leading to the establishment of successful manufacturing activity. Substantial results require a long-range program.

5. Economic values and trends are the sound bases for a community program. The need for increased industrial activity is seldom permanently satisfied. We must continue to expand. National prosperity is dependent on prosperity at the community level. This need offers the local chamber a challenging field of usefulness.

Appendix to Chapter X

THE INDUSTRIAL SURVEY

The industrial survey should be a complete inventory of the facilities, assets and limitations of the community. The following is a proposed outline of the topics to be covered by such a survey. It may, of course, be expanded or contracted to meet the requirements of the community.

I. Location
   a. County and section of state
   b. Names of nearby large streams or lakes
   c. Distance and direction from representative large cities
   d. Population

II. Transportation Facilities
   a. Rail—
      1. Railroads serving community
      2. Nearest terminals of each
      3. Class freight rates to representative cities
      4. Schedule freight services, elapsed time to representative cities
      5. Passenger schedules, local or at nearest boarding point
   b. Highway—
      1. Highways; federal, state and county, by route numbers
      2. Truck lines
      3. Nearest terminals of each
      4. Class rates and elapsed time to representative cities
      5. Inter-city bus routes and schedules
   c. Air—
      1. Distance to, and class of, nearest airport
      2. Airlines
      3. Schedules; passenger, mail and freight
   d. Water—
      1. Lake, river or other navigable body of water
      2. Dock facilities, and R. R. serving
      3. Steamship and barge lines
      4. Schedules, class rates and elapsed time to representative cities

III. Electric Power
   a. Company serving, name and address of representative
   b. Capacity (obtain data as required from power company representative)
   c. Rates—
      1. Domestic
      2. Commercial
      3. Industrial (submit generally applicable tariff with notation that other more favorable rates

may apply, depending upon load characteristics.)

IV. Fuel
   a. Coal—
      1. Distance to nearest mines, if within trucking distance
      2. Range proximate analyses according to origin producing districts
      3. Freight rates according to origin producing districts
   b. Gas—
      1. Company serving, name and address of representative
      2. Available supply (obtain from gas company representative as required)
      3. BTU rating
      4. Rates (submit generally applicable tariff with notation that more favorable rates may apply depending upon load characteristics)
   c. Oil—
      1. Name representative companies serving the area, name and address of representative

V. Water
   a. Municipal supply—
      1. Source
      2. Volume available for industrial expansion
         (a) raw water
         (b) filtered water
      3. Capacity of plant
      4. Average daily consumption
      5. Peak consumption
      6. Analysis (chemical)
      7. Rates
   b. Industrial—
      1. Streams:
         (a) names
         (b) lowest recorded minimum daily flow
         (c) analysis (chemical)
         (d) temperature, winter and summer
      2. Lakes:
         (a) names
         (b) size
         (c) analysis (chemical)
         (d) temperature, winter and summer
      3. Underground water:
         (a) depths of existing wells
         (b) flow

234 CHAMBER OF COMMERCE ADMINISTRATION

    (c) estimates of potential supply
    (d) analysis (chemical)
    (e) temperature, winter and summer

VI. **Taxes**
   a. Total valuation of land and buildings for tax purposes, within corporation limits
   b. Ratio of assessed value to true value
   c. Bonded debt
   d. Tax rates:
      1. Within corporation limits
      2. Within adjacent taxing districts
   e. Statement showing state taxes

VII. **Fire Insurance Classification**
   a. Within corporation limits
   b. Within adjacent districts

VIII. **Labor Market Analysis**
   a. Population, latest census and present estimate within 10-mile radius
   b. Analysis of composition (male and female; native born white, negro, foreign born white)
   c. Employment by existing industries
   d. Wage rates, range, male and female, skilled, semi-skilled and unskilled
   e. Latest "Labor Market Information" report by State Employment Service
   f. Statement of Labor Laws

IX. **Existing Industries**
   a. List of companies
   b. Products

X. **Agriculture** (Information available from Agricultural Extension Service)
   a. Number and average size of farm in county
   b. Types of soil (soil map)
   c. Agricultural production
      1. Grains—
         (a) average production principal types
      2. Fruits—
         (a) average production principal types
      3. Vegetables—
         (a) average production principal types
      4. Dairy—
         (a) raw milk production
      5. Livestock—
         (a) beef
         (b) sheep
         (c) hogs

INDUSTRIAL ACTIVITIES

6. Poultry—
   (a) chickens
   (b) turkeys
   (c) other fowl
   (d) egg production
7. Processing plants

XI. **Climate** (Information obtainable from nearest U. S. Weather Observer)
   a. Average annual mean temperature
   b. Highest and lowest temperatures recorded
   c. High, low and mean temperatures by months
   d. Average annual precipitation—
      1. Rainfall
      2. Snowfall
   e. Average number of clear, partly cloudy and cloudy days
   f. Direction of prevailing winds
   g. Average relative humidity

XII. **Civic**
   a. Area of town
   b. Type of municipal government
   c. Schools and colleges—
      1. Number
      2. Number of teachers
      3. Enrollment
   d. Libraries—
      1. Number
      2. Number of volumes
   e. Churches—
      1. Number
      2. Denominations represented
   f. Hospitals—
      1. Number
      2. Number of beds
   g. Municipal services—
      1. Fire
      2. Police
      3. Sanitation
      4. Public health
   h. Newspapers—
      1. Names, daily or weekly
      2. Circulation and area covered
   i. Radio stations—television—
      1. Call letters
      2. Frequency
      3. Power

j. Financial institutions
  1. Banks
    (a) number
    (b) total
  2. Savings and loan associations
    (a) number
    (b) resources
k. Hotels—
  1. Number
  2. Number of rooms
l. Clubs—
  1. Service or civic
  2. Private social and fraternal
m. Other organizations (Community Chest, Red Cross, etc.)
n. Wholesale and retail establishments
o. Produce markets
p. Trade area
q. Percentage of home ownership

XIII. Recreational Facilities
  a. Theatres: Number, type and seating capacity
  b. Parks and playgrounds—
    1. Number
    2. Acreage
    3. Supervision
  c. Swimming pools
  d. Pool and billiard halls—
    1. Number
    2. Number of tables
  e. Bowling alleys—
    1. Number
    2. Number of alleys
  f. Golf courses—
    1. Number:
      (a) public
      (b) private
  g. Baseball and football stadiums and athletic fields
  h. Professional baseball, football and basketball
  i. Amateur baseball, football, basketball and soft ball
  j. Tennis courts
  k. Possibilities for hunting, fishing and boating
  l. Nearby state and federal parks and recreational areas

XIV. Raw Materials
  Data on types and volumes available as raw materials for industry—
  a. Minerals (obtainable from State Geologist)

b. Forest products
c. Agricultural products

XV. **Industrial Sites**

(Data for each site)—
  a. Location
  b. Acreage
  c. Dimensions
  d. Terrain
  e. Location in relation to:
    1. Highways
    2. Railroads and possibility of service by siding
    3. Gas lines (size)
    4. Water lines (size)
    5. Sewers (size)
  f. Sketch (plat)
  g. Photographs
  h. Ownership or agent
  i. Zoning
  j. Flood conditions

XVI. **Regulations and Building Codes**
  a. State and local codes
  b. Factory inspection regulations (State Industrial Commission)
  c. Stream pollution regulations

XVII. **Available Industrial or Warehouse Buildings**
  a. Location
  b. Size—
    1. Over-all dimensions
    2. Total floor space
    3. Number of floors, type and load capacity
    4. Ceiling heights, clearance
    5. Size of bays
    6. Type of construction
  c. Heat, light, power, sanitary facilities, sprinkler facilities, cranes, and power boilers
  d. Railroad sidings (in place or possible)
  e. Loading docks or platforms, truck and railroad
  f. Area of lot, parking facilities, and fencing
  g. Plat of lot and floor plan of building
  h. Photographs
  i. For sale or lease
  j. Ownership
  k. Real estate agent

XVIII. Maps
    a. State highway
    b. County, showing township lines and roads
    c. Municipal street map
    d. Power—general system
    e. Gas—general system
    f. Water system
    g. Sewer system
    h. Quadrangle map, U. S. Geological Survey
    i. Zoning
    j. System maps of railroad serving

XIX. Statistics and Business Barometers

Bank Clearings	Electric Meters
Bank Debits	Water Meters
Postal Receipts	Telephones
Cancellations	Auto Registrations
Air Mail Volume	Factory Employment
Gas Meters	K. W. H. Consumption
Building Permits	Live Stock Receipts
Carloadings	Population Estimates
Port Statistics	School Enrollment

Chapter XI

Agricultural Activities

PRACTICALLY every city and town, large or small, depends to a considerable extent upon agriculture for its livelihood and prosperity. To many communities—as to the country as a whole—agriculture is the single most important industry. It furnishes the basis for the trade of assembly and redistribution of farm products, and it provides the raw materials for a variety of processing industries. In the course of operating their farms, farmers require enormous quantities of feed, fertilizer, seed, motor vehicles, machinery and equipment. As consumers they purchase all manner of consumers' goods. Most of these purchases are made in urban market centers. Hence, whenever agriculture is prosperous, cities and towns fare well. When crops fail, soils are depleted or farm prosperity otherwise impaired, there is an immediate adverse effect on the economy of city and town.

Recognition of the interdependence of farm and city has led many chambers of commerce to become as much interested in the welfare of the farmer as in that of the city dweller. In 1950, some 850 out of a total of nearly 3,000 chambers had some type of agricultural activity, ranging all the way from one or two simple projects to elaborate and comprehensive programs conducted by specialized and completely staffed departments. There were as many as 32 full-time employees who devoted their entire time to agriculture.

The activities conducted by the various chambers include the whole gamut of agricultural problems. They begin with land itself—with erosion, soil fertility and conservation. They include selection of seed and breeding stock, methods of cultivating and bringing crops and stock to maturity, control of diseases and pests, as well as orderly and profitable marketing of farm products. In some areas water and its control is of great importance; in others the chambers of commerce champion balanced farming. Some chambers concentrate attention on particular crops or branches of agriculture, while others work more generally. Many stress the physical, mental and spiritual well-being of farmers. Their programs are concerned with rural roads, schools and churches; with fire prevention and safety; and with rural electrification and telephone service. And last but not least, they seek to contribute to a healthy social life with clean and wholesome entertainment.

DEVELOPING AGRICULTURAL ACTIVITIES

Should every chamber of commerce conduct an agricultural program? A partial answer may, perhaps, be found in the fact that in recent years an increasing number of chambers have launched such programs. Yet, in 1950 there were still many chambers without agricultural activities. To many highly industrialized communities such a program would have been sheer waste; to others it was of major importance. Practice varied even among chambers located in rich farming areas. Some had comprehensive programs, others conducted only a few minor projects, and still others had no program at all.

The diversity of practice is illustrated by the experience of two chambers of commerce. One, located in a great steel center in a relatively poor farm area, carried on a three-fold program. That program included livestock shows, tours for farm groups through industries and cultural institutions, and a comprehensive survey of the agricultural resources of a sixteen-county area around the city. The survey was paid for by the chamber and conducted by the state college. Its purpose was to determine the products that could economically be raised in the area, and to make suggestions for more effective methods of marketing.

The second chamber, located in a medium-sized market center in a rich agricultural area in the Middle West, conducted only a general program designed to maintain cordial relations between town and farm. It also did a limited amount of work with boys' and girls' clubs. The manager of the chamber explained the absence of a more comprehensive program as follows:

"We have not found it possible or desirable to engage in activities related to agricultural techniques. Our farmers in this area are for the most part well educated and very progressive. They have their own highly organized agencies for the advancement of their own procedures. They neither need nor do they welcome interference of any kind in farm improvements."

Two fundamental principles are suggested by these experiences. First, no chamber should ever force upon its community or its membership, activities which it does not wish, for which it is not prepared or on which it cannot be sold. Secondly, every chamber should avoid any activity that merely duplicates work already capably performed by other organizations. The second principle is of particular importance in connection with agricultural programs, because farmers are already served by a great many agencies—public and private. The main function of the chamber in this field is, therefore, likely to be one of cooperating with and supplementing the work of other organizations.

The Informal Committee

The chamber of commerce that plans to break into new ground should do so slowly and deliberately. If a manager believes that his chamber and community might benefit from a program of agricultural activities, his first step should be that of talking with and securing the support of leaders in his own organization, who are engaged in marketing or processing agricultural products. With the support of these men, an informal or even formal committee might be set up to canvass two groups—the farm organizations and the agricultural specialists of the area. Such a canvass should be inclusive. No important farm organization should be omitted. Similarly, the committee should seek the suggestions, opinions and assistance of agricultural and home demonstration agents, representatives of the state department of vocational education, teachers in vocational schools, officials of the Soil Conservation Service and the Triple A, experts employed by railroads and processing industries, as well as any other agricultural specialist who is already working with the farmers of the area and their problems. The suggestions and support of these individuals and organizations may be invaluable to the success of the program.

As a rule, there will be a hearty response to a call to an informal meeting to consider such questions as: What is the present agricultural program of the area? What are its needs? How can they be met? How can the chamber of commerce supplement and fit into the program? The reception of an offer of assistance is likely to be one of friendly welcome. County and home demonstration agents, for example, will almost certainly receive with enthusiasm any offer of aid that promises to dramatize and add color to their activities, or to make available to them the specialized skills of experts from business and industry. The experience of one manager in two different positions represents a case in point. In his first job, in a medium-sized city in the wheat belt, a canvass of the county agents resulted in the recommendation that the chamber of commerce appropriate $6,000 to employ an agricultural commissioner. This man worked closely with the county agents—never duplicating, but always supplementing their programs. In his second job in a Missouri town, a similar canvass resulted in the purchase by the chamber of commerce of a sound recording machine. The equipment was loaned to agents and used by them in the balanced farming program. Interviews with farmers were recorded on the spot and then broadcast by the local radio station at 6:30 o'clock each morning.

One caution should be observed by all chambers of commerce. In approaching the representatives of farm organizations, complete frankness is of utmost importance. Farm leaders are well aware of the fact that no chamber launches a program of agricultural activities from purely altruistic motives. Any chamber that attempts to create the impression of magnanimous benevolence is, therefore, likely to meet only suspicion and apathy. If, on the other hand, the proposal to undertake such a program is offered as one of mutual benefit to farm and city, it may well gain the enthusiastic support and cooperation of farm leaders.

In some cases it may be desirable to supplement the informal meetings with a more formal survey of the agricultural resources and needs of the area. Such a survey should, however, be undertaken only if the agricultural experiment stations or other agencies have not already compiled basic data on agricultural conditions. It may be conducted by the chamber itself or by specialists engaged by it.

Organizing for the Program

The survey and the informal meetings with farm leaders and agricultural specialists may be expected to produce suggestions, opinions and offers of cooperation. It remains to translate these things into action. The next steps will, therefore, be those of creating a formal committee on agriculture, adopting a definite program with a proposed budget, and presenting the proposals to the board of directors for approval.

The size and personnel of the committee on agriculture may vary from one community to another, depending on the extent and character of the program. Some chambers prefer that the committee be composed only of their own members—particularly those who are engaged in marketing or processing of agricultural products and who have special interest in and knowledge of the problems involved. Other chambers invite farmers and stockmen to participate as members of the committee. When this is done, it may be advisable to request the farm organizations to nominate representative farmers for membership on the committee. A total membership of from nine to fifteen members may suffice if the program is small. As new projects are added, however, it may be desirable to enlarge the committee and, perhaps, create an organization of sub-committees to handle specific activities.

Building the Program

Although the survey and the informal meetings may produce a long list of worth-while projects, it does not follow that all of them should immediately be put into action. Most chambers have found it advisable to build the program slowly, project by project. Even when the program has the support of farm leaders, it must be sold to the farmers themselves. This may require considerable tact and patience. There must be no feeling on the part of the farmers that something is being thrust upon them by city folk who do not know too much about it.

Some experienced managers have found it wise to suggest ideas to their rural neighbors and let the request for action or help come from them. Others believe that the best way of reaching the adult farmers is to begin by working with 4-H Clubs, the Future Farmers and Future Home Makers of America, and similar organizations for boys and girls. By supporting the activities of these youth organizations they have gradually succeeded in winning the confidence and securing the interest of the parents. Institutes, contests, dinners and awards for farm women have also paved the way for expanded programs dealing with the land, the crops or the animals.

Financing the Program

Methods of financing agricultural activities vary. A small chamber of commerce with a limited program may appropriate a few hundred dollars in its general budget. Others will set aside as much for agricultural activities as they do for other programs, such as industrial and civic activities. Still others raise special funds each year for particular projects. Even small chambers may have special budgets ranging from two to ten thousand dollars. Many large chambers which support full scale agricultural departments, have found it advantageous to solicit additional subscriptions from or levy special assessments on members who are engaged in agricultural trades and industries.

THREE MAIN ACTIVITIES

Although the agricultural programs of no two chambers of commerce are alike, three activities seem to have gained wide-spread popularity. They are town-farm gatherings, work with farm youth organizations, and agricultural expositions and shows.

Town-Farm Gatherings

Town-farm gatherings may be of almost infinite variety. They may take the form of luncheons, banquets, picnics or dances. Some are of a serious bent, others offer only good clean fun. In some cases the chamber is responsible for the program; in others farm groups and city folk divide the responsibility or take turns in planning the entertainment.

Whatever their form, the ultimate purpose of these gatherings is, of course, to create good will and mutual understanding. Sometimes they may also serve a more immediate function. An annual "lespedeza banquet" is an example. In this case town and farm take turns honoring the winner of an annual lespedeza growing contest. There are many more examples of this type—affairs to present awards for all kinds of projects, to honor master farmers, to launch a new activity or to celebrate its completion.

Farm-town picnics—like banquets and luncheons—may be of manifold kinds. Some chambers provide elaborate entertainment: band music, drum corps, free rides, outstanding speakers and games in which all may participate. They may furnish free pop, candy, ice cream, coffee and milk; while the farm families bring their own lunch and make a day of it. One chamber provides food and contributes $50 to the organization selected to prepare it. A small community is the site of the picnic each year. Invitations are mailed to rural box-holders, and followed up with tickets paid for by the merchants. Another chamber sponsors a "good Indian tribe" of townspeople who stage several pow-wows with farmers and ranchers each summer. They go into the farm districts and take along food, beer and stunts. Other chambers make arrangements with rural church or women's organizations to furnish supper for a joint town-farm affair. They may conduct three or four of these affairs each season.

Experience has demonstrated that farm-town gatherings offer an effective means of breaking down prejudices and misunderstandings. They foster a spirit of cooperation and pave the way for an expanded agricultural program dealing with important community problems. In order to be fully successful, however, these gatherings must be developed into truly joint affairs in which both city-folk and farmers participate actively and enthusiastically.

Work with Youth Organizations

No agricultural activity is more popular and rewarding than work with farm youth organizations, such as the 4-H Clubs and the Future Farmers of America. The justification for this type of activity is twofold. First, it contributes to the development of better farmers and growers; and secondly, it offers a successful method of approach to the adult farmer.

Most of the farm youth organizations center their activities around specific club projects. The boys may raise some type of animal or grow some specific kind of fruits, vegetables or field crops. The girls conduct projects related to cooking, sewing and homemaking—although many of them may also participate in the activities and contests of the boys. Chambers of commerce seek to tie in with these activities. They organize projects and contests, and offer handsome prizes to the winners. They finance the purchase of breeding stock, and make tours to the farms to view the animals or to inspect gardens and farm plots. They attend the sales held at shows and fairs, and in cooperation with packers they raise the bids so that the leading animals are sold at attractive rewards to their young producers.

Some chambers of commerce frown, however, upon too liberal subsidization of auctions. They feel that excessive prices tend to give farm boys and girls an exaggerated idea of the value of their work and that, as a matter of fact, their project is not complete until the animals are sold on the open market. So, instead of bidding for the animals on the spot, some chambers arrange to ship them to the market. They take the owners along on a chartered bus and let them see their animals bought for what they are worth. The trip serves the additional purpose of teaching the boys and girls the operations of a central market and affords the opportunity of visits to packing houses and other places of interest.

In many communities where there is no regular agricultural fair, the chamber of commerce has assisted in the development of 4-H or similar junior fairs. One chamber, for example, contributes $1,000 annually to the junior agricultural show. Another chamber entertains all the junior exhibitors at its ten-county district fair. Each boy or girl is the guest of a local business man. The invitations are personalized and an effective system is set up so that each host or hostess meets his or her guest as they come to dinner. Prizes and awards are announced at the dinner. Adult club leaders come in for their share of recognition. In one community, for example, club leaders and their husbands or wives are guests of the chamber at a dinner during the Christmas holidays.

Farm boys' and girls' clubs are frequently members of state, regional and even national organizations which stage periodic meetings and conventions. Chambers of commerce may again assist by financing the trip of local delegates to these meetings or by acting as hosts to regional conventions held in the community. Similarly, many chambers sponsor judging and demonstration teams and send them to state fairs or to one of the important livestock expositions.

Activities of this sort may sometimes accomplish astonishing results in a very short period of time. For example, a few years ago the merchants of a city located in a vegetable-growing section, found great difficulty in marketing the local potato crop because of its poor quality. The chamber of commerce attacked the problem by working with boys' and girls' clubs. It furnished educational materials and organized potato-growing contests. This work led to the sponsorship of a winter vegetable fair. The result of these activities was a gradual improvement of quality until today, a few years later, the quality of the local potato crop is said to equal that of any other market.

Agricultural Fairs and Expositions

Not so many years ago the old county fair was an almost universal institution in many parts of the country. In some counties there might even be a second or third fair in active trade centers. With the advent of the automobile and good roads many of these fairs were discontinued, leaving only the district and state fairs in the larger trade centers.

In recent years, however, the pendulum seems to have been swinging the other way. Many communities, feeling the lack of a major agricultural event, have successfully attempted to revive their old fairs. Chambers of commerce have taken a leading part in this movement.

Chambers of commerce have also given vigorous support to established fairs. Many of them are under the joint management of town and farm. Chambers of commerce have put up guarantee funds, sold stock to buy ground or erect buildings, given money for prizes, financed bands or other entertainment for special events, put hospitality committees on the ground, and arranged for exhibits in the manufacturers' or similar buildings. Even in the case of state fairs which are usually supported by taxes and financed by admission and concession receipts, the local chambers cooperate by maintaining information booths, arranging for exhibits, and entertaining special groups of visitors.

Some of the great regional events are actively supported by chambers of commerce. The agricultural department of one chamber of commerce, for example, takes responsibility for all junior activities of a great mid-western livestock and horse show. It arranges the details of the parade, and gives special attention to the conventions and meetings of farm youth organizations. It is also the host at a banquet for the demonstration and judging teams, their coaches and leaders.

Some of the larger chambers of commerce in cities in which there is no agricultural exposition, have taken their work out into the state by arranging shows and judging contests in several key points. This method promotes good will between the larger chamber and its smaller city neighbors, gives the latter much of the credit for staging the events, and makes it possible for teams and their leaders to attend with little travel time and expense.

SOME REPRESENTATIVE AGRICULTURAL PROGRAMS

Perhaps the best way of illustrating and emphasizing the broad scope and wide diversity of agricultural activities is to summarize briefly the agricultural programs of a number of chambers of commerce. The diversity of these programs suggests that the successful chamber of commerce molds its agricultural activities to meet and deal with the problems and conditions important to its trading area.

Programs of Small and Medium-Sized Chambers

The agricultural program of a chamber of commerce in a small city of about 15,000 people, located in northeastern Oklahoma, is administered by an agricultural committee and conducted by a number of sub-committees. During a recent year, the total cost of the program was approximately $11,000, of which $4,000 was expended for premiums, awards and grants; $2,000 for an annual trip to a major agricultural exposition; and $5,000 for a dairy improvement program, mostly in the form of interest-free loans to members of farm-youth organizations. The specific projects of this chamber of commerce included:

1. A junior livestock show.
2. A county free fair.
3. A county poultry show.
4. A five-breed dairy show in nine counties.
5. A dairy improvement program.
6. A pasture development program, in which there were 400 entries.
7. Work with farm women's clubs. This work embraced many activities such as cake and egg shows, a flower and vegetable show, as well as food production and conservation contests.
8. An annual farmer and merchants tour.

Perhaps the most outstanding agricultural activity of this chamber of commerce is its annual automobile caravan to some large agricultural exposition. The caravan usually attracts some 150 farmers and merchants. Each car carries three farmers and two businessmen. The chamber committee arranges the itinerary, books hotel rooms, and pays transportation costs. Each person, whether merchant or farmer, pays his own personal expenses. In addition to visits to the agricultural and livestock exhibits, one day is spent in touring industrial plants manufacturing products used by farmers and stockmen in their operations The chamber believes that these trips are worth while not only because of their educational value, but also because they help to break down barriers and to promote lasting friendships and understanding.

Another chamber of commerce, located in a town of 30,000 people in southeastern Minnesota, encourages and promotes the work of 4-H Clubs and similar organizations. Its annual appropriation for this purpose runs about $2,000. A typical year's program and its expenses were as follows:

Calf show (attendance 1,500) Prizes	$125.00
County 4-H club	
Achievement Day (attendance 700) Prizes	311.25
4-H sale, county fair	429.25
Other expenses, including prizes for pasture improvement, home-making, health and dairy breed contests	677.30
4-H clubs in adjoining counties	280.00
F. F. A.	
Field day, annual banquet, and delegates to national convention	114.85
Safety and Labor Saving Show. The largest indoor meeting of farmers in the area. Attended by 5,000	452.72

Quite a different program is offered by a chamber of commerce located in a city of 40,000 people in the fruit-growing section of Washington. This chamber has organized and promoted 4-H pomological clubs. It has maintained two transient labor camps and helped to recruit townspeople for apple picking. It has also campaigned for the eradication of diseased fruit trees. Farther south, in the potato-growing region of Oregon, the chamber of commerce in a town of 20,000 people concentrates its activities on protecting the crop of premium quality potatoes right through the processes of sorting, packaging, shipping, and distribution to the ultimate consumer. It has also attempted to promote industrial processing plants using agricultural raw materials, such as a potato starch plant. And finally, it has paid a great deal of attention to the protection of the water supply of the community, which it feels threatened by a proposed water diversion plan.

A chamber of commerce in a Florida city of 10,000 people has attempted to tackle the problems of marketing brought about by the development of pre-packaging and quick freeze. The chamber serves 2,600 very small farms producing such specialized crops as strawberries and peppers. Its early efforts ran into a wall of suspicion, prejudice and unwillingness to cooperate. By launching a program of intensive work with farm youth organizations, however, the chamber is making rapid progress and is succeeding in reaching the adult farmer.

Programs of Large Chambers

The agricultural activities of large chambers of commerce which maintain full-time departments, are likely to include a variety of projects and may cover an entire state or region composed of parts of several states. The program of a chamber in an important agricultural market-city in the Middle West may, perhaps, be considered typical. The program is developed by an organization of committees and sub-committees with a total membership of 125 men and women. It is administered by an executive committee of 25 members; and carried out by a paid, full-time staff and a number of sub-committees. Each sub-committee, with from ten to twenty members, is responsible for one or more projects. In a recent year the program included the following activities.

1. *Agricultural development and research.* This part of the program was largely the responsibilty of the paid staff. Activities varied from time to time in order to allow flexibility to meet and deal with new problems as they arose.

2. *Crop improvement.* This activity was conducted jointly with the state university and several chambers in out-state locations. It called for crop yield contests, recognition programs, and certificates of merit and awards to outstanding farmers.

3. *Dairy improvement.* In cooperation with other chambers and organizations, the chamber of commerce sponsored seven district dairy shows open to 4-H club members and F. F. A. students. Although the activity was state-wide, excessive travel for the youngsters and their cattle was eliminated by the organization of district shows.

4. *Awards to farm youth.* A junior farmers' committee was responsible for making awards to outstanding 4-H and F. F. A. members. These awards might take the form of trips to state club weeks and conventions. The committee also entertained farm youth at meetings and conventions.

5. *Livestock shippers.* A livestock committee staged an annual banquet and made awards to all farmers who had continuously shipped their livestock to the local market for 50 years or more.

6. *Rural home makers.* In cooperation with 13 chambers in three states, the chamber of commerce entertained 2,000 farm women at 13 district meetings. Delegates were selected at these meetings and entertained at a three-state meeting.

7. *Pasture-forage-livestock.* The chamber conducted a major institute-type meeting with speakers and panel discussions. The meeting attracted 1,000 farmers and managers.

8. *Poultry improvement.* The chamber assisted in promoting and organizing the National Poultry Congress.

9. *Reclamation and irrigation.* The chamber staged an annual pump irrigation clinic at an out-state location. The clinic attracted 600 farmers.

10. *War on weeds.* The chamber conducted a noxious and allergy weed control program.

11. *Student loan fund.* The loan fund for deserving students of agriculture has been operated for twenty years without loss.

Another chamber of commerce, located in a city of 350,000 people in a South Atlantic state, sponsors the usual 4-H activities, corn growing and pasture development contests, and soil conservation and rebuilding projects. One of its main activities, however, is its farm community improvement contest. The contest requires farm families of each community to organize and develop a cooperative program of commuity improvement. Points are given for each of four broad objectives:

1. *Community organization, planning and development.* This part of the contest calls for social, economic, education and religious activities in which the members of the community work cooperatively for the common good. A maximum of 300 points may be awarded for these activities.

2. *Farm improvement and development.* A maximum of 400 points may be awarded for erosion control, balanced feed and pasture programs, use of modern machinery, and similar activities.

3. *Family food supply.* A maximum of 150 points may be awarded for activities promoting the production, conservation and use of food so as to provide an adequate and balanced diet.

4. *Home improvement.* This part of the contest calls for organized activities designed to improve the appearance of farms and homes, make them more livable, provide more comfort and reduce the drudgery of housework. A maximum of 150 points may be awarded.

The contest runs a full year. Awards are made on the basis of on-the-spot inspections by the judges. A total of 45 prizes ranges from a first prize of $1,000 to 36 prizes of $50 each. The contest is sponsored by the Farmers' Club, an organization composed of business and professional men who own and operate farms, as well as of other members of the chamber engaged in agricultural work.

The agricultural activities of the chamber of commerce of one of the foremost livestock and grain markets of the Middle West are planned with three general objectives in mind:

1. Promote good will and understanding between city and farm.

2. Encourage profitable farm production that will increase the purchasing power of the agricultural market and provide farm products for trade and industry.

3. Keep the membership of the chamber informed about agricultural conditions.

In pursuit of these objectives, the chamber employs an agricultural commissioner who travels extensively in a two-state area. It sponsors also a wide variety of activities such as beef cattle and swine contests, a pasture improvement program, a college grain judging contest, a balanced farming contest, a vocational agricultural show and sale, a lamb and wool school, a fat lamb show, promotion of better seed, poultry flock improvement, and auction sales of pure-bred livestock. Its outstanding project, however, is the American Royal Livestock and Horse Show. This show is recognized as one of the foremost livestock expositions of the country. It attracts thousands of exhibitors and visitors from a five-state area. A special effort is made to give recognition to 4-H club, FFA teams and other youth organizations.

The chamber of commerce of a Southern city of 350,000 people engages in most of the common agricultural activities. It concentrates, however, on two major projects. A "plant to prosper" program is aimed at the evils of one-crop farming. It offers awards for the best records of diversification, soil conservation, and home improvement and management. In a recent year 109,000 persons, working 6.5 million acres, were enrolled in the program. The second project is a "save-n'-enrich our soil" competition. In cooperation with a local newspaper and the bankers' associations of four states the chamber offers a total $4,300 in prizes to farmers who follow soil-saving and enriching practices. Both projects are backed by promotional literature that is practical as well as beautifully illustrated.

The organization and activities of the agricultural committee of a Far Western chamber suggest the wide variety of problems with which the chambers of commerce deal. The committee is composed of 140 members and is served by a secretary and three other technically trained men. Its membership includes individual merchants and farmers as well as representatives of general farm organizations, farmers' cooperatives of all types, growers' associations, commodity organizations, the agricultural press, and many government agencies. The committee is responsible for a comprehensive program designed to promote the following objectives:

1. Provision of an adequate food supply for the rapidly increasing population.
2. Development of markets for indigenous farm products.
3. Establishment and promotion of an open livestock market.
4. Suppression of the foot and mouth disease.
5. Promotion of sound land settlement.
6. Development of an adequate water supply.
7. Improvement of urban-rural relations.

Each of these broad objectives calls for specific projects. For example, as part of the effort to improve urban-rural relations the agricultural committee has appointed a sub-committee which works with orchardists and managers to reduce the smokiness of orchard heaters in order to protect urban dwellers from the smoke nuisance.

A great city in the Southwest rates its agricultural committee as one of the strongest in the chamber. Almost 100 top-flight businessmen, all interested in agriculture, make up the committee which is served by a full-time manager. The chamber sponsors also a farm and ranch club with a membership of more than 1,350 "city" and dirt farmers. The chamber's broad agricultural program includes the sponsorship of an important fat stock show and livestock exposition. It has promoted the establishment of soil conservation districts, undertaken an extensive survey of market facilities, and carried on considerable work with farm youth organizations. Among its other activities are dairy and poultry improvement programs, a vegetable show and a rabbit day. A unique project is the effort of the farm and ranch club to raise $200,000 to be used over a five year period for the establishment and operation of a school of agriculture at the local university.

GENERAL FARM PROBLEMS

The preceding brief survey of agricultural activities suggests that chambers of commerce tend to focus their attention on problems that are immediate and important to their local communities. In so doing they may have neglected problems of longer range and of importance to the nation as a whole. Yet, these problems cannot be ignored; and chambers of commerce might well perform a real service to farmers as well as to their own membership if they were to study both local and national situations and attempt to relate the two.

Among the problems that deserve attention by chambers of commerce are consumption trends, changes in dietary habits and their effect on demand. Closely related are the problems of foreign markets as well as the problems of foreign trade policy as it affects agricultural prosperity. Another set of problems of even more immediate importance relates to domestic agricultural policy. It involves the questions of price supports, parity price and acreage adjustment—and indeed, the whole relationship of urban to rural communities. These problems are bound to create division of opinion. Chambers of commerce may, however, contribute to their solution by careful study and orderly debate.

SUMMARY

1. Recognition of the interdependence of farm and city has led many chambers of commerce to become as much interested in the welfare of the farmer as in that of the city dweller.

2. In launching a program of agricultural activities, however, chambers of commerce should observe two cautions: First, they should not undertake projects for which there is no demand; and secondly, they should not duplicate activities that are already satisfactorily performed by other agencies.

3. In order to put its program on a sound footing, the wise chamber of commerce first makes an informal canvass of farm organizations and agricultural specialists for the purpose of seeking ideas and suggestions. Such a canvass is likely to produce offers of cooperation and support. In some cases it

may be desirable to supplement the informal canvass with a more formal survey of agricultural resources and needs.

4. The next step is to organize for action by creating a formal committee on agriculture. The committee develops the program and puts it into practice.

5. Even a good program must be sold to the farmers. Many managers believe that the best way of reaching the adult farmer is to begin by working with farm youth organizations.

6. The activities conducted by the various chambers of commerce include the whole gamut of agricultural problems.

7. Three activities seem, however, to have gained almost universal popularity. They are: farm-town gatherings, work with farm youth organizations, and agricultural expositions and shows.

8. A survey of a number of programs of agricultural activities suggests that each chamber tends to focus its attention upon problems of importance in its trade area.

9. It might be desirable, however, if chambers of commerce were to give greater attention to broad agricultural problems of nationwide importance.

Chapter XII

Governmental Affairs

GOVERNMENT, at every stage—local, state and federal—has become in recent years one of the major concerns of chambers of commerce.

The importance of governmental relations is not new to any chamber of commerce which has faced the problem of obtaining the passage of a city zoning ordinance, or the establishment of a sewer system, or the general improvement of community services. The developments of the past two decades, however, have brought an entirely new phase of this problem onto the doorsteps of the chamber of commerce, wherever it may be.

THE EXPANDING ROLE OF GOVERNMENT

During these twenty years government has doubled, tripled and quadrupled its controls and regulations over business. It has embarked into new fields that require business contributions, not alone in normal taxes, but through new payroll taxes for old age and survivors' insurance, unemployment compensation, disability insurance, etc.

It has added a great many controls and enlarged upon old ones. The drastic regulations of World War II are only part of the picture. Wage and price controls of that period are held as a constant threat over business enterprise even in peacetime, years after the end of the fighting of the war. Minimum wage and hour legislation, laws to enforce collective bargaining, to regulate types of businesses, to establish standards for safety, sanitation and health, etc.—all of which were common before the war—have unfolded into new and startling requirements upon business operations.

The dangerous centralization of powers in our national government and the steady encroachment of the welfare or socialistic state have caused the business and professional man, who makes up the major part of the chamber of commerce membership in every community, to discover more and more that what government does is one of his major concerns. He has a big stake in government and cannot afford to lose.

On the other hand, the rewards of good government are of benefit not only to him but to the community in which he lives. Securing good government, however, is not an easy job. There are no shortcuts to success. But the job can be done if every individual business man will realize that he has an important part in the effort. The opportunity for success is enhanced, if he will equip himself with good organization, well ordered facts, carefully defined plans, realistic understanding and the proper technique for securing results.

Needed: A Voice for Business

The businessman must depend upon his chamber of commerce for information on the demands his government makes of him and for help in alleviating the demands, either in the halls of a legislature or before an administrative body, which enforces and enlarges upon the rules laid down by law. The task of formulating an opinion and arriving at a position on these vital issues is not an easy one, however.

Businessmen are individualists. As a whole, they try to keep informed on state and national issues. They have to be informed in order to stay in business. But, unlike the people affiliated with some organizations, they do not follow leaders blindly. For example, when John L. Lewis shakes his bushy eyebrows and roars that an act of Congress is a slave labor act, hundreds of his organizers and official retainers echo the charge all over the country. Hundreds of thousands of members of his organization will believe his accusation because he has said it is so. But that does not happen generally with a business group. Let the president of the local chamber of commerce or, for that matter the president of the Chamber of Commerce of the United States, make such a charge and analytical, logical minds in the members of a typical chamber of commerce will start to take it apart and explore and determine for themselves whether the charge is a valid one. Businessmen are accustomed to doing this in the operation of their daily affairs and in every decision they must make. Thus, it is of great importance for the manager of a chamber of commerce, or the staff member assigned to a committee, to undertake a completely factual approach to any issue of state or national government that is presented for study.

Problems of Local Government

Local government for many years has been a basic concern of the local chamber of commerce. Most chambers of commerce began as a local public improvement association. The goal was a new park, or sewers, street paving, a municipal auditorium, better traffic control, or railroad grade separations, etc. Today those needs continue, with increased tempo and complexity. In fact, most local government today has become too complex for the average citizen to appraise it or for the uninformed to direct it.

In the past few decades, a tremendous change has occurred in urban-suburban living and the new community relationships brought about by the automobile, the airplane and mass transportation. Local government, even though a jungle of corruption 50 years ago, survived the industrial revolution, the pursuit of frontiers, the immigration from foreign lands, and the movement from farm to city; but today, despite widespread acceptance of higher administrative standards and techniques, is faced with serious problems of maturity. What are some of these problems which are of concern to local government? Here are but a few of them:

The Necessity for Sound Community Development.—Most American cities today are face to face with serious community problems brought about by the absence of planning and control of land development during the past century.

The price for lack of foresight in proper urban development is measured in terms of traffic congestion, unfit housing, wasteful land development, and inadequate health and sanitary facilities.

Can the city of today plan better for tomorrow, or must blunders of the past be repeated again? Can a system of local government be devised which will answer the requirements of a fluid city in terms of modern transportation facilities, proper land use, and adequate metropolitan services for protection against crime, disease, fires and unpleasant living conditions?

Is the structure of local government confined to present corporate boundaries of cities, towns and townships capable of meeting the demands of modern urban-suburban living?

The Desire for Public Improvements.—World War II left in its wake a tremendous backlog of demands for capital improvements—for new schools to house the increased population of the post-war years, for additional parks and playgrounds, improved streets, better sewerage systems, modern city buildings and properties. Which are the most pressing and how to finance them on a sound and equitable basis is a problem of first magnitude.

The Selection of Public Personnel.—Another important problem of local government is that of selecting and training the more than 2,000,000 employees who perform the local public services—the policemen, firemen, teachers, engineers, inspectors, social workers, and so on through a long list. How they were selected and managed a century ago may not have mattered so much. Life then was simple. Government was simple. Today governmental services are complex and important to the happiness and safety of a community. A poor police department means the growth of the underworld. Inefficient firemen penalize business and endanger life. Poor teachers cripple a coming generation. Unjust taxation robs a city of even a fighting chance to survive in the industrial competition.

City government has become too vital—it pervades daily living too much—to leave to untrained political favorites. A system for selecting municipal administrators and employees far surpassing those now in force in many localities is a need of first magnitude.

Social Welfare and Public Relief.—In good times and bad there are millions on the public assistance rolls and the load appears destined to become heavier as the population grows older. More and more people look to government for help in their insecurity, infirmity, or old age. This problem once was too much for cities alone. The national and state governments have assumed much of the responsibility from sheer necessity and taxable ability. But in spite of enormous federal and state grants, local units still carry heavy public assistance loads—and some grim reminders in the form of debts of the tremendous burdens of the thirties. In the meantime, the federal indebtedness has reached unforeseen magnitudes and schemes for further enlarging the scope of public welfare increase in number and magnitude. What is the answer to this national enigma and wherein lies the responsibility of local government?

The Tax Problem.—There is also the eternal problem of paying the bill—of meeting the cost of local government. At a time when federal and state government have usurped most fields of taxation, most American cities face pressing financial dilemmas. Crippled with inelastic and inequitable tax systems, faced with increased demands for services, hampered by mandatory state legislation, plagued with the problem of inflation, and in several instances groaning under heavy debt, cities face grave difficulties of raising money and of spending it most effectively. What is a sound tax system, and how should the load be distributed equitably among the various levels of government?

Efficiency in Government.—Interest in efficient and economical government arises because good citizens want honest and intelligent administration of their city as well as of the state and nation. Businessmen believe in economy and efficiency in their own business and want these standards applied to their government. Further, the reputation of a city or state for good government is an asset that helps business, just as it helps everything else.

The first requisite of efficient government is the proper form of governmental machinery. Good operators are needed to run any machine; but if the machine itself is not the right kind, even a good operator has trouble in making it do what it should. Chambers of commerce can do very effective work in seeing that the structure of government is sound.

The trend has been toward a simplification of city and town governments and the abolition of party politics in local affairs. Chambers of commerce and other groups have conducted successful campaigns for single and smaller legislative bodies, centralized power in the office of the chief executive, fewer elected officials, elimination of duplication and unnecessary functions in government, consolidation of administrative departments, higher personnel standards and county consolidations. Such improvements in the structure of government have inevitably led to greater efficiency and economy.

THE NEED FOR FACTS

If citizens are to judge these and other problems of their local government intelligently, they need facts on its operations. If civic organizations, such as chambers of commerce, are to aid in securing better government, they need the facts for appraisal and direction of their work. If the facts are available and understood, then citizen efforts to improve government stand a good chance of success. But as leaders in community development, members of a chamber of commerce can't expect to judge government unless they, too, have the facts concerning it.

How are the schools functioning? Are the teachers well trained? Are the boys and girls prepared for useful citizenship? Is school equipment adequate? Are the teaching methods up to date? These are a few questions that require answers in any appraisal of the school system. It cannot be done without full knowledge of all circumstances. How about the police department? Is the crime rate low? Is there favoritism or fixing? Is the department adequately equipped? Is it using modern methods of combating crime? Is it prepared to prevent crime before it happens? Again, ordinary citizens and the average group are helpless without a study of the fact.

The Role of the Chamber of Commerce.—Thus there is a great and crying need for chambers of commerce to secure facts and to get them straight. As a man in touch with civic progress in his community, the manager needs to know about civic progress everywhere. To do his job he must therefore become a clearinghouse on information which pertains to government—information which may be used by and for the entire community. What if the police department is studying reassignment of its personnel for most effective use? How can he help? There is the experience of scores of cities, at his fingertips, so that he can profit by the mistakes or successes of others.

Should the chamber of commerce be interested in taxes? It would be an unusual business man supporting a chamber of commerce who did not believe the organization should at least have some knowledge of the use to which government places its tax money. In order to determine whether or not the proceeds of taxation are being utilized most effectively in the community, facts are needed. This does not mean chambers of commerce should be organized groups to cut taxes. Many of them have aided such reductions, but this certainly should not be the prime motive.

The true value of a real tax program is to seek a full dollar's worth of service for each dollar that can reasonably be made available, not to save taxes so someone can have four mink coats and more trips to Miami. To be effective, the chamber does not have to turn itself into a tax-slashing group or one for graft chasing or spectacular investigations.

Cooperating with Public Officials.—The aim should be one, first of intelligent cooperation with officials for improving government. For a disinterested, skeptical public the need is a quiet, earnest effort for improvement. The chamber of commerce might find, then, that it has secured itself a position as liaison between citizen and official—an interpretive force for tax gatherer and taxpayer, voter and vote getter. Many, if not most, improvements in local government have come about as a result of effective work with public officials—not by fist shaking over the back fence, not by "turning the rascals out," but rather from the determined cooperative efforts of citizens armed with the facts. The chamber of commerce manager thus has an urgent need to be able to talk to officials in their own language and to command their respect.

He will never do so if he seeks the center of the stage, and tries to become the hero of any civic problem. One of the rules he must always remember is: It is the elected or the appointed official who must make the eventual decisions, and take the blame for their failure or the credit for their success. The manager's job is to work with the official, supplying facts and organizing public opinion through educational processes.

The skeptic might say, "What of the attitude of the officials? Won't they ignore facts and continue as they wish?" Most organized groups doing an effective job on public administration have made the important discovery that a majority of public officials, even the most maligned, want to do a good job. Officials, generally, are having difficult budget troubles. Most welcome means of making tax money go farther.

City officials frequently report that there are improvements they want to make in methods but that there is uninformed opposition and the citizens are asleep. Here is where the chamber of commerce, armed with the facts, can help officials by interpreting the situation to the public and providing an intelligent public support for a needed change.

Informing the Public.—Some officials may refuse to cooperate on recommendations. In that case, no alternative remains but for chamber of commerce officials, supplied with the facts, to lay the full story before the public. Once citizens are informed and awakened to the true needs of government, they will act. Officials come and officials go. Administrations come and administrations go. But if the chamber of commerce is equipped with information and stands solidly upon facts instead of prejudices, it will become recognized and will go on permanently year after year as an authority in this field. It will not be long before there will be hardly a nook or cranny of local government that has not somewhere had the powerful searchlight of citizen research upon it.

CITIZENS' CONSTANT INTEREST

The need for improving government will never cease. It must keep pace with the modern tempo of economic and political life. There is still need for new and better charters, for new concepts of public management, for new understanding of federal-state and local relationships and for more effective use of the tax dollar. Any chamber of commerce with a constructive and comprehensive program for promoting good government and finding the most equitable plan of financing it will have a long and busy future.

Obviously, there are differences in the degree of effort that may be extended into this field of public administration and governmental research by different chambers of commerce. In the larger organizations—where a specialized staff is possible—the effort may be a continuous one, utilizing the best tools of research. There may be technical and engineering knowledge applied to specific problems of street paving, budgets and tax rates, sewerage, health and sanitation improvements, etc. Formal studies and public affairs bulletins may be prepared at timely intervals, with full use being made of complete statistical tabulations and visual presentations by charts which graphically and succinctly tell the story.

Develop Interest.—In the smaller organizations, it may not be possible for the manager to become specialized in every field of local government. He can't spread himself too thin in his program of work. Here the margin of success will depend upon finding and developing key members for important projects in governmental affairs. In many communities, good government has become an avocation of otherwise busy citizens. The business man who develops a keen and analytical interest in his government is an invaluable asset to any chamber of commerce—large or small. While experience and background are desirable, many chambers of commerce make the mistake of choosing the superintendent of schools as the chairman of the committee to examine the school system or the mayor or other high official as leader of a study group on local government. At the outset, objectivity may be lacking. Underlying all this effort to improve government—on a large or small scale—is the necessity of a prodding, inquisitive mind which falls back upon good logic, common sense and the security of factual, unbiased knowledge.

Rewards May Not Be Spectacular.—Whether it is the large or small chamber of commerce that is working for improved government, the results will not always be spectacular. It ordinarily will mean going to work on rainy mornings; doing hum-drum tasks that have to do with tax rates; hearing the demands of a citizen for more attention in his end of town; observing how public employees work or don't; answering a school girl's request for material in writing a social science paper; preparing publicity that has to do with some purely local matters; then going home to dinner in an over-crowded bus, after which there is a talk to some business women's club on "some problems of our city government." For the busy chamber executive who has a concern for governmental affairs, life's work is not made up of beautiful sunsets, tropical breezes, fair damsels to be rescued or dragons to be slain.

The Value of Routine Interest.—There is value even in routine work and interest in government. Just sitting on the city hall steps has been said to be of preventative value—that public officers and private pressure groups think twice before acting if they know their conduct will be subject to citizen scrutiny and suitable publicity.

It is difficult to appraise the worth of such community service because it is impossible to know of, and to measure the probable cost of things that don't happen—treasury grabs that don't take place, official favors not granted, unfair contracts not made, selfish legislation not introduced. Such negative activity cannot be valued but it is certain that such citizen concern with government 365 days in the year instead of only on election day, pays for itself many times over, and further, if properly publicized helps to make election decisions more intelligent.

A Word of Warning.—The continuing search for improved government, for efficient operations and economy carries with it a solemn and important obligation. Chambers of commerce must be consistent by refraining from proposing new expenditures, if their demand is for reduced taxation. The consequences of a new spending program must be considered alongside of any demands for new improvements or additional services. The statement or belief that it is "somebody else's money" or that "we must get our share" is a prominent and popular fallacy nurtured and promoted by the obvious and enticing features of state and federal grants for local projects. "We're for economy, but . . ." is a dubious and devious line of reasoning for a chamber of commerce. Such organizations that demand economy on the one hand and stand in line, tin-cup in hand, for "free" or "easy" money for some seemingly desirable project on the other, which the state or federal government has shown willingness to support, jeopardize the whole movement for sound, economical government.

LEGISLATION—STATE AND NATIONAL

The progressive centralization of activities and powers in Washington and in the state capitol has caused business men to become keenly aware of the vital stake they have in the normal legislative processes. They want to know what is going on and they want to be in a postion, when occasion arises, to voice their opinion.

Few chambers have the means or feel the necessity of direct representation in Washington, or for that matter in the state capitol. It is, however, possible for them to form a strong legislative committee on state-wide issues, or a national affairs committee on national issues, to keep themselves fully informed and to find a vehicle through which to communicate their opinions and wishes.

Here, as in the instance of work on local administration,

importance of the factual approach needs to be recognized. The chamber should not be hasty in committing itself on any legislative program, where there is a hint of prejudice or bias. There is every need for careful investigation and realistic understanding of all issues under consideration. Objective presentation of well-ordered facts is to be desired over pure "propaganda" or the wining and dining of legislators.

Forming A Committee on Legislation.—The technique of forming a committee to operate either on state or national issues is about the same. The first move is to select a good general—the right man to lead forces. The chairman must know the issues. He must know something about the psychology of public officials and about public life in general. The job calls for plain hard work without any let up. The chairman, or any member of the committee concerning legislative affairs, must be a go-getter with intelligence and stamina to bounce back from reverses and work diligently for the final result with patience and understanding. As many as possible of this type of personnel should be used in the formation of the committee membership.

Local chambers certainly will want to use the excellent bulletins and consulting service of the Department of Governmental Affairs of the Chamber of Commerce of the United States. The services rendered by this national organization provide up-to-the-minute news on actions in Congress and also offer significant analysis and interpretation of pending legislation.

There are certain fundamental principles for a committee on governmental affairs to follow if it is to function efficiently and effectively. Of course, detailed procedures may vary, but basically a committee upon legislative matters should follow these concepts:

1. *It meets as often as occasion demands.*

   It is not enough to just keep abreast of developments or to attempt to do a month's work in one session. A committee, to be effective, must keep ahead of important issues as they develop. It must be **prepared to act** the moment any piece of legislation under consideration becomes "hot".

2. *It gets the information.*

   The committee must be kept posted on the issues by the presentation to it of clear, concise and informative material which can be used as the basis for a working program.

3. *It studies the issues.*

   Many state and national issues do not require detailed study. Many can be ignored. It is desirable to screen the legislative problems so that only the important ones require the attention of committee members. It may be desirable that individual members be formed into sub-committees so that they may specialize on the major issues as they begin to appear in the legislative mill.

4. *It prepares the arguments.*

   Committee members themselves certainly should know all the arguments, pro and con, about each issue. Even with presentation of the conclusions to the entire organization, it may be desirable to present a complete analysis of the issues.

5. *It states its position factually and honestly.*

   Chamber of commerce managers must realize that pressure blocs now exert great influence upon legislation and national policy. Men of more or less expert mind and experience have developed techniques for the use of these groups both to cause their legislators to act and to influence public opinion as a force to act upon the legislative or executive mind. The scramble for power offers the temptation to use half-truths, and even distortions of facts to mis-lead. The chamber of commerce has a primary obligation to rest its case on indisputable facts. Whether presenting its opinions to the public, to a legislative committee or an individual legislator, it must rely upon authoritative data, whose reliability cannot be questioned. There is a public concept of lobbying that should be far from the fact so far as chamber of commerce legislative work is concerned. The idea that legislators are easily influenced by entertainment and gifts is rather widespread. It is not a correct picture, though lobbying groups may resort to such tactics. Chambers of commerce should be scrupulously honest and fair in their dealings with public officials, at every level.

6. *It marshals public opinion.*

Taking a position, or passing a resolution, is not enough. The views of the organization must be communicated to others, and especially to those who make the decisions, or help make the decisions. One of the best techniques is by direct communication—by letter, by wire, or telephone or by person—and by as many informed people as possible. This means that the position of the chamber of commerce, to be really effective, must be supplemented by the individual efforts of its members.

Keeping members informed on public issues and getting them to act is an important adjunct of committee work. Then informing the public generally and getting over the story of each piece of legislation and how it fits into the whole problem of the proper relationship of government to the traditional system of free enterprise follows.

Thus, chamber of commerce activity in governmental affairs is an important phase of the vital program of selling the opportunities of a free and virile America. There is no place for failure or half-hearted effort.

SUMMARY

1. Government on the local, state and national levels has a direct effect on business that justifies governmental affairs being included in every Chamber of Commerce program.

2. Local government is concerned with sound community development, public improvements and trained public employees, that can give efficiency in government.

3. Cities and schools face difficulties in raising sufficient revenue for operations because of limiting state legislation and the sources of taxation usurped by state and federal government.

4. The first requisite of efficient government is the proper form of governmental machinery. Chambers of Commerce

cannot logically participate in political contests but they can effectively campaign for an improved city charter or a modern state constitution.

5. Facts are the first essential a Chamber of Commerce must have to do intelligent and effective work in any of the three fields of governmental affairs.

6. Co-operation with public officials is necessary for success. The Chamber of Commerce manager should never seek the center of the stage. That place belongs to the elected or appointed public officials who must make the decisions in public matters.

7. The Chamber can often serve city officials and the public by helping to create a public desire for something the officials want to do but hesitate to recommend.

8. Citizen interest in government is a full time job. The work is never completed. No chamber manager can cover the whole field. He must find and develop leaders for important projects.

9. Working for improved government is not always spectacular, but constant interest may have retarding effect on pressure groups or wavering officials.

10. The Chamber is the medium through which businessmen may voice their opinion in Washington. Today every chamber needs committees on state and national legislation when taxes and government controls are a vital part of every business.

Chapter XIII

Civic Activities

CITIES have individual characteristics and standards of living that vary as widely as do the characteristics and living standards of individuals. The standard of living for individuals and cities is not alone determined by income. To a large extent the combined will of the people in the community determines whether or not it is a good place in which to live and do business. This is of paramount interest to a Chamber of Commerce engaged in commercial and industrial development since an undesirable community can neither hold its population nor attract new industry and new people.

DEFINITION

Civic activities, as treated in this chapter, are closely allied with the preceding chapter on governmental affairs. Historically, many of today's Chambers of Commerce had their origin in trade associations or boards of trade; but, likewise, many in smaller towns have been born of a desire of citizens to improve the civic aspects of their community. Civic activities can be defined best by naming some of those most common to many chambers, such as community chest, park and playground improvements, municipal band concerts, centennial celebrations, public health programs, bond issues for public improvements, fire and police protection, insurance rates, and many others of similar nature.

Why Engage in Civic Activities?

Everyone living in a community has either inherited it or chosen it as a place to live. They should have pride in their home town. The perpetuation of this goodly heritage involves a responsibility, yet civic pride should not be so intense that it blinds leadership to the shortcomings of the community, As a matter of fact, the city may fall far short of its responsibilities to provide for health, comfort, education, recreation and other features of good community life.

To encourage their citizens to know what their city can be and should be and to foster projects to help achieve the goals that are established, Chambers of Commerce engage in civic activities. As the complexities of modern living increased, the demand for participation of Chambers of Commerce in the civic field was intensified, until today it is difficult to find a live, representative, progressive Chamber of Commerce which does not include civic work as a part of its activities. Some of the reasons for this are:

1. A trend of city governments away from politics to a more businesslike administration that is more responsive to business men's suggestions.

2. A broadening point of view of businessmen as to what is involved in the field of commerce and industry. They have discovered that their business prosperity depends to an increasing degree upon desirable living conditions in the community.

3. A more general realization that public service and social work should be conducted on sound business lines, and that the way to bring this about is to get into these fields and help and not to stay out and criticize.

4. A growing appreciation on the part of public officials of the fact that community prosperity and happiness depend upon the prosperity of commerce and industry, and vice versa.

5. The effect of modern conditions upon the community, every element being drawn more closely together and being permitted to see the advantages of combined effort in a common cause.

Other contributing factors might be enumerated. These examples will indicate, however, why the business man has a greater tendency to put himself in the other man's place, to try to understand things from the other man's point of view, to endeavor to work with others, and to realize that each man's prosperity and welfare are affected by the general welfare of those with whom he is associated. A broad understanding of these facts on the part of business men, and a willingness to work together on civic projects, help to create a better understanding of business and its problems on the part of the public generally and of elected officials more specifically.

Such has been the transformation, and the causes therefore, in the interest which every right-minded businessman should have in civic work. Formerly, his participation in these matters was very slight and inclined to be blind and sentimental. Now, it is active, intelligent, constructive and resultful.

It is no longer a question as to whether a Chamber of Commerce should act on civic questions. The affirmative holds sway completely. The important question is what policies a Chamber of Commerce should pursue within the field of civic affairs.

Scope of Civic Activities

Civic issues have become so numerous that it would be folly for any Chamber of Commerce to attempt to include all of them in its program. To do so would spread the work too thinly and would create an impression on the public that the organization is a community busybody. The result would be a scarcity of worthwhile accomplishments and a lessening of influence.

The Chamber of Commerce should participate in civic activities only to the extent that it can do a thorough job, and it should engage only in those activities which are timely and which are of direct importance to business. That, after all, is its field. Therefore, those civic matters which have a bearing upon the conduct of commerce and industry are most definitely within the scope of activity of a Chamber of Commerce.

The activity of the Chamber of Commerce in civic affairs furnishes a striking example of the value of organization. The average business man can himself do little to protect and advance his interests in these matters. As an individual, his efforts would be largely futile. A well-organized commercial group is an effective leader and spokesman for business men on civic issues. It represents the united business community. To strength of numbers, it adds the standing, influence and prestige of its members. This combination gives it the power to command attention and to get results.

Guides to Participation in Civic Affairs

The Chamber of Commerce should observe certain guide posts in its participation in civic affairs if it is to maintain a well-balanced program of work. A few general rules that are probably applicable to Chambers of Commerce of all sizes may be observed in this connection:

1. It is important to deal only with essentials. Unimportant matters and the interests of a single group or trade should give way to civic issues important to more general elements in the business community.

2. It is necessary to avoid the danger of spreading an organization's efforts too thin. There is neither manpower nor resources to deal effectively with all community problems. The tendency to try to effect a modern Utopia in each year's program is an alluring temptation to be avoided.

3. A Chamber of Commerce should devote its attention to civic matters which have an important relation to business. The more intimately any civic matter relates to business, the greater the contribution which business men can make toward its solution.

4. A Chamber of Commerce should not duplicate the activities of existing agencies, if they are doing effective work or can be made effective. It may, however, occasionally supplement most usefully the work of another organization by presenting the point of view of the business element in the community.

5. A Chamber of Commerce should never engage in the personal side of public affairs. Experience has clearly shown that when a Chamber interests itself in elections or appointments of public officials, its effectiveness is soon reduced, if not destroyed.

This is probably the most appropriate place to discuss a false accusation often hurled against Chambers of Commerce. When they become active in civic matters in such a way as to oppose, or displease, public officials or others, the charge is often made that the Chamber of Commerce is getting into politics. The accusation is almost sure to be made; and it does have an effect, even on the organization's members, and especially on those who do not agree with the stand the Chamber of Commerce has taken. Altogether too many members are frightened off by this charge. The Chamber must always be able to prove that such charge is without foundation.

The best answer is to show that the Chamber of Commerce clearly differentiates between the administration of public affairs, in which it has a right to deal, and political contests which hinge upon the election or appointment of particular men or women. Any fair-minded public will readily understand and sympathize with the reasons why a Chamber of Commerce takes an interest in the issues of the community that have a direct relation to business, and, once that understanding is established, the accusation falls.

Practical Limitations in the Civic Field

Some of the most effective work of a Chamber of Commerce is of a type that must be kept on a more or less confidential basis if it is to be successful. Seeking a new industry is a good example. This sometimes creates a problem for the manager in his constant responsibility of keeping the membership and the public sold on the value of the organization to the community. Civic activities, on the other hand, lend themselves better to publicity and often create a more immediate and larger amount of favorable comment than do commercial and industrial activities.

It is advisable, on the other hand, to bear in mind that in civic projects, there are hazards and possibilities of failure equal to those in commercial and industrial activities. This fact should serve as a reminder that caution is advisable but not as an argument against taking up civic activities, since there are many opportunities for constructive accomplishments.

Things Upon Which Success Depends

Success in civic activities, to a much greater extent than in other branches of Chamber of Commerce work, depends upon public support. If a Chamber of Commerce is to secure and retain public support, it must acquire a reputation for:

1. Obtaining the essential facts before expressing an opinion.

2. Conducting its studies and reaching its conclusions without bias or preconceived ideas.

3. Refusing to be led by interested parties into activities that are ill-advised.

4. Being always able to show that it has utilized the resources of brains at its disposal to reach an intelligent decision.

Whatever the facts may be, it must be expected that the hoarse-voiced demagogue will accuse the Chamber of Commerce of the opposite of these virtues. He feels that the Chamber is not a friend of his, and it becomes his objective to discredit it and to attempt to minimize its influence. The best way to accomplish his purpose seems to him obviously to be to accuse it of bias, of being led and influenced by people who have selfish interests to promote, of not having obtained the facts, and of being untrustworthy generally. That is a much easier course for him than to undertake to combat the arguments of the Chamber of Commerce.

The fact that the demagogue adopts such a course of action should neither discourage nor alarm. It is only one of the inevitable incidents of engaging in civic work and is not, in itself, a matter of great importance. Happy is the manager who has sufficient faith in the work he is doing to ignore the vocal but illogical rantings of such critics.

To enjoy this assurance, the manager must be sure there are no foundations for the statements and accusations of the demagogue. It is not enough that the Chamber of Commerce is fair and without bias. It must be obvious that:

1. The matter was approached with an open mind.

2. There was a conscientious attempt to get all the facts.

3. If controversial, both sides of the controversy were adequately considered.

Neither good intentions nor even a desire to get the facts are enough. The way in which the Chamber of Commerce has obtained the facts, the manner in which it has put them together, and the care with which it has reached its conclusions, must prove that its good intentions and laudable desires have been backed by the proper amount and the right kind of work.

Unfortunately, there is all too frequently some foundation for the statement often made by politicians and public officials that "in public affairs the biggest fool in the community is the successful business man.'' When there is foundation for this statement, it rests on either one or both of two things:

1. An unwillingness on the part of the business man to spend the time necessary to get the information he should have, and such as he would feel that any other person ought to have if he were going to express an opinion on business matters.

2. An innate feeling that, because he has been successful in business and knows more about it than other people, he also knows more about everything else than other people do—or, at least, that his opinion with reference to them is entitled to special respect and consideration.

There is no use in denying that too often Chambers of Commerce believe they have the correct information when in reality they have only been impressed by the arguments of interested parties and have accepted without challenge the statements made by them. There seems to be some evidence that Chambers of Commerce are making considerable progress toward the more substantial position of more thoroughly investigating issues on which they act. It is becoming less common for a Chamber of Commerce to pass upon some civic problem merely because somebody in whom the board of directors had confidence sounded convincing in a plea for the action. At one time an aggressive and influential member could often commit the Chamber of Commerce to his way of thinking with surprising ease. Similar efforts to obtain the support of Chambers of Commerce are still made—but less frequently with success.

Actual Results the Final Goal

One of the most damaging indictments that can be made against a Chamber of Commerce is that ''it is a good starter but a poor finisher.'' Too often this accusation is true. Getting a thing started is easy, but completing the job frequently involves long, hard work. Rare indeed is the organization whose records do not show a number of activities that were started with wide-spread publicity but allowed to fade out into failure.

Constructive accomplishment is the goal of all Chamber of Commerce work. It is the measure of the success of the organization. In civic affairs, the task of getting results is more difficult because success depends to a certain extent upon bringing to the organization's point of view men who are not naturally as sympathetic or friendly as fellow business men.

One of the things a manager should learn and remember is that little is accomplished by the passage and publication of a resolution with no subsequent action. If a civic question is deemed of sufficient importance to warrant Chamber of Commerce action upon it, then the organization's position upon it is worth fighting for. Once a decision has been reached by a committee, and the approval of the board of directors obtained, every reasonable effort should be made to get the position decided upon adopted by the appropriate body.

Less work is required, of course, for some activities than for others. Civic projects are of different degrees of importance, and vary in character. The underlying situations are not always the same. The application of ordinary common sense coupled with experience and training will usually reveal which matters should be emphasized and how many may be undertaken at one time. The same qualities will also indicate which activities can best be accomplished quietly and which require intensive publicity. A Chamber of Commerce should not make the mistake of using blatant publicity for every activity.

PROCEDURE FOR CIVIC ACTIVITIES

Because civic activities bring the organization into closer relationships with the general public and with elected government officials, more or less specialized problems arise in this field. Here many members are willing to do committee work because of a personal but not financial interest. The variety of civic activities permits using them effectively on committees.

Effective Committee Service

In the civic program the best machinery for getting the facts, for analyzing and digesting them, and for reaching a wise decision, is generally acknowledged to be an interested, well-balanced committee. Such committees continue year after year with some change in personnel when appointed at the first of each fiscal year. New members bring fresh ideas. Special committees are assigned special tasks and continue in office until that task is completed and the committee discharged. Special committees make it possible to select those members who are best qualified for a particular job and to get a large number of members into the program of work of the Chamber of Commerce.

A continuous or standing committee which constantly keeps track of things, and which is all the time getting better and better informed as to a situation, is frequently in a position to act almost instantly when the occasion arises. It often can do so in cases where the occasion for action would have passed before a special committee could have been appointed and taken the time to study the situation. There is a place in civic activities for both standing and special committees. The thing to do in all cases is to utilize the method which is the best and most effective under the existing circumstances.

Need for Authoritative Information

Most Chambers of Commerce have learned from experience that the only road to lasting success in obtaining and holding favorable public opinion and in influencing public officials, both of which are essential for the success of civic projects, goes by the route of:

1. Careful research.
2. Judicious drawing upon the experience of other communities.
3. Getting the opinions of recognized authorities.
4. Careful and unbiased analysis and study of the facts obtained.

This is sometimes a long road, and at times the going is difficult; but it is the road to success, and it pays the manager and his staff to see that it is traveled. The Chamber of Commerce should not be diverted from this road by accusations that it is slow and unwieldy. Unless a matter is of sufficient importance to justify this care, it is not worthy of the consideration of the Chamber of Commerce. Reaching a decision on an important proposal without delay is important, but reaching a wise decision is even more important. No urgency, no desire to show by reaching a quick decision that the Chamber of Commerce is a live and active organization—nothing whatever, in fact—can justify failure in this respect.

The following general suggestions as to the obtaining of information may be helpful:

1. Depend only upon original sources of information. Hearsay, rumor and second-hand facts and opinions are dangerous.

2. Acquire an ability to know the proper sources of information. It is not so necessary for a manager to have a great fund of information in his head as it is for him to know where and how to get the facts when necessary.

3. Be thorough, but obtain only the pertinent facts. Avoid wasting time with superfluous information which will confuse the committee.

The questionnaire method is effective in securing information from original sources. When a manager believes a questionnaire is advisable, he should first consult the Chamber of Commerce of the United States to determine if the information he desires has already been compiled. If it has been, it will save time and expense and protect those upon whom he would call, from unnecessary work. If a questionnaire is used, it should be as definite and specific as possible, and should request only the amount of information actually necessary.

Publicity for Civic Projects

The participation of the public in many civic projects makes the matter of publicity of primary importance. Whether publicity should be obtained as a means of getting a thing done is a matter which must be decided in each case. The decision should not depend wholly upon the desires of the Chamber of Commerce or entirely upon the wishes of public officials, although both should be considered. It is frequently true that public officials prefer that there be no publicity, especially in cases where the position of the Chamber may be opposed to their own. Publicity should have a part when it will contribute to the success of a project, and it should not have a part when it may lessen the chances of accomplishing the proposed objective.

Assuming that an activity is a matter on which publicity is desirable, Chambers of Commerce have generally found it better to delay the first public announcement of their position upon a civic matter to make it coincide with the direct appeal to the officials in whose jurisdiction a decision lies. The officials appreciate the courtesy and will be less inclined to oppose and embarrass the Chamber of Commerce.

Public officials may sometimes desire no publicity because that makes it easier for them to disregard and smother the recommendation of the Chamber of Commerce. The decision on the part of the Chamber to use publicity should not be prompted by a desire to make sure that it obtains credit for getting a thing done. Publicity which reflects credit upon public officials as well as upon the organization, when such credit is merited, is usually more valuable.

There is nothing undignified in a Chamber of Commerce's sponsoring a vigorous campaign of factual propaganda in connection with some civic project in order to get results. Publicity in many of its forms may be advisable as a means of informing the public and encouraging its support. Propaganda itself influences public officials, but it is more effective with them when it influences their constituents.

Ability to Secure Public Support

In its civic program, the Chamber of Commerce seeks to influence two classes of people in order to get its views adopted.

1. Public Officials.—They may establish an executive ruling or an administrative policy, or they may pass an ordinance or statute.

2. The Public.—Public support may be necessary in order to influence public officials or to carry out such programs as public safety, clean-up drives or similar campaigns, in which there is public participation.

It is impossible to lay down an exact formula for getting results in civic efforts because public affairs vary in character, and they are very likely to be full of whirlpools and eddies of conflicting and uncertain forces; but some fundamentals or general principles may be agreed upon. In this connection, it is the first responsibility of the Chamber of Commerce to get the most thorough understanding possible of the character, attitude of mind and motivations of the men to be influenced.

For example, public officials may be considered in three classes:

1. Administrators.—City managers and department or bureau heads are representative of this group. They may be elected, but are more generally appointed. They hold salaried positions and devote all or most of their time to their work. Presumably, they are experts in their lines; and although they are subject to the uncertainties of changes in administrations, they may hold office for some considerable length of time. While they are not directly responsible to the voters, they are keenly responsive to public opinion.

2. Executives.—This includes governors, mayors, commissioners and other such officials. They are elected by popular vote, devote all or most of their time to the work, and receive monetary compensation. Such positions require executive ability, but frequently those elected have had little experience in this field. Their experience usually has been such as to develop more of a legislative than an executive type of mind. Thus, they are frequently hesitant to make a decision, and are likely to be swayed more by public opinion than by arguments and facts.

3. Legislators.—These officials are almost always elected, and more frequently give only a small portion of their time each year to the work and are not generally paid much for their time and service. Successful business men are not found in legislative positions as frequently as they should be. Legislative positions are sought more frequently for the prestige or political power that goes with them, than for financial gains or from a sense of duty to the constituency. Because they are interested in re-election, legislators are very conscious of public opinion.

Public officials of all three classes are frequently critized by businessmen. Such criticism may or may not be justified. It should be remembered that everyone is governed in his general attitudes by the facts and circumstances which surround him. By being more tolerant, business men may gain a better understanding of the viewpoints of public officials.

The good will and support of their constituents mean as much to public officials as retention and support of customers mean to businessmen.

The thing of importance in this regard is not whether the attitude of mind of the public official is wrong or right but that the Chamber of Commerce should recognize the fact that the average office holder thinks along different lines from those of the majority of its members. It is well to remember, then, that if things are to be accomplished, those who have the power to decide must be approached, and the facts and arguments presented, in a way which will fit in with their thoughts and attitude of mind and environment.

There are four principal motives which, singly or in combination, influence the decisions and action of public officials. They are:

1. Desire to serve.
2. Desire for personal honor.
3. Desire for power.
4. Desire for personal gain.

Public officials decide their positions largely by their answers to these questions:

1. It is right? The Chamber of Commerce has an opportunity to present facts and arguments to help determine the answer.
2. Does public opinion demand it? The right kind of publicity may help to mould the opinion held by the public.
3. What is the personal gain? This may be divided into two classes—financial and honor. No worthwhile civic organization would attempt to use the financial benefit urge, but they should recognize that other interests do use it. On the other hand, if a public official gets a job done, he is entitled to honor, and the use of this urge on the part of a Chamber of Commerce is justified.

Responsibilities of the Manager

In civic activities as in practically every other phase of Chamber of Commerce work, it is the responsibility of the manager to supply direction as well as some measure of supervision. However, he should not be the one to issue public statements or to present the facts and arguments in a case for these reasons:

1. It is not effective for the manager to present the case. Public officials are inclined to look upon him as a hired man of the organization. It is much more impressive for a businessman who has been sufficiently interested to take the time voluntarily away from his business, to make the impression.

2. The fact that members of the committee, or officers of the organization, are expected to make the presentations also has a tendency to make them more thorough in their information.

3. Mistakes or mis-statements made by a business man are much less likely to injure the Chamber of Commerce permanently than if they were made by the manager.

4. The opportunity to appear before public groups to present facts and arguments is one of the rewards for volunteer committee workers.

The manager's part should be that of supervision so that the preliminary work of the committee is done thoroughly and well, the facts and views of the committee are in shape for effective presentation, and the right man is delegated to present them. There is also, of course, much incidental and supplementary work which properly falls to the lot of the manager.

Cooperation with Other Agencies

The aid of other groups in the community is frequently necessary in civic projects. In seeking such support, the Chamber of Commerce should try to make its request in the same way that it would like to be asked. It should never insist upon another group committing itself on matters that are outside of its scope of work, ask for hasty decisions without opportunity to obtain essential facts, or conduct overaggressive efforts among its members to stimulate an artificial demand.

Many short-sighted organizations believe that if they support a proposal urged by another organization, that in itself is sufficient reason for the subsequent support of their proposals by these latter organizations, without reference to the merits of the case. It is an embarrassing request to deny, but one in which the Chamber of Commerce cannot afford to acquiesce.

In soliciting the support of other organizations, the Chamber of Commerce should be diplomatic, show every consideration for their desires, and should studiously avoid an attitude that would embarrass or antagonize.

Organizing a Project

While it is not possible to design a formula which will supply a model for any and all types of civic projects, it may be advisable to suggest a somewhat general outline as a guide to the manager in organizing his own projects—

1. *Objectives.*—Reasons for sponsorship of project. General aims and community benefits that are expected to be accomplished.

2. *General Policy.*—A long-range educational program or a campaign or drive to accomplish certain results within a given period of time. Type of cooperation to be sought from other organizations, elected officials or the public in general. Policy with reference to assembling information and to giving out publicity.

3. *Procedure.*—An outline of the various steps in the development of the project, in the order in which they are expected to occur.

4. *Committee.*—Number and type of members. How selected. How organized. Major functions of the committee. Kind of participation expected.

5. *Suggested Activities.*—If the objective is general, there may be a number of specific activities that will be advisable in carrying on the complete program. As for example, a safety campaign may include traffic, industrial and home safety programs.

Some projects may necessitate large organizations of workers and involve many steps in their development. Such activities should be outlined in detail in order that no essential features will be left out of the plans. Other civic activities may not, on the other hand, require all of the steps suggested above. The fact that should be emphasized, however, is that every civic project should be carefully planned and should be directed toward as definite goals as is possible.

PUBLIC WELFARE ACTIVITIES

Here are some of the more common types of civic activities. This list is not intended to be inclusive; nor should it be inferred that activities not mentioned are to be looked upon as outside the scope of Chamber of Commerce work. In every community there are different factors which make it necessary for the local Chamber of Commerce to adjust its civic activities to its local needs.

The same forces which have brought about profound changes in the relations of government to business in the last twenty years have also altered the status and affected the welfare of many individuals and groups in America. Social change has created community-wide problems as well as opportunities for the Chamber of Commerce to render advisable service in the field of public welfare activities. It should not be the purpose of the Chamber of Commerce to duplicate the services of established social agencies, and each agency and each need should be considered in its relationship to other agencies and needs and to the community as a complex whole.

Education

In the field of education, there are problems to which the Chamber of Commerce can contribute the knowledge and ability it has at its command. If educational subjects are taken up intelligently, the results obtained can easily be traced back to show a benefit to business.

A good public school system is an attraction to individuals and industries contemplating location in a community. The schools train workers of the community and teach the fundamentals of citizenship. Furthermore, schools spend a considerable portion of the taxpayers' money. The Chamber of Commerce should feel free to place the schools under the same scrutiny as other political sub-divisions; and from the businessman's point of view make sure that the curriculum is designed to meet the needs of an industrial civilization and that the economies of good business practices are observed in the administration of the schools.

In some communities education committees devote their attention to special phases, depending upon the points of strength and weakness of the school system. Some Chambers of Commerce feel that their most logical activity in education is to concentrate on endeavoring to improve the training of pupils for commerce and industry. Others place emphasis upon vocational guidance and placement, while still others devote their activities to comprehensive school surveys in which the school costs are closely analyzed to ascertain whether the greatest efficiency possible is being reached.

College and university communities have opportunities for additional activities in the field of education. Such activities may include:

1. *Personnel.*—Membership of faculty members in the Chamber of Commerce supplies an excellent contact between that profession and business. Furthermore, faculty members can render valuable service in meetings and on committees where specialized information is needed.

2. *Promotion.*—During the school year, a college or university sponsors many activities which bring people to the community from outside. The Chamber of Commerce can well join in such promotions, on the same basis that they encourage conventions and tourists.

3. *Legislation.*—Although care must be exercised in this field, the Chamber of Commerce may be helpful in getting before legislative groups facts and reasons for adequate appropriations to maintain state schools and to carry on specialized activities such as research projects.

4. *Alumni.*—Active alumni associations are frequently important adjuncts to a higher educational institution. The local Chamber of Commerce through its members who are alumni of the local college or university may be instrumental in maintaining a live and worthwhile alumni association.

Charity and Character Building

The many social agencies in a community, such as organized charities, settlement houses, hospitals, and character-building organizations, must depend upon the generosity of the public for a considerable part of their financial income. As in all lines of human endeavor, there are varying degrees of effectiveness, efficiency, and honesty among social agencies. Most of the established agencies in a community are above reproach so far as honesty and integrity are concerned, but they may or may not be operated along sound business lines.

Since charitable and character-building agencies look to business for much of their support, it is natural that Chambers of Commerce have found that they have a direct relationship to such social agencies. The activities of Chambers of Commerce with respect to solicitations for these agencies may be divided into two general classes:

1. *Information.*—Determine whether a specific agency is well conducted and worthy of support. Such an agency should be incorporated, managed by a local board which holds regular meetings, publish regular reports, have periodic audits by public accountants, raise funds in an approved manner, and cooperate with other agencies in promoting economy of social work in that city.

2. *Endorsement.*—Since many businessmen do not care to analyze such information as the above, they want some organization such as the Chamber of Commerce to endorse social agencies. Such endorsement can be given safely only on the basis of complete facts and careful analysis. This endorsement should be by one of the strongest and most representative committees in the organization. Names of members may or may not be made public.

Because of the number of solicitation problems coming before them, many Chambers of Commerce have taken the leadership in organizing Better Business Bureaus or in sponsoring ordinances for the city to establish a solicitations commission. Since solicitations are a definite part of the cost of doing business and because there is constant threat of fraudulent solicitation, it is a definite responsibility of the Chamber of Commerce to handle this problem or to see that it is adequately cared for in the community. Not only must a service be provided to give information on solicitations, but the public in general and businessmen in particular must be educated to avail themselves of this service.

Recreation

More and more attention is being given to the relationship between recreational facilities and the welfare of business and industry. While individual companies may meet some of the recreational needs of their employees, the major responsibility falls upon the community. As a community problem, of importance to business, it becomes a matter of concern to the Chamber of Commerce. Here again the approach is primarily one of study and recommendation with some possibility of actual sponsorship of recreational projects.

Community Chest

Chambers of Commerce have had a leading part in the creation of the community chest as a means of more efficient financing of charitable and character-building agencies. A community chest seeks to raise the money to be used by member organizations, usually by a single annual appeal. The funds raised by this central agency are distributed in accordance with budgets prepared by member organizations and approved by the central agency, in advance of the solicitation of funds. A study of the result of community chest campaigns over a period of years indicates:

1. More money for member organizations has been obtained than had been obtained previously under individual solicitations.

2. The number of contributions has been enlarged, though the larger givers still continue to bear the large share of the burden.

3. The cost of raising funds has been reduced.

4. The time of voluntary campaign workers has been reduced.

Those who advocate the community chest plan insist that social work is bettered by it. More money is expended; social work is planned intelligently; duplication is eliminated; uniform budgeting is established with many resulting economies;

strong agencies are permitted expansion according to their merits while weak agencies are strengthened; and directors and paid workers, freed from money-raising worries and duties, devote more of their efforts to social work. In the early days of the community chest, many possible disadvantages were cited, but most of these for the average city have been overcome or proved unfounded.

The character of agencies financed by public contributions has changed greatly in the last decade. Increased governmental assistance to needy people has reduced the demand for this type of charitable work while the character-building organizations have increased in number and volume of work. Perhaps the greatest change is the increasing number of national organizations created to relieve suffering from various human ailments such as heart disease, cancer, infantile paralysis, rheumatic fever, etc. An association to relieve the sufferers and to conduct research looking to prevention or permanent cure has a strong appeal to those whose families have suffered from a given disease.

At this time, 1951, community chests have been weakened by numerous campaigns for funds to support agencies not included in the chest. Leadership and manpower capable of soliciting funds have been greatly overworked. Mail requests are so numerous that most of them are ignored without regard to their merit. In many cities movements are under way to consolidate these many campaigns with the community chest, or to in other ways reduce the number of campaigns for public subscriptions.

Health and Sanitation

In this field the possibilities for activities are broad, and the wise Chamber of Commerce will confine its work to those that give promise of being more directly related to business and that are not being handled efficiently by other organizations. The purpose of the organization in its health conservation program may be summarized thus:

1. To further the development of sound public health work.
2. To stimulate and promote needed improvement in community health services.
3. To assist in the reduction of preventable illnesses and unnecessary deaths.

Spasmodic projects in this field are merely palliatives, and they effect little in the nature of permanent improvement. The chief value in this field lies in the permanence of the work and its success in obtaining the whole-hearted support of the authorities and the cooperation of the public. The program of public education for health and sanitation work can be based on three fundamental premises:

1. To attract and hold the interest and attention of those not now interested in personal and public health and hygiene.
2. To impart reliable information to all who are interested.
3. To inspire those now engaged in public health work to greater achievement.

The problem of health and sanitation is an economic one as well as humanitarian. Business and industry are more likely to gravitate to a community which has a record of health progress and to stay in a community where every effort is made to keep that community healthy. Cleanliness and attractiveness in a city are business assets of no small value. Clean-up and paint-up campaigns, improved water supply and sewage disposal systems, industrial hygiene, better public health service, adequate hospital facilities, and progress in health regulations are examples of activities in this field that may well be a concern of any Chamber of Commerce.

Housing

There are two distinct aspects of the housing problem. One is associated with poverty in general—the failure of the economic system to achieve a sufficiently well-balanced distribution of income to permit all families to obtain the necessities of life. While this phase of the program is not to be ignored, it is somewhat outside the scope of the Chamber of Commerce, and is not peculiar to housing any more than it is to clothing or food.

The second aspect of the problem is a more specific result of urban and industrial disease. The industrial organization may not be equipped to produce the kind and amount of houses needed by the community, and there may be local conditions which discourage rather than encourage adequate housing for the population.

As a matter of great and immediate public concern, housing is a problem of importance to many Chambers of Commerce. Its solution is important not only to the well-being of individuals and families, but has become essential to the soundness of cities and basic industries. It is largely a local problem. Activities of the Chamber of Commerce in this field may be built around the following aims:

1. The removal of legal obstacles in the way of the community's ability to produce houses.

2. The establishment of rational building codes, zoning and land-planning regulations within which free enterprise may be enabled to operate on a sound basis.

3. The encouragement of the building industry to take positive action in reorganizing itself to take up the responsibilities and opportunities before it.

4. Some attention to state or federal aid for families hopelessly beyond the reach of housing as supplied by private enterprise, since they cannot be left with safety to the community, to the squalor and degradation of slums.

Activities in this field may include investigation of mortgage laws, building codes, rational zoning ordinances, city plans, and the whole subject of local taxation. This problem is not always concerned with building more houses. Overbuilding may prove as serious a problem for a community as underbuilding. It is the concern of the Chamber of Commerce to see that actual housing needs are met, and that they are met in such a way as to solve rather than to create other community problems. In this connection a survey might be made to determine the housing needs of the community.

MUNICIPAL SERVICES

Garbage disposal is directly related to public health and sanitation. A sewage system for collection and disposal of the city's waste, that is sanitary and odorless is essential to any city. The economic problem relates to the use of a fee system or of financing the program out of public funds. The Chamber of Commerce should not enter too deeply into the technical questions involved unless it can obtain the services of competent engineers, but it can be very effective in getting things accomplished along these lines by the application of plain business common-sense.

Police protection is, of course, a responsibility of local and state government. Failure to provide necessary protection creates not only a social problem but also a problem to business and industry. In the event of a possible breakdown in law enforcement that threatens the welfare of business operations, it is well within the scope of the Chamber of Commerce to initiate the necessary activities to again assure adequate police protection.

Fire prevention is a worthwhile project for any Chamber. Fire losses create problems for commerce not alone as a result of the actual losses from specific fires but also because insurance rates are determined by such loss ratios.

Since it has been demonstrated that cities can prevent fires and since it has been demonstrated that dollars and lives are saved by a continuing fire prevention program, many Chambers of Commerce include a fire prevention committee as a regular part of their organization structure. The National Fire Waste Council, the National Board of Fire Underwriters, the National Fire Protection Association, the Mutual Insurance Companies, the International Fire Chief's Association, the Insurance Department of the Chamber of Commerce of the United States and other similar agencies stand ready to help any manager who desires to formulate a fire prevention program.

A water supply that is pure, dependable and adequate is a community's most important utility. Not only does it mean health and comfort to the people of the community but it also has a direct relationship to the possibilities for developing business and industry. Chambers of Commerce have proved their effectiveness in sponsoring activities to secure necessary improvements in existing water supplies and to obtain completely new sources and systems of supply.

CITY PLANNING

City and town planning is as old as communities themselves, but its public appreciation even in America has not yet reached an acceptable stage. Stated in its simplest terms, it means creating a program which, when carried out, will put a community in a position to make all of its facilities adequate for what is demanded of them, with reasonable regard for the future. Planning presents a city or town with a program or an ideal.

1. It aims to co-ordinate every element in the physical development of the community so that each may function properly and adequately to serve to the fullest the needs and comfort and health of city dwellers.

2. It aims to create and foster in the minds of all citizens a sense of the entity of the community and the relationship of the various elements, thereby promoting a spirit of real community cooperation.

In general terms city planning includes zoning, but in the final analysis zoning is to be considered a necessary supplement to planning. City planning has to do with the proper projection and development of public and quasi-public areas, such as streets, parks, wharves, railroad right-of-ways, etc., while zoning has to do with regulations governing the development of private property. Among the important items in a city plan are:

1. The street and trafficway system.
2. Water mains, sewers, etc.
3. Railroad and transit right-of-ways and stations.
4. Relation of land and water transport.
5. Park and playground systems.
6. Location of public buildings.
7. Location of various type housing.
8. Location of various type industries and businesses.
9. Off-street parking areas in all sections of the city.

The city plan provides for orderly instead of chaotic or haphazard conditions. It furnishes a system of well-planned thoroughfares to facilitate traffic and to connect all sections of the community as well as highways connecting the city with the country. It differentiates between major and minor streets for the sake of economy and outlines a complete system of boulevards. It suggests in a broad way the requirements of a comprehensive local transportation system, and gives consideration to the requirements of the central business district as well as other business and industrial sections.

Zoning is the adoption by ordinance, under authority of the state, of definitely described kinds of districts within the city. These are use, height and area districts. Each kind of district is then divided into classifications. Use districts are residential, commercial and industrial. These may be, and in some cities are, sub-divided. Residential, for example, may be sub-divided into those districts where apartment houses are permitted and those which are reserved for single-family homes. Height districts vary from the greatest permanent height in the old central business area to height limitations in single-family home district. Area districts prescribe the proportion of lot which may be occupied by buildings.

No argument is needed to convince the Chamber of Commerce manager that his organization should take the lead in obtaining for the community a complete and well-considered plan. The following steps may be suggested:

1. Find a leader and make him chairman of a group of representative public-spirited citizens who are interested and who may follow through on this activity for a number of years.

2. This committee should next absorb all the information it can about city planning.

3. Legal powers the city or town has with respect to appointing a planning commission and what powers the commission would possess must be determined.

4. Determine whether the work should be started by a private or public body, and see that funds are provided to pay for the technical work.

5. Publish a preliminary report or survey and give it wide distribution.

6. The report should be prepared as soon as possible after the preliminary report has been fully discussed, and the support of the public must be enlisted.

7. The plan must be put into effect, step by step, by public authorities, but it remains a responsibility of the Chamber of Commerce to encourage public officials

to prosecute the work as vigorously as conditions may warrant.

City planning is good business for any city, and the city administration should be sold on this fact. Where no planning exists, it may be necessary to pay for technical services from Chamber funds but eventually this cost should be borne by the city. The widening of streets, the construction of public buildings and numerous other public improvements in future years may be very costly if there has been no planning, and the damages to adjoining property runs high. When the city, itself, is sufficiently sold on constructive city planning to finance it, the chances of following the plan are much greater.

No plan should be final. It should be a goal toward which the city works; but time may bring changing conditions that dictate logical changes.

Street Traffic

The full effect of motor car transportation on city traffic has been realized in the last decade. Few are the towns and cities that do not have at least one traffic light. Many have parking meters to collect the nickels and pennies from customers who have come to town to trade in the retail stores. Most cities do not fully use their streets to move the congested motor traffic, although the years after World War II have seen the enforcement of more regulations against street parking. The provision of more off-street parking, establishment of more one-way streets and construction of limited access trafficways are helping to reduce the local traffic problems. The establishment of shopping centers removed from the downtown area also tends to reduce congestion but brings with it problems for the larger retailers. The trend is to follow the customer, and many of the stores in residential shopping centers are branches of the larger downtown stores.

With the increased use of the motor car and the added time for recreation provided by the five-day and forty-hour week, more people have moved outside the city limits and the city's tax receipts have suffered. Few cities have solved this problem. Its importance is a challenge to the Chamber of Commerce and city administration.

SAFETY ACTIVITIES

A good safety program should have a definite place in every progressive Chamber of Commerce, if it is not already adequately handled by a local safety council. Not only will it save life and limb and property, but it will help to sell the Chamber of Commerce to management, labor and the entire citizenship. Accident prevention work is conducted for the good of all and as such provides a common meeting ground for all races and creeds. Such a program, conducted efficiently by a Chamber of Commerce, is certain to make friends and thereby enlarge its influence for good and service to the community.

Traffic Safety

No man, woman or child is entirely free from the threat of traffic accidents. Necessary traffic improvements, impartial law enforcement and traffic engineering are essentials to traffic safety. Committee activities may include streets and highway markers, traffic signals, drivers' license law, junior safety councils, school-boy police systems, safety essay contests, safety parades, and other such projects.

Industrial Safety

Industrial safety work gives the Chamber of Commerce an opportunity to work with a definite problem of industry and to contribute to the reduction of one of the costs of production. Industrial accidents not only mean lost time but also increases in insurance rates. Industrial safety activities may include:

1. Encouragement of safety measures inside the plants, such as correct illumination, hazardless controls and protective alarms.

2. Suggestions to reduce fatigue by step-saving control buttons, automatic regulation of speed and temperature, and other measures designed to keep the employee more alert.

3. Promotion of more healthful working conditions, with provisions for clean air, comfortable temperatures, good drinking water, and draft elimination.

Regular industrial conferences, work through foremen's clubs, and other such measures may be the means of carrying on programs of industrial safety.

Public Safety

The field of accidents is not limited to the street or highway and the factory. The accident prevention program may be carried into the home, the school, the office and the store. Public safety activities may be largely educational, but efforts in this direction may be carried on through almost any type of publicity media. After-work safety programs for employees are important.

TRANSPORTATION ACTIVITIES

Next to food, shelter and clothing, transportation is probably the most essential need of the ordinary person. While work in this field may or may not be included in the civic program of most Chambers of Commerce, it is discussed briefly here since its general aspects were not considered in other chapters of this book. Some Chambers of Commerce have well organized transportation departments, while others confine their work in this field to the efforts of a transportation committee.

Aviation

Recent years have seen a marked increase in the aviation activities of Chambers of Commerce. This work includes in addition to airport improvements, such projects as better air mail and passenger service, extensions of commercial airline service, airport terminal improvements, and other requirements for adequate air service for the city.

Highways

Work in the interest of better highways has long been a major activity with most Chambers of Commerce. For many smaller organizations, highway promotion has been the activity which has been most important in the eyes of many local businessmen. Improvement of existing highways, the building of more direct highways, bridge and overpass or underpass improvements, state and national route designations, and many similar goals are sought by the highway committee of the average Chamber of Commerce.

Local Transportation

Of immediate concern to many local firms are problems of local transportation, and in the program of many Chambers of Commerce will be found provisions for such activities as the following: street improvements, highway routings through the city, street widening projects, the opening of dead-end streets, parking meters, street car and local bus routes and schedules, etc.

Railroad, Bus and Truck Service

Since projects in this field are usually closely allied to the work of the traffic bureau, in organizations having such a division, they are usually handled there. In other Chambers of Commerce they are supervised by a committee. Adequate freight service by railroads and truck lines, and satisfactory passenger service by railroads and bus lines are, of course, important to the commerce and industry of any community. The maintenance and improvement of these services should be fostered by the Chamber of Commerce.

Postal Service

While satisfactory postal service is definitely a matter of convenience to the general public, it may prove to be either a definitely competitive advantage or disadvantage for many firms doing business throughout the trade area. Delays in mail delivery are detrimental to the service of local distributors, and may result in business going to their competitors in other cities. A periodic survey of postal service may well be suggested as a worth-while activity for a Chamber of Commerce.

SUMMARY

1. As Chambers of Commerce acquire a more definite outlook as community organizations in addition to their basic commercial design, they give increased consideration to civic activities.

2. Civic projects of a Chamber of Commerce should be of community-wide importance and should generally have some relationship to business or industry.

3. Constructive accomplishment should always be the goal in any civic activity, although in this field the task of

getting definite results is frequently more difficult than in commercial or industrial projects.

4. Committees handling civic projects should get all information available that is pertinent to their activity, should draw upon the experience of other communities as well as the opinions of authorities, and should make a careful and unbiased analysis of the facts obtained.

5. Most civic activities have a definite community relationship, and their ultimate success depends upon the ability to secure the support of public officials in particular and the general public as well.

6. Constructive accomplishment is the goal of all Chamber of Commerce work. Too often Chambers of Commerce are good starters but poor finishers.

7. Widespread trends in social changes have created new community problems and have paved the way for more extensive participation of Chambers of Commerce in public welfare activities.

8. Civic development activities designed to make a community a better place in which to live and work form another general classification of civic projects.

9. Public construction projects are of community-wide importance and many of them are directly related to commerce. Therefore, they come within the purview of this chapter.

10. Conditions of modern living have greatly increased the possibilities for accidents, and safety activities have gained a definite place in the program of most Chambers of Commerce.

Chapter XIV

The Manager and His Job

THE CHIEF paid executive of the chamber of commerce goes by various titles such as secretary, general manager, vice-president and even president. In the present chapter—as elsewhere in this book—he will, however, be referred to as the manager. The discussion will deal first with the job and then with the man.

THE JOB OF THE MANAGER

The by-laws of most chambers of commerce attempt to define the authority and responsibilities of the manager. In order to obtain a realistic picture of his job, we may, therefore, first examine some of these provisions. In one organization the legal authority for employing the manager is stated as follows:

> "The government of the chamber, the direction of its work, and the control of its property shall be vested in a board of directors consisting of . . . members. Upon their election the directors shall meet, qualify and elect from their own number a president and vice-president. They shall also annually elect a treasurer who may or may not be a member of the board of directors. *They shall also employ a manager and fix his salary.*"[1]

The by-laws go on to define the responsibilities of the manager in the following provisions:

> "The manager shall be the chief administrative officer of the chamber."
> "He shall be responsible to the board of directors for the proper conduct of all departments and the work of the persons employed by the chamber".

Taken together, these provisions establish clear lines of authority and responsibility. The directors are elected by the members and are responsible to them for the general conduct of the chamber's affairs and for the management of its

(1) Italics added.

300

property. The directors, in turn, hold the manager responsible to them.

> "It shall be the duty of the manager to conduct the official correspondence, preserve all books, documents and communications, keep books of accounts, and maintain an accurate record of the proceedings of the chamber, the board of directors and all committees."

This is a clear statement of important duties. But the by-laws go farther, stating that:

> "He shall so manage the affairs of the chamber as to promote the objectives of the chamber."

This provision is, at the same time, an order and a challenge to the manager. He is being told to keep the chamber on the right track—and to remember always what the chamber is and what its proper functions and objectives are. Within those bounds it is his duty to push ahead so as to make the chamber a functioning and effective organization.

> "The position of the manager and his assistants shall be bonded in the amounts approved by the board and the fee or fees shall be paid by the chamber."

In the best interests of everybody concerned, the manager is bonded. That should be true also of every other person on the staff who handles organization funds. In fact, many chambers take out blanket surety bonds covering all their employees.

> "He shall draw and have countersigned warrants for all moneys to be paid by the treasurer."

This is an authorization for the manager's office to draw checks to be countersigned by a designated officer. In many chambers the signatures of any two of the following officers are required to validate checks: the president, the vice-president, the treasurer and the manager. In others, checks may be signed by the manager alone.

> "He shall submit a financial statement and a written report on the year's work at the close of each fiscal year."

In actual practice, most managers submit monthly or at least quarterly reports to the board on chamber finances. These reports may, however, be informal. The annual financial report, on the other hand, is usually that of a certified public accountant who has audited the books of the chamber. An annual audit by a competent, disinterested person is a must, and whenever possible it should be made by a certified public accountant. The report on the year's work should be a comprehensive review of the chamber's activities and accomplishments. It should also set out the needs and the problems of the chamber. The manager's report to the board usually serves as the basis for the president's report to the membership.

The by-laws of some chambers of commerce contain a final provision stating that:

"The manager shall devote himself entirely to the affairs of the chamber."

Such a provision applies, of course, only to those managers who are employed on a full-time basis. It is inserted in the by-laws simply as a safeguard to ensure that the manager will not undertake other activities that may interfere with his services to the chamber.

The Content of the Job

Although the formal provisions of the by-laws provide a skeleton outline of the manager's job, they do little more than suggest its many-sided content. The overall task of the manager is to plan, initiate and direct the operations of the chamber in such a way as to ensure the necessary support—in terms of both manpower and money—to enable the organization to carry out its functions in the fields of industrial, commercial, agricultural and civic development. In fulfillment of this assignment, he must undertake a wide variety of duties and responsibilities.

The manager must realize the importance of having a definite program of work for his chamber. He must know how to formulate it. Because such a program of work serves to direct the activities of the organization and to define its goals and accomplishments, the importance of this phase of the manager's work can hardly be overemphasized.

The manager must know the basic principles of chamber finance, and be well acquainted with the procedures that must be followed in order to secure the funds needed by the organization. He must know how to handle membership committees, and how to plan, organize and conduct membership campaigns. He must have thorough knowledge of accounting, collection methods and other practices that will result in maximum income.

As chief executive of the chamber the manager is responsible for the actions of all employees. His job is that of hiring, training, supervising and—if need be—firing. He must develop an adequate organization, assign functions, define lines of authority and responsibility, and set up efficient systems of operation.

One of the important responsibilities of the manager is that of committee management. If the chamber is to function effectively, it must have an adequate number of active committees. The information, guidance and stimulation they require in order to do their work well, must come largely from the manager.

He must also work in harmony with his board of directors and officers. It is his duty to provide them with the factual information upon which their actions must be based, and to advise them correctly as to what is and what is not sound organization policy. His relations with directors and officers must be on a friendly and dignified plane.

Because meetings are an essential element in chamber operations, the manager must know how to plan, arrange and conduct them. This applies to meetings of all kinds, large and small. More than anyone else, the manager will be responsible for the success or failure of these gatherings.

In the administration of the chamber, the manager must maintain sound public relations. Every chamber may be said to have a four-fold public relations responsibility. It must make friends for the chamber itself, for the city in which it is located, for the business and professional men and institutions of that community and for private enterprise in general. In order to accomplish these results, the manager must appreciate the importance of favorable public opinion, know the principles of good publicity and have a keen sense of news values.

Perhaps the most important responsibility of the manager can be summarized in two words: furnish leadership. The successful manager is one to whom men look instinctively and confidently for leadership—not only in everything the chamber undertakes, but also in many other community affairs. In order to do his job well, the manager must have the knack of implanting ideas in the minds of others so that they accept them as their own; he must know how to organize and motivate without appearing to manage; and he must be able to accomplish results in such a way that a major share of the credit goes to others.

As a Career

Chamber of commerce work has afforded many a man an interesting, challenging and rewarding career. Like every other vocation it has some limitations. Chamber of commerce work usually means long hours, heavy responsibility, countless details and the expenditure of a great deal of nervous energy. It means all the perplexing difficulties of pleasing a large number of people. Enemies can be made, sometimes very easily and in spite of the manager's best efforts.

If one were to ask them about it, most managers would probably say that their greatest problem is that of maintaining the interest of businessmen and the public in the chamber of commerce. Without such interest no chamber can expect to secure the moral, financial and manpower support that is essential to its success. To create and maintain that interest the manager must be able to sell the chamber as a vital and useful instrument of business and community development. It is no easy task to do so; but it is a task that offers real challenge.

It has been said that because of the hazards involved, there is too large a turn-over among chamber employees. It would be idle to deny that there is a considerable turnover, but it is probably due to several factors. It is inevitable that some of the men who undertake managerial or staff positions, should be unequipped to handle the job and, consequently, fail to make good. Others discover that they do not like the work and, therefore, seek other employment. Then there are many who begin in a small chamber, advance as far as they can in that organization, and then move on to a larger chamber where the opportunities and the remuneration are more attractive. As a result, the length of service of managers in the smaller organizations is, on an average, less than that of the executives of the larger chambers. On the other hand, there are a great many managers who have cast their lot with small-city organizations. To them, salary may be less important than the service that they can perform to their community. They may prefer the unhurried and well-ordered life of the small town to the bustle of the big city. Because they perform valuable service and live happy lives, they may be considered as successful as any manager of a metropolitan chamber, although their success is of a different kind.

Although turnover is still considerable, it is probably less today than it was a decade or two ago. The number of managers who have been in the profession for more than twenty-five years, is increasing each year. These men constitute a very sizeable group. One manager has a service record of fifty years and several have completed periods ranging from thirty to forty years. In part, the decreased turnover reflects the maturity and greater stability of the chambers themselves. In part, it reflects a growing appreciation of the advantages of chamber of commerce work.

These advantages are many and important. The work is varied and interesting. It seldom becomes monotonous. The wide range of projects and activities and the great diversity of problems afford the manager the opportunity of exercising all his skills and ingenuity, and making use of all his past experience. The position is one of prominence and influence in the community. It brings the manager in contact with leaders in all walks of life and places him in a position to take part in almost everything that goes on in the community.

One of the finest aspects of the profession is the spirit of helpfulness that prevails among its members. Chamber managers like to and do help each other. They gladly exchange ideas and experiences; they are pleased when someone else adopts methods and practices which they have found successful; older men go out of their way to encourage beginners. Willing and friendly cooperation has not only lightened the load of individual managers and contributed to their success, but it has also increased the proficiency and enhanced the standards of the profession as a whole.

Many believe that the salaries of chamber of commerce managers compare favorably with those of other vocations calling for similar degrees of skill. Be that as it may, the chamber of commerce executive will secure satisfaction and compensation also from sources other than his salary check. The privilege of working with others in pursuits that contribute to the general welfare; the planning and execution of projects that will stand for many years and be used by everyone; the stimulation and inspiration that come from daily contacts with the finest people of the community—these and other intangibles must in the long run pay large dividends in real satisfactions.

Salary

What salaries do managers of chambers of commerce receive? To prospective and present managers this is, of course, an important question. The salary may well be the factor that determines whether or not a man should enter the field or, if he is already in chamber work, whether he should remain.

Chambers of commerce can afford to spend only a certain portion of their income for salaries. If they spend too large a proportion, insufficient funds will be available for other purposes with the result that the effectiveness of the organization may be seriously impaired. For the country as a whole, total salaries average 55 per cent of the total chamber income. The proportion varies, however, by geographical areas as well as by the size of the organization and the size of the community.

The manager's salary is, of course, only a part—albeit sometimes an important part—of the total salary bill. It ranges from a maximum of almost 45 per cent of the total income of small-city chambers, to a minimum of 7 per cent of

TABLE II

MANAGER'S SALARY AS A PERCENTAGE OF TOTAL CHAMBER INCOME, BY SIZE OF COMMUNITY

Population of Community	Manager's Salary as Percentage of Chamber Income
Less than 5,000	41%
5 to 10,000	43
10 to 25,000	38
25 to 50,000	31
50 to 100,000	27
100 to 200,000	19
200 to 500,000	11
More than 500,000	7

the income of metropolitan organizations. The majority of salaries range from $3,000 to $6,500 per year, with a few going as high as $25,000.

In recent years a number of the larger chambers have provided additional compensations. Some of them have, for example, introduced pension plans, and the movement appears to be growing. In some cases the plan is a contributory one, in others the entire cost is assumed by the chamber. Some chambers sponsor also low cost group life insurance, hospital insurance and other benefits.

Manager or Assistant?

Men interested in a chamber career often ask, "Should I try to get a job as a staff assistant and then later, after I have gained some experience, seek a position as a manager? Or should I try for a management position right at the start?"

There can be no pat answer to such a question. Hundreds of men have started as managers—and have succeeded. Many others began as staff members and have advanced into managerial positions. Much depends upon the age and maturity of the man, his willingness and ability to assume responsibility, his financial requirements and many other factors. One man may in the long run be far better off if he starts under the tutelage of an experienced manager. Another may have sufficient maturity and resourcefulness so that he can strike out on his own.

There are, however, more job opportunities for managers than for assistants. A recent survey of 2,600 chambers shows that more than 1,900 of them have incomes of less than $10,000 a year. Possibly a thousand of these small chambers do not even have a full-time manager. They depend upon a volunteer or a part-time person to fill that position. The others are one-man organizations. They may employ one or two full-time girls who serve as stenographers and clerks, but they offer little or no opportunity for the young man who wishes to enter chamber work by the way of a staff assistantship. Only 169 chambers reported incomes in excess of $25,000. Some of them employ one, two or three men in addition to the manager. A few are large departmentalized organizations in which each division has its own manager and staff.

The manager of a one-man chamber must assume full responsibility and participate in all its activities and projects. He must be a jack of all trades. On a two or three-man staff some degree of specialization is possible, but each assistant is usually made responsible for several assignments. For example, the assistant manager of a small chamber may handle retail promotion, publicity and perhaps one or two other tasks. In a departmentalized organization there is room for greater specialization. Although a particular department may handle more than one major assignment, its staff is presumed to be particularly skilled in and devote most of its time to one field. For example, the staff of the publicity department would consist of men trained in that field, even though the department might also be responsible for certain civic activities.

The greater degree of specialization in a large organization offers, of course, the newcomer the opportunity of developing particular skills. The small chamber, on the other hand, offers the advantage of diversity of activity. It may, therefore, be the best training school for the young man whose ambition it is to seek a managership of a small organization.

How To Get a Job

The man who wishes to enter chamber work and the manager who seeks a better job, are concerned about how to find the desired opening. Information about vacancies may reach a man in various ways. He may read a newspaper story telling about the resignation of a manager in his hometown or elsewhere. He may have friends who are members of chambers of commerce in other cities and who inform him about openings, that occur. By talking to the manager of one chamber, he may learn about a vacancy in some neighboring city. If he has completed one of the several courses for chamber of commerce executives that are offered by universities, the school may suggest his name to an organization looking for a new manager.

There is one central agency that provides valuable service in this connection. It is the Commercial Organization Department of the Chamber of Commerce of the United States, located in Washington, D. C. For many years that department has maintained an informal placement service for the convenience of men who are seeking positions as well as for chambers that are looking for capable executives. A man may file his personnel record with the department and if investigation discloses that he has the required qualifications, his name will be submitted to chambers that have asked the assistance of the department in filling vacancies. Not all chambers call upon the Commercial Organization Department for assistance, but many do. The placement procedure followed by the Department is that which has been approved by American Chamber of Commerce Executives.

The six division managers of the National Chamber are also frequently called upon to suggest names of competent men. Some state chambers of commerce and some state associations of chamber executives are in a position to be of some assistance in establishing contact between the man and the job.

From whatever source an individual may obtain leads about vacancies, it is important that he make application in the proper manner. Usually the candidate writes a letter of application addressed to the president of the chamber or to the chairman of the committee that may have been appointed to find a qualified man to fill the vacancy. Such a letter must, of course, be well written. Either as part of the letter or, perhaps better, in an attached statement the applicant should furnish a personal history; i. e. he should give all essential information about himself and outline his education, experience and other qualifications. He should also supply references to whom the chamber may turn for further information about the applicant. The letter should reflect a genuine interest in the job, the chamber and the community.

Few chambers of commerce hire men without a personal interview. An applicant should, therefore, make every effort to secure such an interview and—once secured—he should make the most of the opportunity. The purpose of the interview is to enable the employer as well as the applicant to size up the other fellow. How the candidate acts and what he says must, therefore, have an important bearing on whether or not he is employed. Perhaps the best advice that can be given, may be summed up in two words: be yourself. Don't talk too much; but whenever you talk, say something. The chamber of commerce is interested in finding out whether the candidate knows chamber work, understands the problems and possibilities of the community and is in agreement with local aspirations and philosophy. It wants to know whether he is a good organizer, a self-starter and a man capable of carrying through to completion those things he starts. Talk about these things, not about the weather. Ask some intelligent questions. Sometimes one question is more eloquent than ten statements.

Should There Be a Contract

Should the manager enter into a formal employment contract with the chamber? It is done in a few cases, but the vast majority of executives feel that a formal contract is neither necessary nor desirable.

When a manager is employed by a board of directors, the usual procedure is for him and the board to agree on the date when he will commence his duties, the salary that he will receive, and other conditions of employment. These are usually incorporated in a motion that is adopted by the board, and such a motion constitutes the only contract. In some cases there is a definite understanding as to future salary increases—the amounts and the dates when they will go into effect.

In these negotiations more depends on the integrity of both parties—the manager and the chamber—than on any formal document. The chamber needs a competent manager and in its own interest, the board of directors is usually willing to do everything in its power to secure and hold such a man. Neither the board nor the manager would want to continue a relationship that proved unsatisfactory. A manager who found that he had not made good or who felt he was facing an impossible situation, would want to move on. Conversely, the chamber would not want to be compelled by written contract to put up with a man who proved undesirable; nor would it stand in the way of a successful manager who was offered a better job elsewhere. For these reasons, employment agreements are usually informal. The manager is hired on a yearly basis, and both parties proceed on the assumption that if the executive makes good, he will be fairly treated and paid the best salary the chamber can afford.

THE MANAGER

What kind of a person do boards of directors look for when they seek a manager? There is no exact, comprehensive job specification available. Nor can there be. The functions of the manager varies greatly from one chamber to another. Even in the case of reasonably similar chambers, no two boards are likely to agree completely as to the traits and skills for which they are looking. Nevertheless, there are some attributes that are usually given special consideration by the majority of boards of directors. They appear, therefore, to be basic.

Basic Requirements

First among the basic requirements are those of good health, engaging personality and pleasing appearance. A healthy man is wanted simply because he is more likely to possess the vigor, stamina and enthusiasm that the job requires. He must also be a man easy to meet, a person who is likeable and who likes people. And, of course, he must be "presentable"—that is, he must appear well in any company and be a creditable representative of the chamber and the community.

Every board of directors wants an absolutely honest man. It wants a man of good character, who lives within his income, pays his bills, and behaves himself. It wants a man who enjoys an unblemished reputation wherever he has lived. The board must be able to depend on the manager; and it knows that unless he is reliable, he will not last long in the important job for which he is being considered. Moreover, the man must be industrious and sufficiently tenacious to keep going in the face of obstacles. The managership of a chamber of commerce is no job for a lazy man or for a man who is ready to give in whenever difficulties arise.

Because much of his time will be spent in dealing with people, singly or in groups, he must be able to get along with others, to work with them and to get others to work with him. Every bit of experience that he has had in dealing with other people, especially in groups, will therefore be of value to him. He must possess that indefinable attribute which we call leadership ability. Perhaps it merely means the capacity to plan, to organize and to control—not by exhortation and cajolery, but by supplying positive motivation and inspiration. Certainly, the manager must have imagination and vision, ability to look ahead, to plan and to follow through and finish that which he starts.

One of the most important assets is a generous amount of common sense. Another name for it is native intelligence. It is the capacity for doing the right thing at the right time. A good education is a decided asset, especially if the candidate has majored in subjects that can be used in his work—such as business administration, economics, journalism or English. The ability to express oneself well is much to be desired. The manager should be able to talk clearly and concisely to the board, to committees, to the membership and to other groups.

Business ability is another important qualification. This means, among other things, that the manager needs to know the value of a dollar and be able to handle the financial affairs of the chamber. Finally, most boards want a man who has the capacity for growth—one who will continue to improve himself and become a more competent manager as the years go by. They want a man whom they would be proud to recommend for a bigger job if it should be offered to him.

Self-Improvement

The possibilities of self-improvement are greater today than ever before. First among the available facilities are the six institutes for chamber of commerce executives conducted each summer. The institutes are sponsored by the Chamber of Commerce of the United States, American Chamber of Commerce Executives, American Trade Association Executives, the universities at which they are held, and various state association of executives. Each institute offers short courses in nearly every phase of chamber of commerce management. These courses are taught by men who have long years of practical and successful experience, and who have gained recognition as experts in their respective fields. No manager can attend one of these institutes without bringing back to his job new ideas, greater understanding, and added interest.

The oldest of these institutes is the *National Institute for Commercial and Trade Organization Executives*. No less important, however, are the five regional institutes. They are: *Southwestern Chamber of Commerce Institute, Western Institue for Commercial and Trade Executives, Rocky Mountain Institute, Southeastern Institute for Commercial Organization Executives,* and *Northeastern Institute for Commercial & Trade Organization Executives.*

Associations of Executives

Another facility for self-improvement and for the exchange of ideas and experience is the several associations for chamber of commerce executives. The national association is the American Chamber of Commerce Executives, with headquarters at 1615 H Street N. W. Washington, D. C. The purposes of the association have been clearly stated in its Statement of Principles as follows:

VALUE OF ASSOCIATION MEMBERSHIPS

This supplement has been prepared to expand the section of Chapter XIV of the textbook on CHAMBER OF COMMERCE ADMINISTRATION, under the sub-head "Associations of Executives" (pp. 312-313). It has been felt that further emphasis should be placed upon the statement that "Another facility for self-improvement and for the exchange of ideas and experiences is the several associations for chamber of commerce executives."

Certainly the matter of self-improvement is important. Unlike those in most professions, the chamber of commerce executive is usually the only one in his classification in his community. He does not have the same opportunity of measuring his performance against other local people in his profession as do doctors, lawyers and engineers. Only through association with other chamber of commerce executives does he have this opportunity for evaluating his own standards of qualifications and performance.

The executive serves his community as an "idea man" on civic improvement and community development. To avoid going stale on the job, he needs to tap all available sources of new methods and techniques in his field of service. Association meetings and publications are recurring sources of better ways of doing the organization job.

It is difficult for any executive to keep himself geared to his best efforts. Often he needs new stimulation or motivation to continue to put forth his best efforts. When problems multiply and activities planned with high hopes turn sour, the executive needs inspiration if he is to maintain his dedicated interest in his work. Association affiliation is a constant source of inspiration as well as information.

The chamber of commerce executive should also feel a sense of obligation to his profession. His own fortunes have a tendency to rise or fall with the ebb and flow of the prestige enjoyed by chamber of commerce work. No profession has successfully raised its standards or improved its recognition without the support of strong, effective organized effort. National, regional and state associations of chamber of commerce executives have played an important role in the up-grading of the chamber of commerce profession and in securing for it a more favorable public acceptance.

Therefore, for more self-improvement, for better self-evaluation, for sources of information and inspiration, and for the up-grading of his profession, every chamber of commerce executive should give active support to his professional associations—the American Chamber of Commerce Executives, his own state association, and the regional association that serves his area, if one exists. Not only should he support it by keeping the nominal dues payments current, but he should make his time and talents available to serve when called upon as an officer, or director, as a committee member, or to take a part on the program. In a staff organization, the principal executive should assume the responsibility for encouraging the members of his staff to share his own opportunities for active association participation.

American Chamber of Commerce Executives shall provide facilities whereby members of this association act together:

To develop individual ability for greater service.

To inculcate a discerning sense of organization responsibility.

To inspire adherence to high standards of professional integrity.

To establish in the public consciousness an increasing appreciation of the essential character of qualified commercial organization management.

These purposes of American Chamber of Commerce Executives shall be fulfilled through—

The friendly interchange of ideas and experience.

The enlargement of professional talents through study and discussion.

The encouragement of a spirit of mutual helpfulness throughout the membership.

The dissemination of educational and inspirational material which will accomplish these objectives.

In addition to the national organization, there are state associations in practically every state. They meet once or twice a year, issue bulletins to their members, and serve as media for the exchange of ideas and experience. There are also several regional associations. The New England Association of Commercial Executives, for example, meets quarterly in one or another of the six New England states. The Mountain States Association draws its membership from eight states in the Rocky Mountain Area. Largest and oldest among these regional groups is the Southern Association of Chamber of Commerce Executives whose membership is composed of executives from all the southern states. The manager who fails to join his state and regional groups is denying himself the benefit and pleasure of valuable contacts with fellow workers.

SOME PROBLEMS OF THE PROFESSION

In the performance of their job there are some problems that all managers encounter and must solve to the best of their ability. Among these problems are the question of the amount of public speaking he should do, and how closely he should attempt to work with individual members. There is also the purely personal problem of health. Because of the universality of these problems, each of them will be discussed briefly.

Public Speaking

The ability to speak well in public is a valuable asset to any manager. The very nature of his job requires that from time to time, he must address large and small audiences. The manner in which he conducts himself and the effectiveness of his address may contribute greatly not only to his own success, but also to that of the project or the cause for which he speaks.

But to say that the manager should be a good public speaker is by no means the same as saying that he should everlastingly accept speaking engagements. On the contrary, there are many reasons why he must exercise restraint. For one thing, a good speech requires preparation—time and effort that might be better spent on other things. And in the second place, a manager may easily wear himself out with his local public. Most important, however, is the fact that the manager's place is not in the limelight. The successful manager is one who works quietly and effectively, get things done, and then leaves it to non-paid officers and members to make public appearances and to take the credit for the work accomplished. Sometimes it may be just a bit difficult to handle things that way. A manager is no more than human and, like other men, he enjoys basking in the sun of public acclaim. But a little modesty and magnanimity will, in the long run, contribute greatly to his own success and to that of his chamber.

Whenever the manager speaks, he should do so with dignity. He should be sure of his facts; avoid irresponsible statements. And, of course, his public utterances should be clean. A manager who fails to conduct himself as a gentleman, cannot expect to gain the respect and confidence that are essential to his success.

Calling on Members

New and old executives are often perplexed by the demand that they make regular calls upon members. They ask frequently, "How often should we call?" It is a fine thing to envision the manager calling on all his members at least once a year. But actually it is not possible in most cities. Nor is it advisable. If the manager is to do the job for which he was hired, he will not have a great deal of time for personal calls on members.

Nevertheless, there are certain calls that the manager can make to advantage and for which he ought to find time. There are some occasions when he, better than anyone else, can deal with a slow account, a resignation or a member who is irked because of something the chamber has done or failed to do. There are times also when he will find it profitable to call on a new businessman, or visit a plant, office or store simply to become better acquainted. The point is that because his time for making calls is limited, they should be those which cannot effectively be made by others.

Similarly, no manager should be expected to solicit all new members. If he were to attempt to do so, he would find it impossible to get his work done. A manager can and should, now and then, make a call on a prospective member when his wide knowledge of the chamber is needed to overcome the prospect's sales resistance.

Health

The work of the manager of a chamber of commerce is demanding and nervously exhausting. It is, therefore, essential that he should guard his health. Under the pressure of work it is only too easy to neglect good health practices. It does not pay. Many admonitions might be given, but the following are among the most important:

1. Plan and carry out some form of regular physical exercise, even though it be no more than a good walk each day.
2. Take a good vacation each year. Do not let fancied obstacles interfere with this practice.
3. Find a good hobby and pursue it. It will provide an escape that will be highly beneficial.
4. Guard against mental fatigue. Do not become frightened, excited or worried. Turn often to Him from whom all blessings flow.
5. Have a physical check-up at least once a year.

IN CONCLUSION

The aim of this chapter has been to outline the more important aspects of the manager's job and the essential qualifications of the executive. It is obvious that in a discussion as brief as this, the subject cannot be covered in minute detail. But it is hoped that the reader has gained a fairly clear conception of the nature of the work and the qualities required of a successful manager.

Speaking at a meeting of chamber executives many years ago, Dr. Ralph W. Heilman, late Dean of the School of Commerce at Northwestern University said:

> "In my judgment you are members of a great profession. You are leaders of community action; you are coordinators of your community's forces; you are guardians of the community's welfare; you are builders of your community's destinies; you are missionaries preaching the gospel of industry, cooperation and concerted action; you are pioneers on the far-flung borders of the future—pioneering and blazing the trail for industrial progress."

Since these words were spoken the profession has advanced in terms of professional standards and efficiency. The extent to which it will continue to grow in usefulness and public esteem must depend upon the progress made by the individuals who are its members. For what the prefession is and does, is the sum total of their integrity, ability and accomplishments.

The writer was once asked: "If a chamber manager, or a man who aspires to become one, should ask you to give him your best advice, what would you say?" The answer was: "Strive constantly to improve your abilities, and to do a better job. Make sure that your personal behavior will always merit respect and confidence."

Index

A

Accidents 184, 296
Accounting Records 139-141
Administrative Committees . 71
Advance Solicitation 103
Advance Subscription Committee 95
Agricultural Activities .239-255
   Building Program 243
   Developing 240
   Financing 243
   Importance of 239
   Main Activities 244
   Organizing for 242
   Representative Programs 248
Agricultural Commissioner
   ....242, 252
Agricultural Committee
   ....241, 243, 248, 250-253
Agricultural Fairs and
   Exhibits ..245, 247, 248
Alphabetical File 178
American Chamber of Commerce
   Executives 309
American Industrial
   Development Council.216
American Royal Livestock
   and Horse Show 252
Annual Meetings 65
Appeals, selection of 147
Articles of Association 25
Assignment of Prospects 103, 106
Assistant Manager 307
Associations of Executives
   312-313
Audience, selection of 147
Audits 140
Aviation 297

B

Better Business Bureau 287
Billing Methods 86
Board of Directors 27-29
   Constitution of 27
   Size of 28
   Representativeness 28
   Functions of 28
   Meetings of 29, 64

Budget 129-134
   Advantages of 129
   Approval of 134
   Preparation of 131
Budget Committee 131
Bulletins 151
Buy-at-Home Movement ...197
Buyer's Guide 203
Buying Markets 200
By-Laws 25, 300

C

Chambers of Commerce
   Characteristics of 20-22
   Definition of 21
   Early American 19
   Flexibility of 21
   History of 18
   Modern 20
   Number of 20
   Origin of Term 18
   Principles of 22
Chamber of Commerce of the
   U. S. 128, 204, 216
Charity Agencies 287-288
Citizen Interest 263-265
   Development 263
   Rewards 264
   Value 264
City Beautification 290
City Planning 292-295
Civic Activities 270-299
   Cooperation in 283
   Definition 270
   Factors Making for
      Success of 274
   Guides to Participation
      in 273
   Procedures in 277-287
   Responsibility of Manager 282
   Scope and Limitations 272-274
   Types of 285-298
Civic Development Activities 292-295
Civic Loyalty 270
Club Facilities 127
Collection Calls 87
Collection of Dues 87
Commercial Activities ..186-209

Commercial Organization
    Department, Chamber of Commerce of
    the U. S. 308
Committee Chairmen 75-77
    Appointment of 76
    Board Members as 76
    Duties of 75
Committee Meetings 77-80
    Agenda of 78
    Conduct of 78
    Frequency of 77
Committee on Committees 73
Committee Personnel 73-75
    Appointment of 75
    Selection of 73
Committees 30, 70-80
Communications 171-176
    Contacts Within Office ..172
    Contacts Outside Office ..173
    Correspondence 174-176
    Personal Contacts 172
    Telegrams 176
    Telephone contacts 174
Community Chest 288
Community Publicity
    ....143, 146, 160-165
Confidential Matters 184
Congress of the U. S. 73
Constitution 25
Contingencies 133
Contract 310
Converse, Paul D. 189
Convention Activities ..163-165
Correspondence 174-176
Customs Regulations 206

D

Departments 31
Dinner Meetings 67
Direct Mail 151
Directories
    Income from 128
Division Commander
    ....96, 97, 104, 105
Donations 195
Dues
    Billing for—Collection
        of 86-87, 135
    Effect of Increasing Dues 124
    Income from 121-125
    Method of Determining ..125
    Minimum 123
    Plural Membership 123
    Rate of Dues 122, 124

E

Early Bird Breakfast ..108-109
Education 285-286

Efficiency Engineers 184
Endorsements 184, 287
Entrance Fee 125
Equipment and Supplies ...170
Ethical Standards 84
Evaluation Committee 95, 102
Executing Committees 71
Executive Committee 134
Expanding Government 256
Expenditures
    Control of 136-137
Expenses
    Estimate of 132-133
Export and Import Publications 207
Export Managers' Club 206, 207
External Activities 37

F

Farmers Club 252
Farmers Market 202
Federal Reserve Board 192
Files 177-181
    Importance of 177
Filing Systems and
    Methods 178-179
    Bases for 178
    General Rules of 181
    Methods of Filing 178
    Operation of Filing
        System 179-181
    Principles of Filing 177
Financial Aid to Industry..225
Financial Reports 139-141
Fire Prevention 292
Fiscal Operations 120-142
Foreign Commerce Department, Chamber of
    Commerce of the
    U. S. 204
Foreign Commerce Weekly 204
Foreign Trade Activities
    ....186, 203-208
Foreign Trade Advisory
    Committee 207
Foreign Trade Bureaus
    ....203, 207-208
Foreign Trade Information
    204-207
Foreign Trade Round Table 207
Four-H Clubs
    ..243, 245, 249, 250, 251
Freight Rates 201
Future Farmers of America
    ......243, 245, 249, 250
Future Homemakers of
    America 243

G

Good-Will Building 203
Governmental Affairs ..256-269

H

Health 289, 315
Health and Sanitation 289
Highways 297
House Organs 149
Housing 290-291
Housing Authorities 291

I

Income
  Collection of 135
  Estimate of 132
  Sources of 121-129
  Amount 126
Incubator Buildings 225
Industrial Activities ..210-238
  Attracting New Industry
    226-230
  Community Attitude Toward 213
  Coordination With Other Agencies 219
  Developing Local Industry
    224-226
  Planning for 215-220
  Service to Established Industry 220-224
  Time Element in 219
  Types of 210-211
Industrial Financing Plans 225
Industrial Location Factors
  211-212
Industrial Prospects ..226-230
  Finding 226
  Dealing With 228
Industrial Reference Service
  204
Industrial Relations 222
Industrial Safety 296
Industrial Survey 215
Insurance 184
Internal Activities 37
International Reference Service 204
Investigating Committees .. 71

J

Jobbing Markets 200
Junior Chamber of Commerce............... 32

K

Kick-Off Meeting 108

L

Legislation, State and National 265-268
Legislative Committees 266-268
  Duties of 266-268
  Formation of 266
Letter Writing Principles 175
Life Membership 125
Local Government 258-260
  Community Development 258
  Cooperation With Officials 262
  Efficiency of 260
  Facts, Important 260
  Informing the Public 263
  Personnel 259
  Public Improvements 258
  Relief and Welfare 259
  Role of Chamber 261
  Tax Problems 260
Luncheon Meetings 67-68

M

Manager 30, 300-316
  Authority and Responsibility of 300-302
  How to Get a Job as 308-309
  Job as a Career 304-305
  Manager or Assistant 307
  Qualifications of 311
  Problems of 313
  Salary of 306
  Self-improvement 312
Marginal Industries 223
Market Seasons 202
Media for Publicity 148
Meeting Book 55
Meetings 52-69
  Arrangements 57-58
  Assisting Chairman 61
  Attendance 56
  Calling 55
  Chairman of 61
  Content of 59
  Follow-through of 63
  Function of 52-54
  Minutes of 62
  Place of 57
  Preparing 54-59
  Special problems 64-68
Members
  Assimilating New 86
  Resignation of 88
  Suspension of 87
Membership 26-27, 81-119
  Anniversary of 85
  Application for 84
  Eligibility for 26

INDEX

Ethical Standards of 84
Life 125
Plural 123
Membership Agreement 85
Membership Campaigns
.... 93-112, 114-119
   Charting the Campaign
           93, 114-119
   General Chairman of ... 95
   Intensive 93
   Leadership of 94
   One Day Campaigns 92
   Organization of 93
   Publicity for 98, 118
   Training Workers for 107
Membership Clubs 91
Membership Committee .. 89-91
   Importance of 90
   Personnel of 90
Membership Contests 91
Membership Department .. 90
Membership Dues, See Dues
Membership Meetings 66
Membership Relations 86-88, 314
Merchandise Selection 194
Mountain States Association
     313

N

National Council of American Importers 206
National Firms .. 101, 104, 117
National Firms Committee 96
National Foreign Trade
   Council 206
National Foreign Trade
   Week 204
National Institute for Commercial and Trade Organization Executives 312
New England Association of Commercial Executives 313
Newspaper Copy 155
Newspaper Publicity .. 155-158
Northeastern Institute for Commercial & Trade Organization Executives 312
Numerical File 179

O

Office 169-171
   Appearance of 171
   Organization of 181-182
Office Administration .. 167-185
Office Arrangement 169

Office of International Trade
   204
Office Staff 182
   Absences of 183
   Courtesy to 183
   Interviews 183
   Personnel Relations 182
   Suggestions by 184
Officers, Elected 29
Off-street Parking 295
One-way Streets 295
Operating Manual 45
Opportunist Plan 38
Organization 1-33
   Principles of 23-25
   Structure of 26-32

P

Parking Facilities 193, 295
Parking Meters 295
Payment of Bills 137
Personal Contacts 172
Placement Service 308
Police Protection 292
Presidents' Conference ... 41-42
Press Relations 156-157
Program Advertising 195
Program of Work 29, 34-51
   Adoption of 48
   Follow-up of 49
   Functions of 34
   Fundamentals of 35
   Methods of Construction
      38-45
   Performance of 50
   Publicity for 48, 144
   Record and Analysis of
      Suggestions 46
   Use of 49
   Writing the program 48
Program of Work Committee 39
Project Committee 40, 71
Prospect Card 82
Prospect File 82-84
Publications 149-150
   Income from 128
Public Funds
   Income from 128
Public Officials 280, 281
   Administrators 281
   Executives 281
   Legislators 281
Public Speaking 314
Public Welfare Activities .. 285
Publicity 143-166, 279
   Community 160, 279
   Fundamentals of 146
   Internal 149-154

INDEX

Newspaper 154-158
Purposes of 143-146
Radio 158-159
Publicity Committee 97
Public Relations 159-160
Public Safety 297

R

Radio Publicity 158-159
Recreation 288
Referendum 29, 44
Reilley, William J. 189
Rents 138
  Income from 127
  Paid 138
Report Meetings ..110-111, 115
Reports 151-154
  Creative 152
  Financial 139-141
  Officers 151
  Preparation of 153
Reserve Fund 133, 135
Resignations 88-89
  Acknowledging 88
  Board Action 89
  Personal Follow-up 88
Retail Competition 197
Retail Events 196
Retail Gravitation 189
Retail Market 191-193
Retail Services 196
Retail Store 194-197
  Hours 194
  Modernization 194
  Merchandise Selection ...194
Retail Trade Activities 186-198
  Organizing for 187
  Financing 198
Retail Trade Division 187
Retail Trade Promotion 193-197
Retail Trading Area ...188-191
Retail Training 195
Returned Goods 195
Rocky Mountain Institute ..312
Round Table Method 43

S

Safety Activities 296-297
Salary 138, 306
Sales Promotion 222
Self-improvement 312
Service Charges 127
Service Clubs 313
Shopping Centers 295
Slum Clearance 291
Small Business Aid to 223
Social Agencies 287-288

Solicitation Commission ...287
Solicitations 195, 287-289
Southeastern Institute for Commercial Organization Executives ...312
Southern Association of Chamber of Commerce Executives ...313
Southwestern Chamber of Commerce Institute .312
Speakers 58
Speakers Bureau 97, 117
Special Committees 72, 277
Special Meetings 67
Special Retail Events 196
Special Subscriptions 125
Standing Committees 72, 277, 278
Subcommittees 72
Subscription Quotas ..102, 123
Suspensions 87
Sustaining Fund 123

T

Taxation and Industry 222
Tax Exempt 128
Team Captain 96, 104-105
Team Organization 96-97, 104-106, 116
Team Workers 96, 104-106
Telegrams 176
Telephone Contacts 174
Television 159
Tourist Promotion 162
Town-Farm Gatherings 244
Trade Associations 22
Trade Lists 205, 207
Traffic Bureau 224, 298
Traffic Safety 296
Training the Worker 107
Transportation Activities ..297
Transportation Companies .207
Treasury Decisions 206

U

U. S. Department of Agriculture 192, 205, 216
U. S. Department of Commerce 192, 204-205, 207, 216
U. S. Department of Labor 216
U. S. Department of State 205
U. S. Department of the Treasury 192, 206
U. S. Soil Conservation Service 241
U. S. Tariff Commission ..206

V

Victory Meeting 111
Voice for Business 257

W

Waste Disposal 291
Water Supply 292
Western Institute for Commercial and Trade Executives 312

Where-to-Buy Bulletins 197
Wholesale Trade Activities
.... 198-203
Wholesale Trade Areas 199-201
Wholesale Trade Promotion
.... 201-203
Workers Kit 108
World Trade Directory ... 205

Z

Zoning 294